In the Bey's Palace

IN THE BEY'S PALACE

Masha Williams

The Book Guild Ltd.
Sussex, England

To Libet, Lawrence, Jane and Jessica
and
In Memory of Alan.

The Book Guild Ltd.
25 High Street,
Lewes, Sussex.

First published 1990
Masha Williams 1990
Set in Baskerville
Typesetting by APS,
Salisbury, Wiltshire.
Printed in Great Britain by
Antony Rowe Ltd.,
Chippenham, Wiltshire.

British Library Cataloguing in Publication Data
Williams, Masha, Lady
    In the Bey's palace
    1. British diplomatic services – Biographies
    I. Title   327.41

ISBN 0 86332 510 6

ACKNOWLEDGEMENT

My thanks for the criticism and encouragement I received at the City Lit.

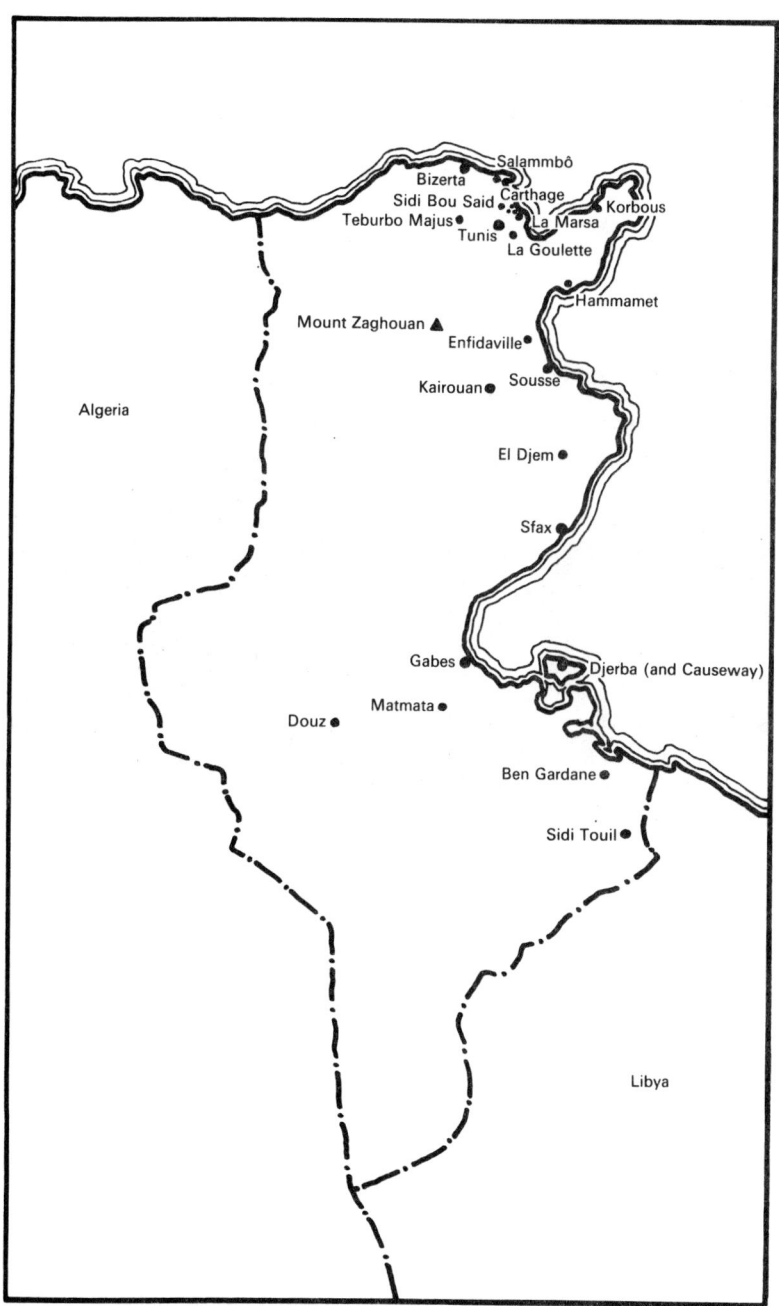

Our palace. The official side.

1

Tunis, 1953

Our Arab Palace! Enormous, gleaming white in the brilliant sunlight. We got out of the car and stared up, overawed, the children clinging to Mavis's hands. Our new Residence! Fifty rooms I remembered reading in the post report. I gazed incredulously at the two cast-iron stairways curving gracefully up to a covered terrace where six twin marble pillars supported stucco-decorated arches. A huge Union Jack swayed above us, gently, but significantly. I took a deep breath. This, I thought, I must turn into a home.

Mr Dismore, the Consul, a square-headed, sturdily – built man, motioned to a line of white-uniformed figures with red sheshias, soft, round caps, on their dark heads, and women in white abas beside them.

'Your staff, Sir,' and he whispered, 'all friendly.' There was martial law throughout Tunisia and I knew that the country was officially a French Protectorate but that the French had taken all authority into their own hands while the Tunisians clamoured for 'Internal Sovereignty'. Tunisians, we had heard, had been attacking and murdering Europeans. Alan, my husband moved down the line shaking each hand, as Mr Dismore murmured,

'Hassin . . . Mahomet . . . Ali . . .'

I followed, scanning their faces, but these men encased in starch with crested brass buttons were reassuring. A tight-lipped Mavis, our governess, came next, then our plump five-year old Libet and finally the four-year old Lawrence.

Mr Dismore again waved a hand. 'We call these the Bey's quarters. They're now used for entertaining. Your living quarters, the hareem quarters, are here at the side. Shall I lead the way?'

We followed him up steps into an adjoining annex, dwarfed

9

Our palace. The official and living quarters.

by the main building, but the size of a mansion. We stepped
into a hallway tiled in blue and white from floor to ceiling;
then into drawing and dining-rooms joined by an archway,
with whitewashed walls, and domed ceilings decorated with
carved and pierced stucco work in delicate geometric designs.
Above hung brass chandeliers. Most Arab houses I had seen
were kept dark for coolness but here, to my delight, all was
light and airy with latticed partitions, inset windows and sun-
filled alcoves. The children, still clutching Mavis's hands,
gazed around wide-eyed, while Alan and I smiled broadly as
we exchanged glances.

Mr Dismore led us to the sleeping quarters, 'Here's the
hareem!' – little doorless dens leading one into the next. One
big room had three doors. 'Your master bedroom, and down
here, we thought, would do for the children.' He led us through
more arched doorways into a larger area containing two small
beds. It was cheerful with blue-tiled walls and a timber-
beamed ceiling in bright yellow, blue and red.

'You can lie in bed and stare up at the lovely colours!' I told
the children as I drew them to me, Libet beaming with
excitement and Lawrence grinning too. I hoped they would
feel at home in this palace of light, air and space as I already
did.

Our drawing-room.

A small room off the children's had a door; here Mavis would have privacy. She glanced at it, obviously relieved.

We were tired, darkness had fallen quickly; we fell into our beds and were soon asleep.

'Mummy! Mummy!' The cry woke me. Lawrence's voice. He was recovering from a hernia operation. I leapt out of bed. The darkness was complete, and there was no bedside lamp.

'Mummy! Mummy' He was sobbing. I felt along the wall for a light switch. I could not find one. I groped my way towards the cries, stubbing toes on furniture, grasping sharp objects.

'I'm coming, darling, but I can't find the way,' I called back. At last the sobs were close but I had run into a wall. 'I'm here, love, but I can't get in.' I rounded a corner, fell over Libet's bed, picked myself up and collapsed onto Lawrence's. I took him in my arms and we comforted each other.

'What is it? Why are you crying?' I asked.

'I don't know,' he sobbed. I rocked him, whispering, 'My pet, my darling, it's all right . . .' till he fell asleep and I tucked him up. Now I had to stumble back through the darkness. Mavis slept through it all.

A knock on the door woke us. Sunlight was pouring in through the intricate wrought-iron window bars that threw strange, long shadows. My clock said a quarter past six. Work at the Consulate, Mr Dismore had said, began at eight. Alan sprang out of bed and hurried into the bathroom next door. Then he peered through the third door and exclaimed,

'My clothes are all laid out! This must be my dressing-room.'

What a joy to find ourselves for the first time in a home with trained servants. In Baghdad and New York we had had to search for accommodation.

'Sunlight is pouring in here too,' Alan shouted. 'It gives on to a back terrace and there's an enormous tree below buzzing with bees.'

I dressed hurriedly. So much to explore, and I decided I'd do that before seeing to the running of the house. But what a house to run! Suddenly I went cold inside. Starting all over again . . . everything strange, in a country in turmoil! Quickly I stifled such thoughts. Here it will be different and it's so beautiful, we'll be safe and I'll manage.

We sat down to an English breakfast. The children, propped up on cushions, were unnaturally silent as dark hands placed cereals and boiled eggs before them, then whisked away the plates. They ate everything without a murmur and I was relieved. Lawrence was still pale, listless and without appetite.

Hassin, the head 'boy' was waiting on us. He had greeted us with 'Bonjour, Monsieur!' and 'Bonjour Madame!' To my surprise he spoke literate French so we could communicate. The children stared up into his face, till Mavis, her delicate features stern, admonished them with,

'Get on with your breakfast!'

Nerves, I thought. A young north-country girl, so reserved, flung into this Arab world. Mavis, tall and slender, had been with us a fortnight but I still had no idea what she was thinking and the children did not yet turn to her spontaneously.

Hassin smiled at the children, showing startling white teeth in a pleasant, regular-featured face. He was big and broad-shouldered but his movements, as he hovered round the table,

The terrace.

were quiet and his big hands gentle. He was in no way frightening. The children smiled back at him.

'I must go now.' Alan kissed us good-bye and was gone.

'Come! Let's explore!' I cried. We knew the residential part of the house, though we had to search through the maze of rooms to find the way out. I wanted to enter the main part by that magnificent curved double stairway. The terrace ran the length of the building and was tiled from marble floor to the intricately painted ceiling. Five immense Italian-styled panelled doors in blue, white and yellow led into the Grand Salon.

Mavis gasped. It was the size of a banqueting hall and high up on the blue tiled walls oval windows of coloured arabesque glass cast jewelled patches on the white floor. The children skipped into them, danced and shouted 'Look at me! Look, Mummy! Look, Mavis!' Their faces, bare arms and legs were

13

bathed in colours of the rainbow.

'It's fantastic,' Mavis breathed and she was smiling at last, her pretty face alight. The children ran to her and she put her arms round them for the first time. 'It's a dream of a palace!' she exclaimed.

'And our home,' I added. The vast ceiling, thirty feet high at least, was of dark blue velvet with tiny bulbs like stars embedded in it. Hassin who had appeared beside me told us 'To change the bulbs we have to call the fire-brigade!' He stood relaxed, already one of us. Beside the Grand Salon were the official dining-room and drawing-room with blue tiles in a wavy pattern and inset ceilings in brilliant colours.

A car drew up. We hurried after Hassin back onto the terrace. A plump lady with reddish hair had arrived and behind her one child after another tumbled out. They scrambled up the stairs, chatting and laughing.

'Hullo, Mrs Williams! I'm Winnie Dismore. We've come to help you settle in. These are our children, Anna, Leo, Martin, Poppy and Jackie.' They smiled, hugged our two and shook my hand.

'We've been through the house,' I told them. 'Now show us the garden.'

The children were off down a long corridor, sweeping Mavis along with them. I followed with Mrs Dismore – Winnie I already called her.

'I do hope you'll like it here,' she was saying. 'We love it.' Such a warm person, I thought. We would be the only two home-based wives in the Consulate. It was encouraging to see that such a motherly, typically English woman with her snub nose and plain cotton frock was at home in these Arab surroundings; so evidently were her fair-haired, blue-eyed, long-legged children.

On the back terrace I was looking at Winnie but suddenly I could not see her chin. I blinked, rubbed my eyes . . . no . . . it couldn't be . . . it mustn't be . . . imagination, that was all . . . but then her mouth disappeared. Those frightening symptoms! But not now . . . The unpacking . . . the servants . . . Lawrence . . .

'Winnie,' I whispered, 'I'm a bit tired. I'd better rest.'

'Of course,' she assented. 'We'll take Mavis and the children home with us. Our house is on the beach, and we'll give them lunch. That'll give you a chance to sleep. Come everyone!'

All nine of them bundled into the car and, arms waving,

drove off. I walked slowly back to our room. A migraine in this lovely palace while outside sunlight dappled the garden! I flung myself on my bed and covered my face with my hands. A migraine here and strife throughout the country.

I lay rigid, eyes tight shut as the glittering zig-zags spread slowly outwards. It had all been too much. Lawrence's operation going wrong . . . how he screamed! The hospital sister shouted at me, 'Keep him down! Keep him still!' Lawrence struggling with the cot bars to reach me, sobbing, hot with fever. I clutched him, lifted him out. He clung to me 'Put him down! Keep him quiet!' How could I? I put him back and fled, his screams pursuing me. Ashamed, miserable, unable to cope, I ran away.

Zig-zags right across now.

Everything went wrong. The hospital kept him longer. Our flight to Tunis had to be cancelled. Our hotel rooms were taken. Where to go? All that luggage . . . a friend offered his house. Alan brings a sick Lawrence. He sobs, 'Mummy, why didn't you tell me about the hospital?' I reply, 'The sister told me not to, she would do it better herself. But in future I'll always tell you. I promise.' Mavis arrives, reserved, probably frightened. Libet cries, won't stay with her. Lawrence up but clings to me. We leave for Tunis. In Paris French airline on strike. Fly to Lisbon and there that first migraine. Terrifying. Zig-zags, splitting headache, vomiting. Alan out checking flights. I lie in bed in the hotel in the dark. Next morning better, but headache overwhelming. Fly to Madrid, change for Algiers. African heat hits us. Change again for Tunis. Greeted by press, flash-bulbs, French officials, prominent Maltese. I keep smiling, praying vomiting won't start again.

The zig-zags are over at last and now the headache starts up and grows fiercer every moment. I clutch my head. If only I had an icepack!

Why can't I stand things going wrong? Others do, but so soon after the strain of New York . . . Those parties, dinners, banquets, crowds, noise, airless rooms, faces and faces, always new. Too much food, too much drink, too many cigarettes, and I must always say the right thing, be official and smile, smile, always smile.

I lay still.

'My poor dear!' Alan was home for lunch. 'Do you want anything to eat?' My stomach heaved, I ran for the bathroom and kept running, sweaty and wretched all day long.

15

By evening my head felt better but I tried not to move. What a start to a new posting! What were the children doing? Was Mavis managing? I had not seen the cook.

Alan came in and sat on my bed. 'Don't look so worried. You'll be all right soon. It's not the end of the world.' He was holding local newspapers. 'Want to hear these? About our arrival?' He grinned.

'Go ahead,' I muttered.

'I am apparently a member of the *Jeunesse diplomatique*.' He was pleased with himself. 'But that fellow who tried to get a statement out of me, he's detailed all the impedimenta I was carrying, umbrella, mackintosh, binoculars, brief-case, the lot. Wanted to make a fool of me, and he describes me as large, smiling and greyish.' Alan laughed. 'So much for the 'young diplomat'!' I had to laugh too and immediately felt more normal.

Next morning I was up and eager to explore once more, with only the remains of a headache.

'Take it easy,' Alan advised as he left for the office.

Mavis and the children led me to our swimming pool. The children rode their tricycles down a wide alley lined with tall palms which ran through the centre of an eleven acre estate. Eleven acres all our own! It seemed incredible. The pool, a deep irrigation tank, was filled with brackish water. An iron ladder to which the children could cling, ran down the side. Mavis dived in cleanly and we could see her slim figure weaving in and out under the water like a fish. I lay in the cool water, recovering, the children in rubber rings splashing and giggling round me.

As we returned to the house, Hassin came running to meet us.

'Madame, Fatma, the cook's wife, is having a miscarriage. She's very feverish.'

'A doctor, Hassin! Who's the doctor?'

'Dr Tabone, but he lives in Tunis and has no car.' We were twelve miles from Tunis.

'I'll ring the Consulate.' Hassin put me through and Alan promised to send a car to fetch the doctor.

Hassin led me to a bare, whitewashed room where Ali, the cook and Fatma lived. The only piece of furniture was a huge bed, Ali's bed. Fatma lay on a mattress on the floor. I knelt beside her slight figure wrapped in sheets. Tears of pain streamed down from her huge black eyes. I pushed the mop of

16

Children on tricycles in our alleyway.

The author with Libet and Lawrence in the pool.

black hair off her face and held her hand tight. A short, stocky man stood motionless by the door, arms hanging at his side, shoulders hunched – Ali. There was shouting, the door flew open and in burst a crowd of screeching women, arms waving out of their white abas. From the village, I presumed. They pounced on Fatma and I left, colliding with the doctor, a plump, short Maltese who nodded and hurried into the room.

When he came out, he sighed. 'It's difficult treating Arab women. I'm not allowed to examine them or touch them or even look at them. I can only ask questions. She'll be all right though. She's lost her baby. I suspect that's what she wanted. Now she must rest, she's not strong.'

When he was gone, I called for elevenses, coffee and biscuits, to recover from the shock. Hassin began, 'Madame, the refrigerator has broken down and the milk has gone sour.' In this heat! The temperature was in the eighties.

'Oh Hassin, what shall we do? How do we get it repaired?'

'I'll call the man.' He smiled reassuringly. We had tea with lemon from our own orchard and the children had lemonade. As we were enjoying it, Hassin reappeared. 'Madame, the windmill that works the pump for the tank has broken.'

'And no more bathing! What do we do about that?'

'Joseph, the farmer, usually sees to it. He works part-time in the garden in exchange for the farm.'

'Then please ask him to do so.' I hoped Hassin would not reappear.

At lunch Alan said, 'I trust you're taking it easy.' I told him about Fatma, the refrigerator and the pump and I exclaimed, 'Hassin's an absolute treasure. He copes with everything.'

'Let's hope he copes successfully,' Alan retorted. 'Things are breaking down in the office too.' We were silent. Apparently the price of beauty was high.

After the siesta, Mavis suggested I go into the garden with the children while she unpacked. 'It's quiet and peaceful. It'll do your head good.'

At the side of the house, the garden wall was lined by a towering hedge of cactus, covered in soft baby cacti like tiny green balls. I picked one and threw it into Libet's pudgy hands. We started throwing the green balls at each other, the children prancing about. We collected handfuls of them. Then Libet began rubbing her hands, my palms itched, then Lawrence's. Our hands were covered in fine, almost invisible thorns.

'How stupid of me!' I exclaimed. 'Come children, we'll wash them away.' We washed and washed but we could not get the thorns out. Libet's round face had grown very red from the sun – both children were very fair – so I covered her face with baby oil. Evidently we had to suffer the itching, so out we went again. Libet was suddenly enveloped in a cloud of flies and they settled all over her face. I rushed her indoors and pushed her face into a basin of water, washing away flies and oil. Unconcerned, she still smiled as she peered up at me, her face redder than ever. I smothered it in powder.

Still itching, we set out on a tour of the garden. In the olive grove, I cried, 'Look children! A great mound. Let's climb up it.' From its top we looked down on row upon row of ancient olive trees, with silvery leaves, their old gnarled trunks twisted into weird, antediluvian shapes.

'*Descendez*! Get down! Quick!' Hassin was shouting, eyes wide with fear, waving his arms, '*Descendez*!' I seized the children's hands and, heart pounding, we climbed down.

'What is it, Hassin?'

'This is an old well, Madame. It's full of German and Italian ammunition. It's cemented over but the cement has cracked. It's not safe. Thank God you did not fall through.'

Enough adventure I decided. 'Come children. Let's go in.' Mother had not proved a very sensible guide and I told Mavis,

'It wasn't exactly quiet and peaceful out there but strangely it's cured my headache.'

As I recounted the day's adventures to Alan, I wondered, if that's what happens in one day, what will the future hold?

2

We settled into a routine and began our official life. The tank, pump and refrigerator were working again. Cleaning was easy even with only two servants. Hassin and Mahomet, our 'second boy' merely hosed down the tiled walls and marble floors. Mahomet was a short young man, very dark-skinned, with a thick mop of dark hair, heavy features and a long nose. As he swung the hose with muscular arms, he frowned up at me from under bushy brows and I could only smile back as he spoke nothing but Arabic.

I did accounts with Ali. The servants' quarters were grouped around an inner courtyard. I sat at the long kitchen table with Ali standing beside me. He informed me that Fatma was better and was recovering at her mother's, then he reeled off from memory a long list of purchases, giving amount and price, which I took down in a notebook and then paid him. I was astonished that he remembered all these half and quarter kilos, but Winnie assured me that illiterate Arabs have phenomenal memories. Does writing blunt the memory, I wondered?

'Of course,' Winnie went on, 'he gives himself a percentage. My cook takes less, but as the Consul-General's cook, Ali would lose face if he didn't add more. You have to accept that.' Other Tunisians trooped in and out of the house doing the laundry, the ironing or something else but I had not yet sorted them out.

Winnie took me in the consular car to Tunis. On the way I was admiring flamingos with their fragile, spindly legs and hook-like necks on a lake and, at its edge, a herd of camels that lifted their heads for each swallow, when the most abominable stench hit us.

'It's a sewer entering the lake.' Winnie informed me. We had to hold our noses and this we and our guests had to do every time we drove past.

In Tunis, 'This is the main square,' Winnie explained. 'It adjoins the Medina, the native quarter through that dark

21

archway. All goods for the Arab market pass through here.'
Men in striped ankle-length shirts wearing sheshias or cloth
wound round their heads wheeled cartloads of melons and
tomatoes; others, thongs across their foreheads taking the
weight, stooped under great loads of vegetables; two men
balanced trays of large fish on their heads and were followed by
a boy wheeling a pram full of eggs. As we crossed the square we
dodged heavily loaded horses and donkeys trotting in and out
of the stream of cars. The noise was terrific, yet inside some
empty barrels men lay fast asleep. 'Weary and burdened'
crossed my mind.

French officers in smart, white uniforms and stiff, round
kepis strolled nonchalantly through it all. A group chatted in
the middle of the square, ignoring swerving cars and cursing
drivers.

'The masters,' Winnie said. 'The Tunisians are the under-
dogs. They claim that according to the Treaties they have a
right to 'Internal Sovereignty'.'

'Sovereignty!' I thought. Hardly! They're so primitive!

Winnie pointed upward. There, dominating the whole
scene, including the French officers, was our Union Jack at the
top of the British Consulate-General, an imposing, white
building beside the gaping mouth of the Arab souk. I imagined
the new Consul-General (Alan had just been promoted) at his
desk, surveying this chaotic world below.

Someone plucked at my sleeve. I turned and gaped. I was
staring straight into the dark face of a man without a nose – just
a hole! I stood rooted, shocked. A crowd of beggars behind him
displayed horrifying deformities. I fell back, pulled my sleeve
away, turned and with a sickly feeling inside, ran into a large,
glass-fronted French shop skirting the square. French ladies in
elegant, light suits and high-heeled sandals were tripping
around the counters. In Baghdad I never got used to the
beggars. I tried not to feel their pain, their hunger and
isolation. Why should they suffer so? A kind God? Hardly! I
envied Winnie who, though she followed me, chatted on,
taking them in her stride. I'll do all my shopping in French
shops, I decided, though conscious and ashamed that I was
running away.

The children were slipping easily into this strange world,
though Lawrence still shouted with glee, when running
through endless arches, he recognized his own room. They
began morning lessons in the shade of a big tree and I could not

resist peeping at them and listening. I heard Lawrence laying down the law, 'I know that four plus four makes eight, so now let's do four plus four makes nine.' Mavis smothered a laugh. Later when she showed them pictures of Africa, Libet said with her gentle smile, 'I suppose in central Africa Daddy also wore no clothes.' I crept away.

The children quickly learnt to say *Bonjour* and *Merci* but Hassin's nine-year old sister only spoke Arabic. Hedia, bare-footed and woolly-headed, pranced out of Hassin's two-roomed bungalow in the garden. The children scrambled into an enormous banyan tree whose five huge low branches leant outwards, forming a big cavity. As they all pushed each other, Libet shouted, '*Schweya! schweya!*' (gently! gently!) and some-thing that sounded like 'Mind-your-ears' which made Arabs nod and smile. Lawrence only made deep, guttural noises at them.

They played together till Hedia threw a stone at a little grey cat. Libet seized her arm and cried, 'No! No.'

'Yes! Yes!' Hedia laughed and to tease Libet, struck Hassin's puppy on the head with a stick. I intervened and stopped her.

With tears in her eyes, Libet sighed, 'I wish Arabs were not cruel to animals!'

I put my arm round her. 'I know, darling. We'll try and stop Hedia.' But I had to tear myself away and get on with my own job.

We gave a cocktail party to meet the consular staff. I had couches and chairs brought on to the front terrace for I could not bear to be indoors when the evening was balmy, the air herb-scented and while the wind sang in the trees. After New York's airless rooms I revelled in this outdoor world. I felt sure our guests felt the same.

Alan and I waited for them, seated on the vast terrace, its colourful ceiling ribbed and embossed, and so high that, owing to the echo, we had to shout at each other. Our guests mostly Maltese, came up the great stairway, dressed in neat, white suits. There were two Vellas, AP so-called, the Pro-Consul, short, grey-haired with a huge stomach, and Vincent, the accountant, tall, dark with a wife and several tall daughters. The only English member was Joan Cavell, Alan's secretary. They seemed a pleasant lot but before I could make out who was who, the lights went out.

'The tramways have started a twenty-four hour strike,' AP Vella announced, 'so the electric light will be cut off till ten tonight.' I did not see the connection but we all nodded.

The last rays of the sun lit up refreshments and drinks, but when the sun set, we sat in darkness talking to barely visible shadows till our guests decided it was time to leave. I gazed up at the large moon, drank in the warm, scented air. 'Alan,' I exclaimed, 'they were great, taking it all in their stride. I like your Consulate staff.'

We went to bed by the light of one candle as Hassin could not find any more. Mavis was caught above the kitchen courtyard and, as she later told us, 'I looked down and two white eyes glared up at me. I was scared and was about to run when a deep voice said, 'Mahomet'. His dark face was invisible!'

Alan was busy calling on the French officials, beginning with the Resident-General, the man who ruled Tunisia, reputedly with a rod of iron, General Viscount de Hautecloque. He sounded forbidding. Next Alan was taken to the Bey, the nominal ruler of Tunisia, in his Carthage Palace.

When Alan returned for lunch and kissed me, he smelled of perfume. 'From the Bey's hand,' he told us, 'and it won't wash off.'

'How did it go?'

'Well, nothing romantic,' he began. 'I was introduced by de Choiseul, a long-nosed French aristocrat, French chief of Protocol, and General Tahar Maoui, the Tunisian Chief of Protocol, a vast man, with rimless glasses and a moustache. His main job, I'm told, is to place his great bulk between the Bey and any would-be assassin. I was given six instructions: to wear a dark suit . . .'

Lawrence interrupted, 'Why, Daddy? Why dark?'

'Dark is more formal than a lighter colour – to make three bows, one on entering, one half way to the throne and one just before shaking hands . . .' Libet giggled. 'To refrain from crossing my legs or feet . . .'

'But why, Daddy? Why shouldn't you cross your feet?'

'Showing the soles of your feet or shoes is insulting to Arabs. Just you remember that, young man . . . to speak only when spoken to.' He glared at the children. 'To make three bows on the way out and not to turn my back on the Bey.'

'Did you do all that?' Lawrence was wide-eyed.

'Yes, and I must have looked damn funny! All went well except that the Bey came further to meet me than I expected and my third bow nearly caught him on the nose.' We enjoyed that.

'What's the Bey like?' I asked.

'He's slight but dignified, about seventy-five, white hair and beard, dark glasses, white suit, no tie. He would only speak Arabic though Choiseul says he speaks perfect French. He was polite but cool. He's the only Tunisian authority left. The French are threatening to depose him if he doesn't knuckle under. (Poor devil! I don't envy him.) They've already deposed the Sultan of Morocco. We sat in a stiff row on one side of the throne, the Tunisian officials on the other. After ten minutes of stilted conversation we were out again.' The children breathed deep with excitement, while I sighed, poor old man.

We were interrupted by Mr Dismore rushing in and blurting out, 'Le Breton has been drowned – the American Vice-Consul!'

'How dreadful!' I cried. 'What happened?'

'The children, I mean the new American Consul-General's children, insisted on bathing and got into trouble.'

'But they only arrived this morning!' Alan exclaimed.

'Yes. Le Breton went in to help and was carried away. The warning flags were out. We all know the sea is dangerous if there is any movement at all and le Breton did warn them but, with waves only four feet high and the children experienced swimmers, the parents let them go in. Immediately they were knocked off their feet. Le Breton got the two girls out but when he returned for the younger boy, he was carried away. The boy scrambled out. When they reached Le Breton, they tried artificial respiration for five hours but he's dead.'

I felt for the Hughes family. What a tragic start to a new posting! As we had come from the States I longed to help. I rang Mrs Hughes and suggested sending the children to us. She was controlled, business-like and agreed. I rang Winnie and asked, 'Please send the children over. That might help.' They came immediately.

Sixteen-year old Anna took charge. 'Martin, you, Poppy and Jackie go into the garden and play there with Libet and Lawrence. Don't come in here.' We were seated in our 'hareem' drawing-room. 'We'll send the boy out to you when he comes.' The children scuttled off. 'Leo, you and I will look after the two girls. How old are they?'

'Thirteen and fifteen, I believe.'

I went to meet them and brought them in, Mary fair, plump

25

and apparently self-confident, Judy thin and dark following her sister. I knew how shattered and guilty they must feel and I started to put my arms round them but they looked such sophisticated young women in their well-cut cotton suits, hair permed, lips and nails red and this made me as controlled as they appeared to be. Anna quickly stroked down her own unruly mop of hair as she stood up.

'I'm so glad you've come. This is my sister, Leo.'

Leo, shy, conscious of her crumpled cotton frock, hesitated then offered her hand. There was silence as they stared, not exactly approvingly, at each other.

'My brother, Rusty, is ill and hasn't come.' Mary explained and then again, silence.

'Sit down, girls,' I said. They sat, Mary and Judy side by side, stiff-backed, children still but already braced to face the world, putting up a screen like young diplomats.

Anna swallowed and pulled herself together. 'You'll find it strange here at first, but if we can help . . . What school have you been to?'

Should I leave them or stay? The frown on Leo's face and the strain on Anna's kept me there.

'Would you like to bathe? There's a pool here.' Leo suddenly burst out. The American girls stiffened, stared at her, Judy's lips trembling. 'Oh, I'm sorry . . . of course . . . wasn't thinking . . . forgive me!'

Anna stretched out a hand towards Judy but then let it drop. Instead she jumped up. 'Let's go into the garden.'

'I'll call you,' I said, 'when tea is ready.' At least, I thought, we're helping them to pass the time and only time will allow them to forget.

They were not allowed to forget. The press suggested that American children are uncontrollable and that these had killed Le Breton. However, a doctor at the hospital, a friend of Alan's, told him that the post-mortem showed that Le Breton had had a heart attack and he had probably suffered from a weak heart without knowing it.

'Mr Hughes is terribly upset,' Alan reported. 'He fainted as he went up the steps to call on the Resident-General. One misfortune after another!'

'How humiliating for him,' I exclaimed.

'His wife is furious, he says, because he wants to get out, to resign and go home.'

'And ruin his career, his future?' She must be the stronger of the two, I thought. Alan went to the Memorial Service for Le Breton and then on to the airport to see the coffin off to the States. It was harrowing for the whole Hughes family.

'I've decided to call on the clergyman who took the service,' Alan went on. 'I'll ask him to convince Mr Hughes that the Consuls here all wish him to stay and that it will all blow over. I'll also try and persuade the press to publish the autopsy results. That will exonerate the children.'

It did blow over and though I had only met those young, sophisticated girls, I felt close to the whole family. Their first days had been even more harrowing than ours!

3

Alan announced, 'It's the British Legion Gala tonight. They're raising money for their charities.' I caught my breath. Here it comes . . . from now on, day in, day out, one event after another. My job – to receive and to be received. Then quickly I told myself – nonsense, socializing was deadly in New York, so I'm panicking here, a Pavlov reaction, but with swimming and the garden I'll manage.

But I bathed and dressed in silence; the new white cotton evening dress dotted with tiny black stars I had longed to wear, I now hardly noticed, but Alan was humming to himself.

The Gala proved to be out of doors, not in an airless hall. My spirits rose. Alan and I were seated at either end of a central table with other officials, mostly elderly, bald men in white suits. The sky was clear and wide, a big moon and brilliant stars shone down on us while a cool breeze fanned our faces. I knew no one and I did not catch any names but the orchestra was loud so there was no need to talk. I leant back in my chair, listened with pleasure to the chatter in French and looked round.

The girls were very feminine in their long brightly-coloured gowns, with their big, expressive eyes and shiny, blue-black hair. They swung rhythmically back and forth as they clung to their partners on the dance floor. I wish I could dance to, I thought, but my rôle was to preside and be seen.

Most people were speaking Italian and I realized why when the guest singer was wheeled onto the stage, an Italian film star, Luciano Tajoli, a polio victim. As he lifted his face to that dark sky and sang, his sad, sugary tenor moved us deeply. His deformity forgotten, together with him we mourned for the suffering of the whole world. When he stopped we were left with a feeling of great beauty. There was a roar of '*Encore! Encore!*' He sang again and again and each time we were carried away, filled with nostalgia.

Later he joined our table. I found it hard to look at his

28

deformed body. The audience rushed up to greet him; they surrounded him, pushing, pressing up against him. Suddenly his wheelchair swung back and he fell into the crowd. I jumped up. Such a frail body . . . but three policemen ran up, thrust people aside and raised him. He was unhurt and joined us again, smiling triumphantly.

The policemen stationed themselves behind his chair and shouted, '*Dansez, Bon Dieu, dansez*! *Allez-y*!' (Get on. Dance for God's sake!) The crowd danced but always round our table. I tapped out the rhythm with my foot as we sat on and on into the night. Neither Choiseul nor Alan knew which of them was the senior and should, according to protocol, leave first. Finally when my watch showed two in the morning, exhausted, I got up and we left.

That was amusing, I thought, and it's a promising start.

The Maltese formed the greater part of the British colony. The 'United Maltese Societies' greeted us with a reception. I put on a sleeveless, white dress and a new flower arrangement on wires that clasped the top of my head.

In a low-ceilinged hall to the strains of 'God save the Queen' we were led to the top of a long table. Our hosts, all men in neat suits and ties, stood on either side. Alan had warned me that I would be the only woman present but added that the Maltese would be offended if I did not turn up. We sat down. They did not speak English and were shy of talking at all. Their President told me in French that these men were all veterans of the Second World War. I looked down the table. They were humble folk of varying hues, some with Arab features, yet here in Tunis, they had volunteered to fight for us, British. They risked their lives, were prepared to die! My war years in London were still a painful memory and I was filled with a warm feeling of gratitude. I hoped their loyalty had been officially recognized.

It was hot, we were deafened by the efforts of the 'Duke of Connaught's Own (Brass) Band', and we had to drink sweet champagne. My head began to throb. Alan rose to speak, and in French. He was out of practice. As he rushed along, I thought he must be feeling the heat too. I tried to smile my thanks when I was presented with a large bouquet but I felt sick. Another migraine? No! But was it or not? There were no zig-zags, just this painful bar across the forehead. I was desperate to get away. At last Alan got up. I clung to his arm as we marched out to the band's last strains.

Back home, I tore the flower arrangement off my head. The throbbing stopped. It had been pressing too hard on my temples! I flung the flowers angrily into the wastepaper basket. Alan laughed.

Maltese celebrations followed each other. On the Maltese National Day we attended a *Te Deum* in the twin-towered Cathedral of St Vincent de Paul with its gold mosaic-studded façade. I was haunted by fear of a migraine and my first thought was, would there be fresh air and space? In the Cathedral the ceiling was high and the doors were left open. I relaxed.

Three chairs had been placed in front, one for Alan, one for the French Resident-General's representative and one for the Bey's. There they stood, the first two bare-headed, the Tunisian, General Tahar Maoui, his head covered out of respect by his silk-tasselled sheshia. I liked to see them together, representatives of rival nations and rival religions, especially after what we had heard of Tunisians attacking white 'colons' (French settlers). Here Frenchman and Tunisian stood together with Alan between them.

This pleasant train of thought was shattered by Archbishop Perrin of Carthage. He had praised the Maltese for their piety but then, as an example of their heroism, he launched into a description of how they swam out at night to ships of the invading Moslem fleet – here his voice rang out – 'and cut the throats of the infidels.' The last words were flung straight at Tahar Maoui, who seemed unmoved, however.

After the service we all dashed through the traffic across the road where Alan laid a wreath on the Unknown Soldier's grave. Then we took leave of the officials and drove to the Maltese Society rooms for more sickly champagne where we sat under a large Union Jack and a portrait of the Queen while Alan made another speech. Driving home I remarked, 'The Maltese are easy to get on with but they're darker than Tahar Maoui who has a white skin.'

'So has the Bey,' Alan said. 'The original Tunisians were Berbers – white-skinned nomads.' So why look down on them? I wondered.

As we neared home we noticed car drivers pointing to our house and laughing. Drivers invariably glanced up at the flag to see which way the wind was blowing. We looked up. The flag was dancing, up and down, up, jerk, and down again.

'What the Hell?' Alan cried. 'Cutajah, hurry up!' Cutajah

30

was our Maltese driver.

Alan jumped out of the car, ran into the house and up to the roof. I ran after him. We found Lawrence and Mahomet pulling on the ropes, hoisting the flag up and down, rocking with laughter.

'What do you think you're doing?' Alan demanded.

'Playing,' Lawrence replied. Alan turned on him.

'You do not play with the Union Jack. It's disrespectful. The flag represents Britain. It shows that this house is part of Britain and no one can touch us here, can harm us. If it's lowered, at half mast, it means someone is dead. People might thing the Queen had died. Do you understand?' and he added, 'In any case it is Government property.' He shook his head at Mahomet. The two came down, eyes lowered, in silence.

The Maltese held their annual party in our garden. In the morning I heard unintelligible shouting; men were putting up trestle tables, stalls and bunting. At three in the afternoon a special train brought about five hundred Maltese to the station at the bottom of our garden, called *Consulate Anglais* – an official stop on the track from Tunis to Carthage. We watched the Maltese pour out, form into a procession and march down the alley behind the drums and brass of our friend the 'Duke of Connaught's Own band.'

The women, all in black, with weather-beaten, wrinkled faces, settled on folding chairs under the trees where they remained, hands folded in their laps.

'They don't seem to be having much fun,' I said to Dizzie, as Mr Dismore was generally called.

'To sit quietly in the fresh air, far from the heat of the city, in the shade of beautiful trees is luxury for them.'

'Are they that poor?' He smiled ruefully and I sighed. They had pleasant, serene faces. Was it resignation that gave them dignity? They beckoned to Libet. She skipped up and beamed as they stroked her yellow curls.

The men handed round soft drinks and cakes, then hovered in groups downing beer. The children held races down the alley. First they bunched up in a brig crowd, then they were off, lashing out, knocking each other down, yelling and laughing. The crowd cheered them on '*Allez! Allez!*' then '*Bravo! Bravo!*' They clapped and all was good-natured fun. Our children clung to Mavis, too shy to join in with these toughies. The children then stood open-mouthed as they watched a conjuror. Libet bought a ticket in a tombola saying to Mavis, 'I

31

always win' and she did – a lamp.

Alan addressed the company from the front terrace. His voice over a faulty loud-speaker reverberated, '*Mes amis . . . amis . . . is . . . ,*' grew more and more strident, rose to a high-pitched screech and all the babies burst into loud wailing. Their mothers hushed them even louder and excited children rushed terrified to their parents. Quickly Alan finished his speech, the echoes died down and calm was restored.

In the evening we left the young to enjoy themselves and went indoors. We could hear the thump of feet as they danced foxtrots and waltzes on the front terrace to the tunes on a radiogram. As our clocks struck eight the band burst into 'God Save The Queen' and our guests departed. Dizzie appeared later, 'Well, you'll be glad to hear it was a great success.'

4

Next morning Alan and I came out onto the terrace for the dismal task, as we thought, of clearing up.

'It's incredible!' Alan exclaimed. Everything was back to normal. 'The trestle tables, the stalls, they're all gone!'

I ran to the flower beds. 'Look! My precious freesias and zinnias are all intact! and I thought those children toughies, and look, there's not a sweet paper or any rubbish anywhere!' Five hundred people had left in the dark the night before and now, early next morning, not a trace left.

'Good for them!' Alan exclaimed.

I smiled to myself. These first events had passed and no migraine. They had been out-of-doors and I could manage that, or so I thought.

Before we were officially accepted we had to attend the French welcome-dinner in our honour and to call on our consular colleagues.

I felt both excitement and the usual nervous flutter (plunging into the unknown) as I stood before the mirror in my black taffeta evening dress with its tight bodice and long, billowing skirt which swished as I moved.

As we swept into the grounds of what proved to be another Beylical Palace, sentries presented arms. We stepped through graceful arches with long vistas but we saw nothing as elegant as our Grand Salon. It must rankle with the French, I thought complacently, that we British live in the more spectacular palace. I donned the diplomatic mask as we entered the reception hall and became the Consul-General's wife.

De Boissesson, the Minister replacing General de Hautecloque, greeted us. Rotund, bald-headed with a pleasant, kindly round face, he introduced us to a glittering gathering of French officials in smart uniforms, chests covered in medals and elegant dignitaries in evening dress. Their wives in long, backless gowns, displayed embarrassing décolletages. Most were titled, though I understood that titles were banned in

France. But a title is not something people part with lightly, I supposed; it turns a nobody into a somebody.

'Tunis must be a haven for the fallen aristocracy,' Alan muttered. For the next few years, I realized, we would be mixing almost exclusively with these socialites.

We sat down to table, De Boissesson on my left. The conversation, in French, darted back and forth, clever, witty, concerning art, music, and the theatre – politics were evidently taboo. I spoke French, as I thought, fluently but as guests parried and cut with lightning speed, my 'When we ... ' dangled unheeded in the air.

The women competed with the men, laughing coquettishly, with graceful gestures, gazing up into the men's faces. But all the time the guests were conscious of De Boissesson, as though they held court around him, their careers at stake, while he sat silent, plump fingers tapping the table.

The Americans and the Greeks were officially honoured at the same time.

Mrs Hughes, whom I had not met before, sat opposite me, but she made no special gesture towards me. Tall, angular, with a determined chin, she looked an ambitious woman who would promote her husband on every occasion. But even her penetrating '*En Amérique* ... ' failed to cut into the conversation.

Mr Hughes, further down the table, needed encouragement, I decided; he drooped. His shoulders sagged, as did his moustache, but every time I looked his way, his blue eyes smiled back.

The Greek lady, very feminine, watched us trying to edge into the talk and her lips twitched with amusement. As for her husband, he expressed himself exclusively with thick, black eyebrows, that shot up and down, together or separately in a most intriguing way.

We foreigners gave up trying to contribute our thoughts and concentrated on the rich, highly flavoured food. Wine flowed and the conversation turned to absent colleagues. I murmured 'miau' to myself at the subtly expressed spitefulness.

As we drove home Alan asked, 'Did you enjoy it?'

'Yes. It was fun but all this glamour . . .' I was thinking of those beggars in Tunis. Differences there always will be, I realized, but they should not be so acute.

Alan's Humber Super Snipe had at last arrived. We set out on our courtesy calls, flag flying from the car's shining bonnet.

Police and the military saluted. I grinned at Alan.

Calling on more senior Consuls-General was a useful way of getting to know them individually. We started with the Turk, Uzel, and sat on his marble terrace, the lights of Tunis twinkling below. He was a short, stubby man with a large, bald head. His wife, a monumental figure, answered in monosyllabic, halting French, but the Consul-General spoke it fluently. He enlightened us on the local scene and painted a grim picture.

'The situation is dangerous. Martial law, demonstrations banned, leaders of the Néo-Destour, the nationalist party, arrested.' He waved short, stubby fingers. 'General de Hautecloque shows no mercy. He let loose the Foreign Legion in the Cap Bon area and they massacred the locals, women, children ... two hundred dead and numerous wounded. The whole country is in a state of mutiny, farms attacked, assassinations.' My heart beat fast. Shades of Baghdad with that ever-present undercurrent of tension, only here the French and not we, were the target. Nevertheless I peered into the night. Was someone lurking out there? The Consul-General went on. 'The French are going in for see-saw politics – concession, repression, concession, repression. They say the communists are back of it all.' Communists? I doubted it. In Baghdad, when the hungry filled the streets demanding bread, it was the communists. Now here ... perhaps to gain our support ... they know Britain's paranoid fear of a communist threat to the Mediterranean.

The Consul-General leant across to Alan and whispered, 'De Hautecloque has been recalled. I heard it today. We'll see what the next man will do. It's difficult. The Néo-Destour agree that France should retain Foreign Affairs and Security. Paris agrees, but the *colons* refuse to consider any concessions. They descend on Paris, talk of a communist threat, Paris panics and all concessions are cancelled. The answer is murder!' I shivered. He leant back, folded his hands over his stomach and announced, 'When we ruled North Africa there was law and order.' I had forgotten that for some three hundred years Tunisia had been part of the great Turkish Empire. This Turk looked smug.

As we left I shook him warmly by the hand. I had imagined Turks to be uncouth, primitive.

'That was useful,' Alan remarked. 'He knows what's going on.'

We exchanged calls with the Hugheses. There was quite a

35

gathering at their house.

Mrs Hughes held forth. 'We don't know anyone here and it was that lonely for my poor girls, but now they've met two teenage sons of the Beylical family. Mary, my eldest, goes cycling in the park with one of them.' I was 'hipped', as Alan called it. 'Don't know anyone' after I had introduced them to the Dismore girls! Evidently only young men were welcome and only royal at that!

Mary was only sixteen and Arab boys were not used to going out with unveiled, unaccompanied girls. 'Do you think it safe for Mary to go out alone with this Arab boy?' I ventured to ask when the others had left.

'Of course. Why not? Arabs are just as good as us.' A reproach from an American to a colonialist Britisher! But their customs are different, I thought.

When Calista, as I now called her, returned my call, on leaving she shook my hand and said, 'Thank you so much for your kind visit.' I was annoyed; the woman was not thinking what she was saying and she talked in set phrases. Obviously I meant nothing to her. Then I told myself – I'm being mean and petty. She's distraught by the drowning. She's starting a new life in a new place and needs our support. But I still felt a little 'hipped'.

We had now performed our first duties and I felt immersed in the Tunisian scene. The rest of the world hardly existed. Coming back home to our palace, I felt secure. We were isolated, several miles from even the little village of La Marsa and I liked it that way. I could unwind. London wasn't watching and there was no one to criticize. I could be myself.

Alan phoned from the Consulate. 'A whole lot of naval chaps are to spend two hours here. I've got to take them to see Carthage. Then I'll bring them home for tea.'

'What naval chaps?'

'The First Sea Lord, the Permanent Under-Secretary, an Admiral, the Under-Secretary at the War office and his secretary.'

Chaps! The First Sea Lord . . . so much for our isolation! Strange how disappointed I felt. We were not completely on our own, of course not. I wandered out onto our beautiful terrace. I stood in the midst of that blaze of colour and thought – this isn't mine. This home isn't ours. It's all Government property, and it came out suddenly – I too am Government property! Then, quickly dismissing that nervous flutter welling up again, I went to tell Ali to prepare a sumptuous tea, a real spread, and I instructed Hassin to lay it out on the front terrace.

He hesitated. 'Is it wise, Madame?'

'Yes. Why not? It's the most impressive spot and we've had tea there before. But punctually, please Hassin. It must be ready by four.' Meals had not been punctual, the servants having little sense of time.

At four Hassin hovered on the terrace while at the foot of the stairway I greeted the tall, large men in neat, dark suits, with hearty voices. Alan, eager to impress them, pointed out the marble tablet on the wall, 'Here . . . Field Marshal Viscount Alexander of Tunis . . . established his HQ after XVIII Army corps under his command liberated Tunis 7 May 1943.'

'You're living in a monument,' boomed the Admiral. We mounted the stairway. I stopped, bewildered. On the terrace the long table was black. What had happened? I hurried up. A plague of flies! Every plate of sandwiches, cakes, biscuits was covered with solid lumps of flies. What was I to do? I seized Hassin's cloth and waved it frantically.

'Quick Hassin, more cloths. Call Mahomet.' Together we beat off the flies while the hearty voices died down and our guests drew away from the table.

'Please sit down. Do,' I urged. Our first visit from London and this would happen! While Mahomet stood guard against more flies, I seized a plateful of sandwiches, now free of flies, and thrust it at the guests, talking the while to distract them. 'How was Carthage? Was it interesting?' Reluctantly they started nibbling at the edges. The Admiral answered in monosyllables. Hassin offered him a cream-covered chocolate cake, Ali's best. Slowly he put out a hand and took a piece; others felt obliged to follow suit. Below my chatter there was silence.

They were in a hurry to catch a plane but I insisted they should see the Grand Salon. I must blot out memory of the flies, I thought. Impressed, they gazed at the exotic ceiling and walls and fingered the coloured tiles. Before leaving Alan had to show them to the bathroom. He led them through a door but a moment later, they all filed back again. Alan whispered to me, 'Can't find the way.' I pointed to another door and they filed through it.

When they had left I asked Hassin, 'Why so many flies?'

'The wind, Madame. It depends on the wind.'

When Alan returned from seeing the VIPs off at the airport, he explained, 'I haven't been to that part of the house yet.' He sighed. 'We seem to have messed things up completely today!'

I was tired, yet that night I could not get to sleep. At last as light began creeping in, I dropped off.

Libet pranced into the room and woke me.

'It's Sunday and only six o'clock!' I protested. 'Go away!'

She wound soft arms round my neck and whispered, 'I don't want to annoy you ever, ever.' I looked at her slanting blue eyes and high cheek bones, her whole face delicately browned – a ripe peach Winnie had called her – and I murmured, 'I'm sorry, it's those beastly flies.' Then I burst out, 'Their faces!'

Alan stirred and said, 'Just imagine what they're saying in London!' and we started laughing.

5

It did not just start raining. A wall of slanting water cut off the front terrace from the soaking world beyond, while enormous rain drops bounced up off the stairways. But inside all was excitement. We were giving our first lunch party for the Wakefield-Harreys who were staying with us. Cyril Wakefield-Harrey was Consul-General in Algiers.

Cyril and Margaret had braved the rain and the *Fellaghas*, as the nationalist fighters were called. Margaret laughed it off. 'The car almost swam through the floods only to skid violently over all the mud,' and Cyril added, 'Even the camels crouched, heads down, behind the Bedouin tents and looked more disconsolate than ever.' The Wakefield-Harreys were evidently our kind of Foreign Service people – ready for adventure – but I knew the tension under which they lived. Algeria was in a worse state of ferment than Tunisia. I hoped to offer them rest, as well as entertainment.

The luncheon was to be held in the main part of the Residence, in the drawing and dining-rooms.

'Is this wise, Madame?' Hassin asked.

'Yes!' Nervousness made me impatient. 'Why not? There are no flies here, surely!'

He shook his head and stared out of the window. 'It's raining very hard, Madame.'

'Yes. But better get the drinks out, Hassin.'

'Very hard. Listen to it hammering on the roof.'

'Yes, yes. But hurry, Hassin. The drinks.'

The drawing-room was bright with blue, pink and red bougainvillia, plumbago and oleander. The long table fitted perfectly into the long dining-room with bunches of freesias running down its whole length. The silver shone, the cut glass sparkled and I donned a new floral silk dress.

I was ready, my stomach tight. The guests arrived, headed by Mr and Mrs Leland-Smith. He was an ex-State Department Officer, now settled in Tunis, a pale, thin man with thick

Official drawing-room.

glasses. She was French-born of a family from Reunion. They were useful friends for Alan, to keep him in touch with local opinion.

The Mediterranean produces stunning women and Mrs Smith was one such. She sailed in, shimmering in green silk. Black, glossy hair fell over her shoulders, contrasting with an almost transparently white skin. Long earrings swung from perfectly-shaped ears and bangles jingled as she joked and laughed. She must be at least fifty, I thought, but she outshone us all. They lived in an Arab-style house surmounted by a great dome – a perfect setting for her. The men crowded round, vying in wit as we sipped our sherries.

Hassin flung open the dining-room door and with a grave bow, announced, 'Madame is served.'

I led the ladies in, chatting as we went, Mrs Smith express-

Official dining-room

ing outrageous views. 'In Reunion life was good. But when slavery was abolished, well, you can imagine, the family couldn't go on living like that!' She made a grimace. 'They had to leave.' But she gave the warmest of smiles to Hassin as he slid her chair under her. Slavery and such a good heart. . .

When we were seated, plonk! a huge drop of rain fell on the table in front of me. Hassin hurried forward to mop it up. We drank our bouillon. Plonk! Splash! heavy rain drops formed a wet patch on the table-cloth. Hassin quickly laid a table napkin over it. Glancing up I saw a wet patch on the ceiling.

In the middle of the meat course, a cold drop slid down my

neck. I started. Then another and another. I dabbed my face with my handkerchief and drew it casually across my neck. Hassin could do nothing. My shoulders were soaked but the flowered dress served as camouflage. No one noticed.

Our guests were talking with animation, downing the white wine, then the red. I smiled and listened, mopping away while Hassin hurried with the dishes and Mahomet whisked away the plates. With the desert I was shivering; the rain was cold.

Drops began to fall further down the table. One fell on Mrs Smith's hand. She looked up.

'Gracious! Its raining!' Drops were falling on other guests.

'So it is!' They cried. Exclamations all round.

'A real Tunisian Party!' Mrs Smith laughed, her cheeks pink from the wine. 'Eating in a palace under the rain! What an experience!' That made the others laugh too.

I led them out into the drawing-room and Hassin closed the doors quickly behind us.

I sat tense, my dress sagging with rain-water while the guests drank coffee still joking, in no hurry to leave. When they finally departed, Alan exclaimed, 'Masha, you're wet through! I had no idea. Quick, run and change.'

'Full marks,' Cyril laughed. 'You bore it without flinching.' I hurried away. In the passage Hassin remarked, 'That roof always leaks when it rains heavily.' Now I understood what he had meant. We placed a bucket under the leak.

Hassin reported more leaks so we rushed around with receptacles, the children fascinated by the loud 'pinging' as heavy drops resounded in the buckets. We climbed on to the roof. A lake covered almost half. Alan cleared choked gutters and built six-inch dams with bits of plaster. He's enjoying it, I thought, playing with plaster and water.

For tea we collected in the drawing-room on the hareem side of the house. Plonk! Plonk! Rain drops began to fall off the central chandelier. Next, fireworks flew out from it and we were plunged into darkness. No lights throughout the house. We sat, exchanging outlandish Foreign Service reminiscences till Hassin brought us each a candlestick.

The children seized theirs and started running down the long, spooky, corridors, then rushing back to us. Suddenly a scream! Candle in hand, I ran towards it. The children stood gazing at Hassin's large bulk cowering against the wall, his face grey in the candlelight. Mahomet beside him peered into the dark on either side.

'What's happened?'

'It's Hassin. We ran up and now he's like that,' Libet whispered, clinging to me.

'Hassin, what's the matter?' He smiled wanly and glanced quickly over his shoulder.

'Madame . . . ' and he fell silent. I remembered how I once came suddenly up behind him, in broad daylight, and he had started up with a great shudder. When he saw me, with that same nervous smile, he had muttered, 'Evil spirits.' The children had startled him. *Djinn* were evidently very real for him and Mahomet, especially in these dark crannies, lit by a flicker of candlelight.

'Leave Hassin and Mahomet,' I told the children. 'They're tired. They've had a hard day. Come!'

'Mahomet can stand on his head on the kitchen table!' Lawrence volunteered.

'Not now, darling. Come!' I led them away with a nod at Hassin and Mahomet. 'Get yourselves some coffee,' I advised.

We dined by candlelight, the servants hurrying, silent, withdrawn. The whites of Mahomet's eyes suddenly fixed themselves on the dark dome above us. We all looked up too. It was eerie. Darkness pressed down onto my back. I could almost feel something hovering over my shoulder.

With relief we withdrew into the small drawing-room. I brought out a pack of cards and, with the children in bed, we played sevens. Sitting close together round the table, candles lighting up smiling faces, each with a glass of wine, we argued and joked as we played. Cyril and Margaret eagerly scooped up centimes, Mavis rocked with laughter as she paid up, Alan leant back, relaxed. This is my kind of life, I thought. Friends gathered together, not all those social engagements; yet so many people envied me my public life. It was ironic.

The Wakefield-Harreys were given a bucket for the night, just in case.

'How did you sleep?' I asked them at breakfast next morning. They exchanged glances and laughed.

'The bucket wasn't broad enough,' Margaret said. 'We kept having to edge out of the bed as the middle was awash!' Cyril was limping; he suffered from rheumatism.

'I'm terribly sorry!' I exclaimed. 'And with your rheumatism!' He shrugged the matter aside. Alan persuaded them to stay another day till the floods subsided, saying,

'It's no fun if you break down. You don't speak Arabic – we

don't either. A crowd of Arabs invariably materializes out of nowhere with primitive ideas about the distribution of wealth.'

When they were finally leaving, I was full of apologies. 'What a time you've had! I am sorry!' But Margaret assured me, 'It's all been fun. I feel much better for it. I haven't laughed so much for a long time.'

The sun was out now. It raised a rainbow haze from the soaking vegetation and a family of frogs was prancing about in the pond that had formed at the bottom of the stairway.

6

The rain continued to beat down but whenever the sun blazed through the clouds, we hurried out of our cold palace and into its warmth. Firs and palms stood unexpectedly green among splashes of red and white shrubs.

Alan, a maniac for chopping and always craving for exercise, began hacking down the cactus hedge towering over the garden wall. According to Hassin it harboured snakes and scorpions. Also it bristled with thorns and Lawrence, who backed into it, had to stand all through lunch.

In old grey flannels and an open-necked shirt, Alan worked side by side with Joseph, the farmer, a silent Maltese, burnt brown by the sun, who scowled permanently. They sliced through stems a foot thick and hauled them, heavy with water, to a wheelbarrow, where Ahmed, our ancient gardener, wheeled them away. Ahmed, rags hanging limply off him, and head bound in a grimy cloth, looked so thin and fragile that I marvelled when he lifted the weighty barrow with ease.

Hassin kept muttering 'Monsieur . . . ' and shaking his head. It was not a reproach but bewilderment – the Consul-General at manual work with natives! But Monsieur was enjoying himself and it certainly made Joseph and Ahmed work harder than they had done for a long time. They tramped all over the cactus branches barefoot, while I pulled out thorns that penetrated right through Alan's thick leather gloves.

'How can they? What about the splinters?' I exclaimed.

Alan shrugged. 'We all adapt. Camels eat the stuff and they're supposed to have sensitive mouths.'

I took the children on a picnic to Carthage, the ancient Punic capital built in 814 BC and destroyed many times over. The guide book I carried also told me that Tunisia had been conquered by the Phoenicians, Romans, Vandals, Byzantines, Arabs, Aragons, Normans, Spaniards, Turks and the French and all had left their mark on Carthage.

It was about three quarters of an hour's walk. We were

crossing a field of stubble when I saw an enormous bull, shaggy hair covering his huge horned head, trotting along our path towards us. I seized the children's hands and darted sideways across the field: the bull came on, ignored us and Mavis, standing still a few feet away, and passed on. Loud barking started up behind us. Hounds, big, bony and scraggy, were racing towards us. It's their field, flashed through my mind, and we rushed back to the path as Arabs in long gowns and head cloths appeared from behind a prickly-pear hedge surrounding a mud hut. I shouted a nervous '*Bonjour!*' They smiled, raised arms in greeting and in harsh voices, called back the dogs.

'I'm not sure I'm enjoying this,' I told Mavis as I thought of all the talk of Arabs attacking Europeans.

She grinned. 'It's all right, I'll go ahead and warn you of any bulls or dogs,' and she strode forward.

I called out '*Bonjour!*' to every Arab I saw; I got a greeting back, and dogs were called off. Bulls apparently were left to wander around by themselves and preferred to keep to paths. Lawrence insisted on showing off by staying near the path as they padded past, but they hardly glanced his way. I grew braver and merely crept round them, Libet clinging to my hand.

We reached Salammbô, a Carthaginian city where an Arab, dressed in the inevitable rags, led us to the two remaining Punic temples.

'They are the oldest temples here,' I informed the children. 'Tanit was their goddess. The people worshipped her.'

The children gazed at the remnants of walls and arches. Inside the main temple stood row upon row of large earthenware urns.

'What are those, Mummy?' Lawrence asked.

'Baby boys,' the guide pointed to them. 'Eldest boy in each family sacrificed to Tanit, the great goddess.' His arms jerked as though to throw something. 'Boiled alive in oil, then put into urns and buried here. Baby boys.'

We stood silent. The sun had gone in. I shivered and Lawrence shrank back against me, clutching my skirt. 'Let's go! I want to go!' he cried. Babies in these urns! Sacrificed! Carthage . . . Punic wars . . . all so long, long ago. History . . . nothing to do with us. But it was real. It had happened . . . here. Had things changed? The holocaust . . . wars . . . sacrifices to new theories, new gods? I put my arm round Lawrence and hurried him away. Mavis and Libet clasped hands and followed.

I led them quickly to Carthage, the ancient city sheltering beneath the modern town. The sun, out again, shed a pinkish glow on the great weathered stone blocks. Huge broken marble capitals and plinths decorated with massive stylised acanthus leaves littered the ground. The children ran their hands over their smooth surfaces. 'It's warm, Mummy!' Libet exclaimed. The glowing whiteness of the enormous marble pillars lining the water's edge stood out against the deep blue of the sea. The children pranced along ancient waterways and under archways calling out to each other.

We were hungry and climbed up to a grassy hillock, amidst stone remnants of a Christian Basilica. We ate egg and tomato sandwiches and gazed down across sprouting green grass and budding wild flowers to the Bey's sprawling white palace below; then on to the vast expanse of warm sea and beyond to the twin peaks of the Bou Kornine, mauve against the blue sky.

Mavis sighed. 'It's so beautiful! I'm afraid I shall forget it. I want to remember it always just as it is now.' I felt the same.

The children skipped in and out among the ruins, chanting, 'I'm in the Basilica!' and 'I'm in the Rotunda!' Libet found a bank of golden buttercups and sat beaming in their midst. The Punic urns were forgotten.

☆   ☆   ☆

Alan and I were invited to dine with the French Admiral in Bizerta, the big French naval base about an hour and a half's drive from us. 'It's an opportunity to see more of the countryside and its inhabitants,' Alan said.

Lawrence clung to my evening dress. 'Don't go, Mummy!'

'It's all right, darling. Mavis will stay with you and we'll be back soon.' Had he remembered those horrible urns?

A rainstorm had flooded the roads. As we crept along, we saw huts swept away and water pouring through villages. I wondered how their inhabitants survived. In the fields nomads were taking down their soaking, black tents.

'They've been here helping with the cereal harvest, but now they're moving south for the olive picking,' Cutajah remarked. He was usually silent and sat square-shouldered in his dark blue uniform.

A group of Bedouin passed us: the men, wrapped in woollen

47

cloth, now soaking and bedraggled, led the way, followed by five camels swaying under heavy loads, six donkeys, four goats, several dogs, numerous children, also dressed in woollen cloth, and finally, the women brought up the rear. Their loose blue gowns and shawls were heavy with rain-water, but bright earrings swung jauntily to the tinkling of their gold bangles, pendants and anklets. They planted bare feet firmly on the prickly stubble.

'They walk all the way,' Cutajah went on. 'Twenty miles a day. And good riddance! Nothing's safe with them around.'

A young woman swung along towards us. She glanced up at me from under strands of dark, wet hair and smiled. Her eyes were mischievous and friendly. I felt very conscious of my white evening dress, the silver fox across the shoulders and the pearls in my ears and at my throat.

'She makes me feel ashamed,' I said to Alan.

'She may be as happy as you,' was his reply.

Suddenly I envied her the vast expanse of sky, her indifference to weather, to her own looks, the freedom of life in the open. Was it my great-grandmother in me? I did not advertise the fact, since we represented Great Britain, but I was Russian by birth and I had a Siberian, Buryat nomadic ancestor, something my family concealed. Siberian spaciousness . . .

We had arrived. Sailors, red pompoms on their caps, stood at attention at the Admiral's gates, saluting as the car, flag flying, swept in. More sailors presented arms at the front door.

Guests in the drawing-room rose as we entered. Most were in naval uniform. The ladies' décolletages stood out from their bosoms in a particularly revealing manner – the newest Paris fashion, I presumed.

Admiral Josan, a tall, slim, distinguished figure with rows of medals across his chest and among them several British ones, greeted us warmly and kissed my hand. As we sat down to table, chandeliers glittered overhead, and candles flickered over the silver. Sailors waited on us and the talk was loud but too fast so, as usual, we failed to join in.

The nine delicious courses and all the wine loosened tongues and the conversation became embarrassingly cynical. Guests openly criticized their government. I turned away, pretending not to hear. I knew I must never interfere in or comment on current Tunisian or French affairs.

Admiral Josan turned to me. 'You British, you're lucky. You can hold your heads up high. You didn't surrender. You held out and won the war.'

'The channel protected us.' I sensed his bitterness.

'No. We collapsed.'

'Perhaps you're too intellectual. You theorized and concluded that the Germans were sure to win so there was no point in continuing the fight. We don't think. We do whatever has to be done. I never thought I'd survive the war. We'd read H.G. Wells with his death rays. But we just carried on.'

'France,' he muttered, 'is humiliated.' He drained his glass. Was that why France clung to her colonies? To restore her dignity?

After dinner we listened to chamber music. At the end of the concert, with a roll of drums, the orchestra burst into The Marseillaise. I stood up. Beside me Admiral Josan remained seated, leaning back in his armchair. So did the guests behind us. A French Admiral deliberately insulting the French Republic! I alone was on my feet! Glancing quickly round I saw that Alan had already been standing with a group of men at the back. What was I to do? Sit down? For France's National Anthem? I could not. Yet to remain standing was a reproach to my host. I dithered and felt foolish. As the orchestra thundered on, I reached for a box of cigarettes on a sidetable as though I might have risen merely for a cigarette. I fooled no one.

At last it was over. I sank back on to my chair, red in the face. Admiral Josan looked away, giving me time to compose myself. He must be a monarchist, I decided, but as for loyalty to one's country . . . and in his position!

When we were leaving the Admiral said, 'It's not safe to drive in the dark. That's when the bandits strike. I'll give you an armed guard.'

'No,' Alan protested. 'We'll be all right, I'd rather not.'

'We'll drive in convoy,' guests from Tunis cried. I noticed each car had an armed solider in the front seat. 'We'll keep together. It'll be safe like that. Line up everyone after we cross the ferry.'

'We're safer without a guard,' Alan told me as we drove over on the ferry. 'Guns are provocative. I don't care for them.'

On the other side of the ferry, the cars lined up. Cutajah took so long over opening the door for us and getting into the car himself, that we were last in the convoy. The cars moved off: the one in front of us started up. Then swish! and it was off into the night, hurtling away at it must have been at least a hundred and twenty miles as hour. Cutajah followed at his own moderate pace. We were alone in the black countryside.

Cutajah exclaimed, 'They'll kill themselves at that speed. The French are more dangerous than the bandits. Madmen!' Now I realized why he had dallied.

Alan was amused and added, 'I was told that when the Bey went on an official visit to France, he said to his entourage, 'My friends, I am going to France. Pray for me'.'

7

Armistice Day. We were driving to St George's Anglican Church. We're celebrating the end of the war to end all wars, I thought, but I felt no relief for here we had been on the brink of civil war. However now a new Resident-General, a civilian, M Voizard had arrived. He had immediately reversed some of General de Hautecloque's repressive measures. He had relaxed some provisions of martial law, lifted press censorship, returned police powers to the civilians and freed some political prisoners though not the leaders of the Néo-Destour. Always only 'some'. Was this enough, I wondered? France had repeatedly promised internal sovereignty. The French press likened these measures to an aspirin that soothed without curing the disease. Nevertheless, assassinations had stopped. Tunisians evidently still had faith in French promises. I felt safe again driving through the city.

'We're in the Jewish quarter, the Hara,' Dizzie told us. We had picked him and Winnie up on our way. 'The church belongs to the London Mission to the Jews.'

Jews, I knew, hated us British. In Baghdad we heard how savagely the Jews in Palestine attacked our forces. I looked out at the passers-by.

As they spotted our Union Jack, they stopped, smiled and started clapping. Others turned and clapped too. Soon we were driving through cheering, clapping, Jewish crowds.

'Incredible!' Alan exclaimed. 'They're applauding the Union Jack!'

'It's the Archdeacon,' Dizzie explained. 'He runs a school for Jewish children, who otherwise would get no education. He's never converted anyone as far as I know, but the Jews love him. He's a local phenomenon.'

We waved back, basking in the Archdeacon's popularity and eager to meet him. I imagined him as some sort of giant-figure with a commanding presence.

In the little church the pews were crowded. We stood up as

the Archdeacon, the Reverend Isaac Dunbar, entered, bowed to the altar and turned towards us. He stooped and his round, balding head was inclined humbly as though in perpetual apology. Hardly a heroic figure but what a gentle smile.

He beamed at the array of Consuls-General, from the USA, Greece and even Italy, a gracious gesture from a former enemy. The French were well represented and so were the Tunisians, headed by General Tahar Maoui – a solid tribute to Great Britain.

Mrs Dunbar sat at the organ, tall and straight with heavy features under her typically British pancake hat with a feather aiming straight at Heaven. She led the singing in a deep, penetrating voice.

The Archdeacon launched into his sermon, partly in French and partly in English, and my thoughts strayed to the stony-faced Tunisians sitting beside their French masters. Were they French supporters, 'collaborators' as the Néo-Destour dubbed them, or were they at heart nationalists? And what of Tahar Maoui himself?

He had eight children to support. Would the Néo-Destour brand him a traitor? Alan said he was no politician. We had called on the Maouis. We had been unable to enter their house by the front-door as the key had been mislaid. The General had to lead us through the garage. Things not working – a Russian touch, I felt! The house, built European-style, was crammed with curios, both valuable and trash, furniture, carpets, immense cupboards, benches. Again it reminded me of the usual chaotic Russian household and I felt a fellow feeling for the Maouis.

We sipped tea in a shady, sweet-scented orange grove and ate sweet cakes and Turkish delight. Madame Maoui, a plump lady exposed most of a generous bosom, partially contained in a low-cut white blouse so that I understood the need for the aba in which Arab women wrapped themselves when going out.

She kept clapping her jewelled hands and first a boy in a long shirt ran up bringing her a fan, then a girl, also in a long shirt, brought a shawl. Madame Maoui did not glance their way or thank them. They ran back and squatted on the house steps, silent, eyes fixed on the ground.

General Maoui saw me looking at them and murmured, 'They're orphans. We're bringing them up.' Orphans? More likely slaves, I thought. Slavery was officially forbidden but these two . . .

The Maouis' eight children joined us, the boys neat in shorts and shirts, the girls in flowery cotton dresses and all with plump, round faces, big, dark, soulful eyes and black curly hair. They draped themselves around their mother, her hands patting their heads, their shoulders, hugging them – a happy family scene. The two 'orphans' looked on. I sighed. The Maouis were hospitable, generous but, I thought, 'They know not what they do,' though probably we too, all of us at times 'Know not what we do.' A depressing thought!

The service was over. Alan and I shook hands with the congregation as they left and we drove home.

'I've invited the Archdeacon to stay with us,' Alan told me. 'On doctor's orders he must have at least a month's complete rest, preferably in the country. Something to do with his heart.'

The Archdeacon settled in easily. The children, in their excitement immediately promoted him with a 'Good-night Archbishop!' from Lawrence and in the morning a 'Where is the Duke of Edinburgh?' from Libet. The Archdeacon was delighted. Dressed in plus-fours he took the children on his first walk. They came back Lawrence shouting, 'We went into a mud hut. Men made bricks from clay and straw,' and Libet cried, 'We looked into a deep well with frogs' noses peeping out of the water!'

Winnie and I had given up shopping in the souk. The crowd jostled, pushed us aside and struck us with their elbows, but the Archdeacon persuaded us to go with him. He led us into the darkest, eerie tunnels. There were sudden smiles as men emerged from behind colourful rolls of carpet, bowed, raised hands in greeting. We were invited to drink coffee from miniature cups, perched on leather pouffes. We watched silversmiths moulding fine silver wire into brooches and coppersmiths engraving intricate designs on brass and copper trays.

'You see, you don't have to be afraid,' the Archdeacon whispered. Tunisians, rich and poor, treated him with the graciousness he invariably aroused as though all were his parishioners. Evidently it was not only the Jews. A real peacemaker, I thought, and I warmed towards him.

Mrs Dunbar visited us one afternoon. 'Would the children like to join our Sunday School?' she asked. 'But it's held every Thursday afternoon.' We agreed. 'Better give them a traditional religious education,' Alan said, 'and later they can choose for themselves.' I knew nothing nobler then the teachings of Christ. They were reluctant to go but when they returned from their first Thursday Mavis told us, 'They were very good, only after the children sang *Praise ye all ye little children*, Lawrence called out, "I know a hymn." '

' "Then sing it to us," Mrs Dunbar said. He stood up and sang in a loud voice, "Oh me taters and me 'ot fried fish . . ." '

As we laughed Alan explained, 'His grandfather taught him that.'

Mavis went on, 'Jackie Dismore excelled too. The children were asked, "What is a shepherd?" and Jackie called out, "A dirty little girl." ' True, it was often little girls we saw watching over sheep.

Mrs Dunbar appeared with another request. Would I take on the Presidency of St George's Fellowship, a monthly gathering of English ladies with prayers and a talk by the Archdeacon? Dinners almost every day, lunches often as well, and this perpetual fear of starting a migraine . . . I had had two more though both had been safely at home. I can't cope with anything more, I thought.

'I'm not Anglican . . . ' I began. 'I'm Russian Orthodox.'

'That doesn't matter.'

'I'll think it over and let you know.' She gave me one of her determined looks through flashing spectacles. I had that sinking feeling again, but why should I be so nervous? The more experienced, the more nervous I became. It did not make sense.

'I can't do it,' I told Alan. 'I'm not religious.'

'It's a chance for English women to meet. They're isolated, some without cars, alone among Tunisians, and with the tension around . . . the church and the Dunbars are a haven for them. Surely just once a month?'

'Oh all right,' I muttered.

One afternoon the Archdeacon hurried into the drawing-room; he had been out for a walk. 'I must go home. There are things I must see to.'

'But you've been ordered to rest,' I protested. He was holding one leg of his plus-fours and they were muddy.

'Is anything the matter?' I asked.

He smiled. 'No, nothing. I just got a bit dirty. I'm sorry to leave so unexpectedly. Forgive me. I'll ring the Consul-General and the children and Mavis to say good-bye. But I'll see you at St George's Fellowship.' He hurried into his room and was soon on his way to our station. I watched him go, disturbed but not knowing what to do.

The telephone rang. It was Winnie. 'Masha! Is that you? A dreadful thing's happened. Anna's been bitten by a dog. On the beach. They can't find it, so in case of rabies, she has to have the sixteen injections!'

'Oh, poor darling!'

'She's very brave. It's me who's upset!'

She was hardly off the phone when it rang again. Calista Hughes. 'Masha! Rusty's been bitten by a stray dog. He stroked it as it was sniffing around our back door. Now we can't find it. He's got to have all those sixteen injections!'

'Oh, poor lamb! I am sorry!'

Had the Archdeacon been bitten too? I rang Mrs Dunbar. 'Yes,' she told me. 'He's with the doctor now.'

'Why didn't he tell me? I could have got the car for him. Oh, I am sorry!'

'He didn't want to trouble you. It's the Bedouin. They're camped all round Leland Smith's house with their animals. But Isaac couldn't identify the dog so he had to start the injections.'

I knew how painful these were with the stomach, soon becoming so sore there was no space for any more. But it was that or the risk of rabies and certain death. I hated to think of it. Poor Archdeacon! Poor Anna! Poor Rusty! Where were the children? 'Mavis!' I called and ran to warn her. Better to keep them at home.

St George's Fellowship. On the way Winnie kept glancing at me and grinning. I implored her, 'Please, don't laugh and don't look at me.' In the church hall the ladies were very English in skirts and twin sets, with pudding basin felt hats. They talked in subdued voices while Mrs Dunbar handed round cups of tea and cucumber sandwiches.

The Archdeacon entered, smiling and looking his usual cheerful self. I opened the meeting with, 'We will start by singing hymn number thirty-six' and I looked away quickly as Winnie was biting her lip. Later I announced, 'The Archdeacon will now address us and tell us about . . . ' Winnie's head was turned away from me. Hysteria was rising in me but I must not laugh. I must not laugh! I tried to listen to what turned out to be a sermon and then speaking quickly I said, 'The Archdeacon will now lead us in prayer.' As we bowed our heads Winnie's plump shoulders were heaving. But it was nearly over. Just one more announcement and with a stiff face I announced, 'Our next meeting will be in a month's time . . . ' I had not laughed. All was well. Nor had I started another migraine.

Mrs da Rin, a young Australian, married to the Italian Consul, came up to me. Slim and elegant, the perfect diplomat's wife, she said, 'You look as though you do this sort of thing daily.' Now I could laugh. Then she added, 'I feel homesick sometimes among all my Italians. That's why I come here. It's a real bit of England.' I told myself we should be ashamed of our hysteria but next time, I knew, it would be just as difficult to control. Why? I wasn't sure.

8

'*HMS Forth*, a depot ship, and six submarines are coming from Malta to Bizerta,' Alan announced as he collected his suit-case for a week's stay in Paris. 'They'll stay five days. The programme is fixed; the office will cope with everything. If you could just arrange our party on the first day, let's say for two hundred, and then a luncheon for the Captain,' and Alan drove off.

Really Alan! I muttered, as I waved good-bye. Just arrange our party . . . the invitations, the food, drink, for two hundred, and the Resident-General will be coming to the luncheon . . . in one week too . . . so simple! I sighed.

I hurried to the phone for help from the office. The phone was dead.

'Madame, the lines are down,' Hassin told me, '*La pluie* . . . owing to heavy rains.' Never mind, I told myself, I'll have to wait till they're repaired. The house felt chilly. I touched a radiator; it was cold.

'There's no more wood or coal,' Hassin explained. With the master away . . . and Arabs have little respect for women. I called Cutajah and tried to speak sternly.

'Please Cutajah, the coal and wood . . . We must have the house warm for the naval visit.'

'Madame, I'm sorry. I forgot. My sister-in-law and her fiancé have arrived. They're getting married.' Cutajah and his family lived in a cottage by our entrance gates. 'All the same Cutajah . . . ' He nodded. '*Oui, oui, Madame.*'

'Madame, Fatma is ill.' Ali had appeared. 'I have to take her to the doctor,' and he vanished. I tried to keep calm but we had a silent sandwich lunch.

Then in the nursery I heard Libet shouting, 'Stupid! Stupid!'

Mavis, 'Don't hit Libet. Turn your back on her and leave the room.' More shouts.

Then Lawrence crying, 'I'm turning my back and leaving

57

the room.'

'Silly! Silly!'

Lawrence ran back and cried, 'Libet I'm turning my back again and leaving the room.' He came running out sobbing. To cheer them up I started chasing them, bent double, swinging my arms, baring my teeth like a gorilla, up and down the long corridors. They ran giggling away. Mahomet started chasing them too but when he bared his teeth he really looked like a great, black gorilla. The children ran screaming to me and clutched my dress. Then to my surprise they ran back to Mahomet, seized his hands, pulled on his arms and stared up into his face, till he smiled and wasn't a gorilla any more.

'Off with you into the garden,' I urged them.

Cutajah was back. 'Madame, the fiancé – he's a petty officer – because he comes from Malta and is divorced, they've been told they can't get married.' He sniffed.

'I'm sorry,' was all I could say. Alan would have to untangle that mess, 'But the coal and the wood, Cutajah?'

Hassin sought me out. 'Madame, my brother-in-law's wife has run away and on her wedding night too.' He was lighting one cigarette from another. I started chain-smoking too. We did not get any tea.

Cutajah again, 'Madame, a telegram. The young man's mother is seriously ill.' He clasped and unclasped his hands adding, 'and he's eating me out of house and home.'

There at least I could help. 'Take this,' and I handed him a token for three hundred francs' worth of goods that Alan had won at a charity. Cutajah went off and later returned but not with food, with a bit of silk, 'Madame, to make a brassière for my wife.'

Winnie rang. She had been to the doctor. 'Masha! It's incredible! I've got a form of epilepsy!' Epilepsy! My worries evaporated. I dropped everything and drove over to her. She was surprisingly cheerful.

'Just one of those things!' and she grinned. 'The doctor's given me pills which should control the *mal* as he calls it. Nothing else to be done, but now Leo is anaemic and has to have injections.' She was more worried about Leo. She's marvellously brave, I thought, as I hugged her – there was nothing I could say – and hurried back to my minor but nagging problems.

Certain items that were not obtainable in the market had to be ordered in advance. 'Hassin,' I asked, 'have the bread, the soda-water and the other things been ordered?' He shook his head. 'Where do we order them?' He shrugged and stared at the ground. I realized that his sister-in-law running away meant humiliation for the whole family.

'Ali, you must decide what you need and order in advance.' He too stared at the floor. Two dejected figures. Fatma had been retained in hospital.

'Please Hassin! Ali! We must put in the orders!' It was some time before I extracted the information and all the time I thought to myself – as if the drinks, and the party itself are more important than his wife's illness. Nevertheless I had to struggle on.

Alan was to return the afternoon before the *Forth* docked. His plane was late; Paris was shrouded in fog. I sat waiting all evening, conscious of the gloom pervading the kitchen. Suppose Alan did not arrive in time and I had to cope alone? I couldn't! No, I couldn't. It had grown dark. An accident? Quickly I switched on the light.

Suddenly Alan pranced into the room with a cheerful, 'Everything ready?'

'Oh, yes,' I answered, wiping away unexpected tears.

Early next morning we gazed at Alan resplendent in his black uniform, high collar and sleeves frogged with gold braid, nine gold buttons down the front, gold braid down the sides of his trousers, plumed hat, white gloves and a gold-tasselled scabbard at his side. When the children tried to kiss him good-bye Alan laughed. 'I can't bend. My trousers are too tight and they're attached to my boots.' He drove off to greet the Navy.

At home we scrubbed, cleaned and cooked, with the Dismore girls and Mavis helping in the kitchen. The children had been sent to play in the garden. As I sat down to learn the difficult French, Arab and British names of our guests, I peered out to see whether they were all right. Lawrence was sitting on a stool, a jar in front of him, milking Libet on all fours before him. Cows were their latest passion. Hedia was rolling hysterically on the grass. The children frowned at her; they took their games seriously. I turned back to my names. Everything was finally ready. In the Grand Salon an enormous log fire blazed, shedding a warm glow over the blue tiled walls; bright stars shone in the blue and gold velvet ceiling. I had massed six-foot oleander branches in the corners. Everything had to be on a massive scale. The long table in the centre was laden with food. Alan had returned and we awaited our guests.

Alan.

The children kept running in with, 'There's a man with a black face in the kitchen' and, 'There's a man with a red hat and a black face.' Our consular staff helping out.

We greeted our guests at the central door. They dropped their voices, overawed by the splendour of the surroundings. Hassin and Mahomet, their white uniforms stiff with starch, threaded their way among them with trays of drink. The girls, in flowered silk frocks, hair shining, carried round platters of food. There was a feeling of expectancy as we waited for the Navy.

When the coach arrived, everyone turned towards the doors. In they filed, young men in smart, dark uniforms, buttons shining, hair plastered down, faces scrubbed and eager. A ripple of excitement spread through the guests. So many officers shook our hands that they flapped up and down mechanically. We counted forty.

As they quickly dispersed, voices were raised, laughter grew louder. Midshipmen crowded, chatting, round the girls; officers with cries of '*Bonjour!*' handed food to the French ladies, in their little black Parisian dresses; senior officers, dredging up school-boy French, with repeated, '*Ah oui!*' laughed uproariously, exchanging jokes with the Tunisian Ministers, impressive, voluminous men in flowing white robes, and red sheshias. The Prime Minister, a monumental figure in their midst, they hovered round the table, helping themselves to devilled eggs and canapés.

'They're only puppets; they don't have any power,' Alan had told me. But who was I to judge them? I was glad they had come. They grabbed glasses of whisky from behind the orange juice that Hassin was proferring them, and cried, 'Good! Good!' as they slapped officers on the back. They also ate ham sandwiches, though Hassin shook his head.

'Monsieur!' Hassin whispered. 'The police have not arrived. No one's protecting the Ministers.' I imagined *Fellaghas* creeping into our garden, up the stairway, bursting into the Grand Salon, shouting 'Traitors' and shooting the Ministers. Alan glanced round the crowded Salon. The Ministers were jammed in by naval officers. He evidently thought them safe enough as he shrugged, saying, 'Too bad! But warn Monsieur Dismore.' Poor Dizzie would now be watching all the doors. A huge, white-robed figure, towering above the throng would be the first to attract attention – the Catholic Archbishop of Carthage. The Naval Chaplain was plying him with food, oblivious of any danger.

I was distracted from such gruesome thoughts by the arrival of the Spanish Consul-General, de Bailen, the doyen of the Consular Corps. He limped into the Salon on two sticks. An old man, he had had several heart attacks. Installed in an armchair, waving his arms, de Bailen demanded a small table, chairs, platters of food and whisky. He leant back and called in a penetrating voice,

'Ah Antoinette. Come here, my dear! What a lovely dress! Giselle! How beautiful you look! Marie so smart, so Parisienne!' The most striking women clustered round him, blushing, their hands in his.

'The old devil!' an officer near me remarked. 'A dago of course.' I laughed.

The noise was deafening, faces were radiant, flushed with excitement. There was magic in the air. I stood in the midst of it all and marvelled. The Navy had charmed them all! After long spells at sea, presumably, to be free on land, in female company and plied with food and drink made them considerate and appreciative; their delight was catching and in their presence the women felt confident and alluring. Winnie, her fair skin flushed, was telling jokes, epilepsy forgotten.

Some youngsters had too much to drink and glasses were crashing to the floor. One officer said laughing to a lady beside him, 'What funny hats those Arabs wear!'

'She's the wife of one of them,' Alan hissed. The officer backed away. A drunken young voice suddenly exclaimed, 'Who's that guy?' A midshipman was swaying beside the Prime Minister. Then quick as a flash he raised an arm and snatched the sheshia off the Prime Minister's head. I tensed, but Dizzie was there. He seized the sheshia, thrust the midshipman aside and stood before the Prime Minister, who had not moved, nor had his Ministers.

'*Votre Excellence*! I apologise. He's drunk. That's no excuse, I know . . . he's young . . .'

There was silence between them, poignant with the clamour all around. Slowly the Prime Minister replaced his sheshia. Then he spoke, 'We were young once!' and he smiled at Dizzie. Two officers marched the midshipman outside.

Alan hurried over, 'Thank you, Sir,' he said.

The Prime Minister smiled broadly. '*Santé*! Your health, *Monsieur le Consul-Général*!'

The invitation had stated from six to eight. It was eleven

before the guests left and half past before the Navy departed in their coach, taking Mavis, Anna and Leo with them. They'll be safe together, I felt sure. A midshipman shook my hand and said, 'I haven't met you, but never mind.' I spared him the usual, 'I'm you hostess.' In any case I was too tired to care.

Years later in the London Underground Alan turned to his neighbour. 'Didn't I meet you in Tunis?'

'By Jove, yes. Tunis . . . I remember . . . We were taken to some sort of club. Magnificent buffet and drinks literally flowed. What an orgy!'

'That club,' Alan said 'was my home.'

☆　　☆　　☆

Next morning Mavis, Anna and Leo were safely back at the breakfast table.

'Mummy, Reggie's giving us lunch on the *Forth*.' Lawrence was prancing up and down beside me.

Mavis explained. 'Lawrence said that he hadn't seen a single sailor, so I brought some of the officers to say good-night to them. I hope that was all right. Commander Cole promised to give them lunch on board today. He's cleared it with Captain Pizey.'

Alan and I had the same thought – the Navy was here to promote good relations between France and Britain but the crew also needed rest and recreation – Mavis would certainly provide the latter.

'All right,' Alan said. 'And you can have the car.'

Libet suddenly clung to me, 'I feel shy without you.' Behind her Mavis spoke softly, 'I feel a bit shy too.' Mavis was still reserved with me but the children told me she was their 'best friend.' They clasped hands and then all three were off to Bizerta.

The children bounced in late that evening.

'I was a good boy,' Lawrence cried, 'I had tomato soup.'

'And the *Forth*?' I asked.

'It's high, high up,' He stood on tip-toe stretching his arms up, 'and such a long, steep, steep gangway and the officers at the top saluted us. They did, Mummy, they saluted us, at attention.'

'Was everything all right, Mavis?'

She was smiling. 'Oh yes. They let the children run wild all over the deck and up and down the ladders and the sailors chased them.'

Lawrence chimed in. 'I stood on the Captain's bridge and was given a telescope. We climbed into a submarine. It's so narrow and everything's neat. They raised the periscope and I could see through it, and Daddy, listen Daddy . . .' Alan had picked up a newspaper. 'They raised the guns.'

Libet rubbed up against me and added shyly, 'They wanted to show Mavis everything and, Mummy, Mavis and Reggie danced and they sang the music.' Mavis blushed, eyes lowered.

Next day – our lunch party. It was for the Navy but the Resident-General had to be guest of honour. I was in the kitchen early.

'Hassin, it's M Voizard's first visit so everything of the best, china, silver, table napkins.' Hassin hoisted up a spotless flag. The roof of the main building was not yet repaired so in our small dining-room Mavis arranged a centre-piece for the table of blue, pink, mauve, yellow and orange freesias. In the kitchen Libet helped clean artichokes. Lawrence talked of torpedoes and periscopes but since no one listened, he went off to play with Hedia.

The Navy arrived first, then the French guests. We waited. Alan and I hovered in the courtyard, nerves under control. I was always straining to achieve the best, for Britain was judged by us. I was too conscious of this and found it difficult to relax and be natural.

The long, black car, tricolor flying, swept up the alleyway and M Voizard, a broad-shouldered man with a balding head, got out with his wife, a plump and genial matron. I led them inside, Mme Voizard chatting all the time, 'It's beautiful here. So good of you to invite us.' I wondered how she fitted into the aristocratic gathering at their Residency.

We sat down fourteen in all. Captain Pizey tried out his French: no one understood but he and the other officers looked very imposing. Everyone except Voizard accepted second helpings. The French Minister, de Boisseson, a circular man, made a cryptic remark as he accepted more helpings,

'Such a blessing that meals are smaller nowadays!'

M Voizard turned to me. I was shocked by his haggard face, grey with deep lines. Had Tunisia done that to him already? He made a surprising remark.

'It's good of you to receive me *en toute simplicité*. Simplicity! The gold-crested plates, the dazzling silver, the polished furniture, the spotless damask cloth and massed flowers everywhere? What did he mean? Perhaps he was alluding to our manner? Alan and I were unable, even on special occasions, to adopt the socialites' artificial expressions and posture. Nor, I thought, could M Voizard himself.

'How long have you had your servants?' he asked. A strange question!

'They were here when we arrived.'

'How long have you been here?'

'Four months.'

'People here don't usually keep their servants that long. You're the first person here I've heard saying 'please' and 'thank-you' to servants. And you address them as *vous* (you). Frenchmen say *tu* (thou).' How could I be so familiar with Hassin? We respected him, Ali too and Mahomet. M Voizard was watching me. 'You can't persuade French *colons* that Tunisians are their equals.' It seemed he shared our feelings, not those of his *colons*.

'I suppose our Empire builders feel the same.' I admitted. 'They're just as fanatical.' I remembered how British friends from Kenya refused to shake hands with Alan because of British preparations for Kenya's independence.

The Resident-General was smiling as he left and he kissed my hands. The Navy, I felt, had gained us his friendship. I liked his open, forthright manner.

We changed quickly and were off for cocktails on the *Forth*. When I put on my silver damask skirt and jacket with tiny, blue birds embroidered all over it, Libet hugged me and exclaimed, 'Oh Mummy!'

The Captain's cutter picked us up. We sped through the foam, the ship's fairy lights twinkling ahead, their colours reflected in the dark water. We climbed up the long gangway and Alan pushed me ahead on to the deck. The Captain and senior officers were saluting, at attention. I held my hand out. They ignored it and stared out above my head. Perplexed and feeling foolish, I turned to Alan. Sailors were piping and he was bowing first in one and then in another direction, at nothing in particular, not at the officers, just into space! What was he doing? What was I supposed to do? I dithered, embarrassed. Alan stopped bowing, the officers' arms came down, faces unfroze, Alan shook the Captain's hand and the officers turned to me and shook mine.

'What was all that about?' I whispered.

'Sorry, dear. I forgot. I should have gone ahead. I have to be 'piped on board' and I salute the quarter deck. You don't count!' and he prodded me in the ribs. I pushed him away and sighed, but officers crowded round and wine flowed. General Tahar Maoui was drinking whisky; 'For the honour of the ship' he explained. I had drunk two glasses of wine at lunch and now refused both wine and tit-bits. I'm no drinker, I decided, such a waste! Everyone was lively, Bizerta was enjoying itself and Alan was relieved.

We stayed on for a cold supper with Captain Pizey. We were exhausted but, taken up with his flow of stories, he did not notice our silence nor that I was not eating. We drove home very late with two officers, one the famous Reggie, who begged for a lift to see Tunis. Tunis was presumably Mavis. Alan sat at the back of the car in the middle, my head resting on his left shoulder, while another young officer slept on his right shoulder.

'I've had more comfortable drives,' he remarked.

It was the last morning of the naval visit and our last chance to make a real success of it. Squeals from the garden; shouting in French, children raced on tricycles, wheeled prams, climbed up trees. Those willowy French ladies I had met had six or seven children. Their young English governesses, whom Mavis had invited, now stood bunched together, transfixed, gazing up at the officers who I supposed had invited themselves and, who, in grey flannels and open-necked shirts, scampered up Lawrence's knotted rope, swung wildly on the rope ladder while Reggie poised high up on a branch swayed dangerously, pretending to lose his balance.

The girls implored him, 'Reggie get down! Don't be a fool!' The young men kept a hopeful eye on Mavis, who tall and slender, carried round lemonade and biscuits and pretended to ignore them.

It was time to leave for the Captain's lunch on board the *Forth*. The officers, back in uniform, climbed with us into the car and we drove off while the girls with long, sad faces waved good-bye. How wise, I thought, that the Navy never stayed longer than five days!

Lunch was a noisy affair. Loud, naval voices and laughter resounded through the confined quarters. I was seated between the *Contrôleur Civile*, the French Governor of Bizerta, a diminutive M Le Mire and a massive Commander Williamson. M Le Mire kept reaching absentmindedly with his left hand for his drink and taking first my white wine, then my red. As soon as the glasses were refilled, he drank them up again. Peeved I turned to Commander Williamson.

'These waiters, they're very dark. Are they sailors?'

'Maltese,' he answered, 'that's all they're good for, being waiters. They're hopelessly inefficient and you can't trust them.'

Back home we had referred to anyone from the Mediterranean as 'wogs' but now to my surprise, I heard myself saying,

'Our war veterans here are Maltese. They're all volunteers.' He shrugged. I went on, 'You want them to do things your way. We would be just as inefficient if we had to do things their way.' He looked doubtful but I persisted. 'You can't look down on them. They stood by us during the war. If we don't accept them as friends and equals they'll break away.' I had not known that I held such views! He shook his head and smiled that superior navel smile. I was worked up.

'The French are making the same stupid mistake. They've built hospitals, railways, schools. They've done a lot for the country but the Tunisians won't stand being looked-down on. Would you? They're treated like helpless children. Of course they're helpless when they're not allowed to show initiative.' I was almost shouting. Commander Williamson made a grimace. Infuriated I turned to M Le Mire.

'Monsieur! You have drunk all my wine!'

He stared at me through his round glasses. 'Madame, forgive me. It was a mistake. Please, here ... ' He passed me his untouched glasses of white and red wine. 'I beg you, drink ... ' I drank the white wine in one gulp and drew a deep breath.

'Here, waiter,' he called, 'fill up for Madame.'

'No, that's enough.'

'Well then, the red wine. I heard your argument. You are upset. Drink this.' He held out the red wine. I drank and felt better.

'I get so heated,' I apologized. 'I pontificate! My husband hides behind his *Times* when I start.'

'There is truth in what you say. Only we are not our own masters ... ' He fell silent.

'I know.' The French received orders from Paris, as we did from London, and we both had to follow them even if we judged them disastrous. He raised his glass, I mine and, partners in frustration, we clicked glasses.

Finally the guests departed full of wine and cheerful talk.

☆   ☆   ☆

Then on to Admiral Josan's cocktail party with uniforms, French and British, on all sides and elegant French wives, but as usual the French talked exclusively among themselves of their affairs.

We stayed on for a buffet supper. Admiral Josan, handsome and gallant as ever, plied me with food and we continued the arguments we both enjoyed.

'France must regain a prominent position in world affairs . . . '

'No!' I countered, 'We must all work together through the UN . . . '

'The UN? It's communist and communism is the great threat, creeping over the whole world.'

'The greatest threat comes from hunger, destitution, despair.'

'People must learn to know their place.'

'Ordained by God, man or by you?'

I was on the point of mentioning Tunisian frustration but stopped in time. However, the Admiral guessed my thoughts. He banged the table with his fist and shouted, '*Nous sommes ici and nous y resterons!*' (We are here and here we stay).

Guests were leaving. I thanked him for the football and tennis matches, the swimming, dancing and all the private entertainment laid on for the naval crews.

'The Royal Navy is always welcome,' he replied with a bow.

'It's always a pleasure to come here,' I told him.

It was late. We had said good-bye to the Captain and officers of the *Forth*. The naval visit was over. In the morning the *Forth* and her submarines would sail away. As we sped home through the night, Alan heaved a great sigh, stretched and remarked,

'Apparently it's been a great success. The sailors had a good holiday and the French thought them *charmant*. They did their stuff admirably.' And I have made two friends in Bizerta, I thought, that is in so far as diplomats can make friends – M Le

Mire and Admiral Josan.

'Thank God it's over,' Cutajah muttered in a hoarse whisper. Driving back and forth to Bizerta had left him sneezing and coughing. But he did not have our sympathy; he had spent every day in the *Forth's* kitchen.

Next morning Alan asked Mavis, 'Any broken hearts, Mavis?'

'No, none.' But she was red in the face. Neither Mavis nor Libet could control their blushes.

9

It was Christmas time and the Americans were giving their first dinner party – an important occasion for them. I was haunted by a petty thought; I was sure Calista would outshine me! She would not have flies on her cakes or rain pouring down on her dinner table. With the power and might of the USA behind her . . . and Great Britain unable even to repair our roof . . . I was tired . . . the persistent migraines and all the nightly pre-Christmas dinners, but then, I told myself, parties are my job, in fact, my life!

We arrived, punctual as usual. Alan had trained me to stand on the doorstep exactly on time, if not earlier. Morrie and Calista met us at the door with the new American Consul Mr Krueger, who stooped to greet us. At six feet five he towered over the six Vice-Consuls hovering behind him.

'I wonder what they're all doing here?' Alan whispered. 'Waiting for the French to collapse so they can move in?'

'I've just spent a year in the State Department,' Mr Krueger told us as he led us into the drawing-room. I immediately thought: to have survived in Washington, he must be *persona grata* with the McCarthy Committee on Un-American Activities. Has he been sent here to spy on Morrie? He and Alan played golf together and had become friends. I hoped Morrie did not have any obvious 'liberal' tendencies. To be 'liberal' was dangerous in the USA with McCarthy combing through the State Department hunting for communists. No wonder Morrie was so silent. I edged away from Krueger.

We chatted in groups, cheerfully, for the country was calm and the French optimistic. We were all in evening dress except for General Tahar Maoui, who arrived conspicuous in a dark suit with a black tie. Calista looked puzzled as she shook his hand. We pretended not to notice but a stickler for protocol, the General gazed round at the others through his thick lenses, then turned to me,

'I don't understand, Madame. The invitation card said

Cravate Noire and he touched his black tie. I explained that 'Black Tie' was a literal translation. It should have been 'Smoking', the term the French used, but I assured him, 'It is of no consequence.' He looked annoyed – the only Tunisian present, and incorrectly dressed.

We stood for a long time waiting for drinks. My back ached and I swung from one foot to the other. At last two servants appeared with trays and offered us sherry but in glasses adorned with prancing cowboys, horses and Indians – the children's beakers. Calista whisked the men and glasses away. Again we waited, the talk faltering. There were chairs but I did not like to sit alone. At last sherry was served in the proper glasses. Then another long delay. Finally doors were opened and we filed into the dining-room.

After a plateful of soup, another long wait. Perhaps the kitchen staff were having little siestas between courses. Calista's loud flow of conversation ceased, her eyes were glued on the kitchen door, willing it to open. It did. A champagne bottle exploded, a cork streaked across the room, hit the ceiling, bounced back on the table and skidded along it. Silence except for giggles from the kitchen. Calista sat motionless, then looked quickly at Morrie, who smiled back, twiddled his moustache but could do nothing, nor could the six Vice-Consuls, who stared at their plates. I tried to keep a straight face; I did not dare look at Alan. I no longer felt tired; this was fun. Eventually the servants entered with dishes of food and we drank the champagne.

Dinner over, Calista rose and led the senior lady, Mme Uzel, the Turkish Consul-General's wife, upstairs to her bedroom. We women followed while the men retired for port into the library. Calista showed her guest into the lavatory. Mme Uzel turned puce, glared at Calista and rushed back into the bedroom, evidently insulted. She flung herself into an armchair and there she remained, monumental and silent. We took turns to go into the bathroom, and then we perched in our sparkling evening gowns on the double bed. We gossiped as though it was normal to spend the evening on our hostess's bed. Periodically Calista tried getting up and looking hopefully, imploringly at the Turkish lady. At last the red spots disappeared from her cheeks, she regained her composure and followed Calista downstairs. We trooped down to the drawing-room. It was empty! No husbands. We sat down and tried to chat naturally, while Calista remained strained and silent.

'Morrie must be very absent-minded,' Alan said later, 'He forgot to return to the drawing-room to join the ladies. We stayed in the library till the Turk decided to leave.'

Calista had a brittle smile on her face as we said good-bye and thanked her for a delightful evening. It was not the moment to joke about the evening but I clutched Alan's arm and laughed all the way home. I felt warm affection for our American colleagues.

☆   ☆   ☆

'We have just a few official functions,' Alan told me, 'and then we'll be free to celebrate Christmas ourselves.' I knew what that 'just a few' meant – a week crammed with official duties. 'Don't look so gloomy,' he went on. 'Anyway this morning we act the 'Lady Bountiful' at the Maltese Home for old folk, run by the Little Sisters of the Poor.'

From the sunny warmth we stepped into the chill of a large hall with bare walls, reeking of disinfectant. Like a prison, I thought. Two long rows of old people sat back to back on hard chairs. Nuns hovered over them; one straightened an old man's jacket, another put a handkerchief to an old woman's nose. The old people sat motionless, silent, staring ahead like dummies. The Chaplain, thin and long-faced, strode to greet us, his hearty voice echoing.

'*Ah, Bonjour Monsieur, Madame . . .* ' He led us round, handing us from a bag over his arm, the oranges, tangerines, bags of sweets, biscuits, tobacco and a few Tunisian mills, which we put into the old peoples' hands as we walked down the lines. One old man stretched out trembling hands, grabbed the orange I held out, and stuffed if quickly, furtively, into his pocket. An orange so precious! I forced myself to smile down at the balding, shaking heads, the rheumy eyes, the drooping mouths and I hurried on. One old woman, blue eyes peering out from a mass of wrinkles covered my hands with kisses. She looked up, smiled and whispered, 'Thank you, dear!' I pressed her hands in mine.

I could not speak as we drove away.

'I know, I feel the same,' Alan said. 'But at least they're off the streets, and they're fed and clothed. The nuns are doing their best.'

'Of course. I couldn't do the work they do.' It's what life has done to them that is so cruel, I thought.

Alan interrupted my thoughts. 'This afternoon the Archdeacon's London Mission to the Jews is having what they call here their 'Christmas Tree'.'

The hall was packed with dark, black-haired boys in blue shorts and white shirts, and girls in blue skirts and white blouses. Lined up on either side of a huge Christmas tree, they gazed wide-eyed at the branches heavy with silver and gold, glistening under candle-light. At its feet the smallest girls squatted in colourful native dress.

The children launched into a carol, singing in French. There were about two hundred of them, but instead of the usual childish throaty sounds, they filled the hall with sweet melody. Coming from the poorest Jewish quarters, they could only have heard music at school. I listened with amazement and delight. In one soft passage some boys squealed up on to wrong notes, but no one giggled.

Mr Dunbar prayed while the children bowed their heads. A boy stepped forward, his chubby face stern. Standing at attention, chin raised, in a clear voice, he shouted out, 'Now when Jesus was born in Bethlehem in Judaea . . . ' Strange, Jewish children reciting the New Testament! A girl took up the tale, her heavy plaits, tied with white ribbons, reaching to her waist. 'And she brought forth her first born and wrapped him in swaddling clothes . . . ' Mr Dunbar followed with his sermon, 'Jesus loves all children.' The school thundered out the Lord's Prayer and sang the tender carol 'Silent Night'.

'They're singing for Mr Dunbar,' I whispered to Alan. 'Look, their eyes are all on him!' They were giving him, I realized, the best Christmas present he could wish for – they were celebrating his Christmas with him!

I stepped forward to hand out the presents, dolls for the girls, toys for the boys. The smallest girl came up first, curtseyed, clasped the doll tight in pudgy hands, grinned up at me and toddled off. The girls now jostled each other in their excitement as they hugged the dolls and smothered them with kisses. The boys bowed, and ran back grinning with their toys. But the happiest among them was Mr Dunbar as he gazed proudly at 'his children', these disciplined, engaging youngsters.

We attended several charity 'Christmas Trees' and then finally the British Legion's party in the Maltese Hall.

Two hundred Maltese children, grouped around trestle tables covered with white cloths, were all shouting as we entered. The loud-speaker bellowed, 'Sit down and quiet please. This is our Consul-General and Mrs Williams. Applaud!' They applauded and we were led to a High table to join the officials. A little boy, his big eyes staring up at me in terror, advanced with a cellophane-wrapped bouquet of red gladioli. He tried to speak into the microphone, 'Madame . . .' forgot the rest and thrust the flowers at me.

Once again I was distributing presents – a heavy parcel for each family. The children and mothers pressed up against our table. The loud-speaker called, 'Mme Azzopardi, eight children, No 37.' A voluminous Mme Azzopardi, a great bun of black hair on the nape of her neck and her eight children, an obvious ninth on the way, battled through the throng to reach me, her friends shouting encouragement, 'This way. No, here! This way!' Finally the family assembled in front of me, and I handed over the parcel. All eight children strained to get a grip on it while officials bundled them out of the hall. Then up came No 36 and six children, with another on the way too. They struggled forwards for their parcel and were herded out.

'We don't want them to compare presents or there might be trouble,' the President told me. 'This way all are happy.' The noise and heat were overwhelming but the excitement on the children's faces was reward enough. I continued to hand out parcels till none were left and the hall had emptied. I imagined Mme Azzopardi, back in her modest home, opening the parcel and the children scrambling for the eight presents. I turned to Alan. 'Christmas must mean most to the poor, don't you think, Alan?' He only grunted, with no desire to think, as I knew he would say – unnecessarily. But I had to express my thoughts to someone.

Now for our own Christmas celebrations. First a Christmas tree. In the office station wagon we drove with Hassin to his father-in-law's market garden. Libet, in a red tunic, white ribbons on her neat plaits, and Hedia, a faded shapeless cardigan over her shift and her hair the usual tangled mess, sat close together, beaming and clutching hands. Lawrence nursed Rida, Hassin's fat, solemn two-year old son, on his lap.

The old man met us, his gown flapping around a massive

frame. He hugged the children and shook our hands in both his. Instead of the usual tumble-down Arab shack with plots of dry earth smothered in weeds, we passed neat vegetable plots and parallel rows of trees weighed down with oranges and tangerines. Every hundred yards a line of cypresses or pines acted as windbreakers.

'The land is hired from the D'Erlanger family, the bankers',' Hassin explained. The old man was illiterate, a humble person yet he had produced such a well-run establishment.

'Tunisians are supposed to be inefficient and apathetic,' I whispered.

'That's what the French say,' Alan murmured back.

'I planted everything myself,' Hassin translated for his father. 'I run it with my six sons and six daughters.' For our Christmas tree we chose the top of a thick, evenly-balanced pine, its healthy green glistening in the sunlight.

We drank strong, sweet tea outside their single-storeyed, flat-roofed white house, with dark slits for windows. The family, lean young men and smiling, black-eyed girls, crowded round. We had to be shown everything.

A new modern bungalow stood obtrusive in that Arab setting.

'I built it for my eldest son's marriage,' the old man told us, shaking his head.

The brothers and sisters shouted, 'His bride ran away on her wedding night!'

'She left her presents behind!' Inside they peered wide-eyed into the hanging cupboards, the chests of drawers and the double bed. 'What more could she want?' Nothing, I thought. She did not want any of it. Used to sleeping in a rug on an earth floor, this modern luxury must have been too strange, too frightening. Poor young bride!

The bridegroom was pushed forward. 'That's him! It's his bride who ran away on her wedding night!' We shook hands with the slender, gentle-faced young man.

To view the sea meant crossing fields. The old man strode ahead shouting. The Bedouin immediately tied their fearsome dogs to their tent poles. I might face these skeletal creatures with more courage, I thought, if I knew what to shout. Ignorance made our life frightening too; I felt close to that bride!

It was time to leave. Alan whispered to Hassin who threw up his hands. 'No! No! Monsieur. He won't take anything. It's in the family, a present for the children.' The family! I was grateful for that word.

The station wagon was loaded not only with the tree but also with leafy branches of sweet and bitter oranges and tangerines. Our host came out of the house and the children gasped. He was holding two baby rabbits, soft balls with silky ears and twitching noses. Smiling broadly, he placed a grey one into Libet's outstretched arms and a black and white one into Lawrence's. Clutching their rabbits, the children held up their faces to be kissed. '*Merci*! *Merci, Monsieur*,' they cried. My ideas of Arabs had suffered a complete reversal.

'Alan,' I exclaimed, 'Arabs are said to be mean. They're so generous!'

☆　　☆　　☆

Christmas Eve. All was bustle and excitement. Hassin and Ahmed, the gardener, staggered into the Grand Salon with the thirteen-foot Christmas tree.

'Ahmed asked why you want a tree inside the house,' Hassin remarked. 'I told him it was to do with the English religion. 'Religion?' he says, 'What's a tree got to do with God?' Nothing, I thought, but what a beautiful custom! The children painted the tree with lime and it blazed, its thick branches covered in tinsel and brilliantly-coloured trinkets, collected in Vienna, Baghdad and New York. I kept them all – treasured links with our past.

We held a staff party with some trepidation; they were such a mixed crowd. We included the RAF liaison officer, his two NCOs, two oil men from Sousse, all unknown to us, and the Greek Consul-General and his wife, newly-arrived, like ourselves.

'I want it to be fun,' I told Alan but in our grandiose surroundings, our guests stood stiffly around, some at attention. I pinned names of famous people on their backs and made them guess whom they represented. One teacher had never heard of Einstein and the RAF lads, of Lindbergh. Embarrassed, they fell silent. I put on the gramophone; girls and young men swung back and forth in the darker corners of the hall. That was better. We opened the buffet consisting of the usual Christmas fare. AP Vella, the fat one, pulled a chair up to the table, settled his large stomach comfortably on his knees and sat eating for the rest of the evening.

Suddenly the Russian in me burst out and I cried, 'Let's dance the *Grand Rond*!' I seized Alan's hand though he made a protesting face. 'Choose a partner!' I shouted. 'Form a big circle! All hold hands!' They obeyed – I was the boss' wife. To the strains of a Strauss waltz I rushed them round the room, winding them round Alan, stationary in the centre. We galloped faster and faster, tighter and tighter till, puffing loudly, all were locked into a knot. 'Raise arms!' I shouted again. Alan dived under their arms and struggled out, unwinding the circle as he toured the room. Bent double, the dancers followed, but Vincent Vella was too big to squeeze through under the arms.

'I can't get out!' he yelled. The others pushed and pulled till suddenly he shot out, skidded, hit the central table and landed in AP's lap. Everyone burst out laughing. Now they were at ease, nibbling from the table, helping themselves to wine. I produced a long piece of paper which they pulled in turn for their fortunes. 'You will make a fortune in 1954.' Even AP left the food and got 'You are greedy!' They called out their fortunes, 'You are drunk!' Finally each received a gift off the tree and then they left chatting, smiling, a good-natured crowd.

'I enjoyed that, Alan, and I think they did too' I insisted, for he disliked what he called making a fool of himself. But he was smiling.

Christmas day. We drove to St George's Church and in the accepted British manner we sat in the front pew with the gloved and smartly-hatted congregation behind us. As they knelt, the children copied the Archdeacon and covered their faces with their fingers. Still in pain from the dog bite, Mr Dunbar kept sitting down and springing up again. Alan read the lesson, loud and clear, as usual and the children joined in singing *Away in the Manger*. The service over, we stood at the door, exchanging 'Happy Christmas!' with the congregation.

We returned to a traditional family Christmas lunch at the long table in the centre of our immense Grand Salon. I felt it important that the children, who would be living so much abroad, should feel British. To the tune of carols on the gramophone we pulled crackers and donned paper hats. After lunch we listened to the Queen and stood for the National

Anthem.

The staff were invited to join us with their families, whom I wanted to meet. Hassin brought his pregnant wife, Zora, a dark-haired, pale young woman, her swollen figure swathed in a dressing gown. Hedia and Rida clung to it. Cutajah brought his plump wife and two sons of twelve and thirteen. Lawrence led in his special guests, too shy to come on their own, Joseph, the farmer, in his best suit, arms hanging awkwardly down, his brother and sister and an unknown woman whom Lawrence referred to as 'the lady in black'. Lawrence often ran down to the farm. I had watched him riding Joseph's scrawny horse, when Joseph ploughed the olive grove. The horse refused to move when Lawrence waved the whip, he would not strike it, but it took off rapidly when Joseph lurched towards it. I asked Lawrence what he did when he went into the farm.

He replied, 'I sit on a chair.' Once he told me, 'Joseph knocked Ahmed down and made him cry, and he went for me.'

Alarmed, I asked, 'What did you do?'

'I picked up the pitch-fork.' Joseph must have been joking, I decided, for they were still good friends.

Our guests stood silent, backed up against the wall, gaping at the Christmas tree, too overawed to stir.

'It doesn't matter,' Alan whispered. 'Don't fuss. That's all they want, to be here, our guests . . . shows we care for them.' Libet and Lawrence distributed gifts which they clasped unwrapped.

'They're shy, Mummy,' Libet whispered. 'And they're grown-ups!' The children handed round sandwiches, cakes and biscuits while Alan brought each a glass of wine, and orange juice for the Moslems and the children.

Cutajah remarked, 'The boys sang carols at school.'

'Oh good!' I cried. 'Please boys, sing for us!'

Cutajah barked our, 'Marcel! Joseph! Forward and sing!' Skinny Joseph hid behind the elder, pudgy Marcel as, giggling, they shuffled forward, elbows covering their faces. Cutajah frowned and shouted, 'Get on with it!'

Marcel squeaked into *Il est né* . . . and Joseph joined in *le petit Jésu* . . . and soon both boys were singing in fresh, tuneful voices. We gazed at the two small figures, dwarfed by the tree, their faces raised, mouths wide open and we clapped enthusiastically.

Beaming, Marcel exclaimed 'I sang well, I did, didn't I?' We assured him that he did. The grown-ups then went home, leaving the children with us. Good-natured Marcel offered his present, a gun, to the others and immediately they all shared their toys, the boys shouting in French, Hedia and Rida in Arabic and ours trying both languages. Marcel and Joseph, who normally never associated with the heathen Arabs, kept exclaiming, 'Oh, I am enjoying myself!' and, 'Oh, how lovely it all is!'

When the children had been delivered home, ours were asleep and Mavis was off with friends, Alan and I slumped into armchairs on either side of the log fire and stared in silence at the leaping flames. A small lamp shed subdued light around us, while the vast expanse of the Grand Salon stretched far away into the dark shadows.

'Its all very feudal!' Alan remarked.

'Alan,' I said, 'we've celebrated Christmas with Catholics, Protestants, Moslems and Jews. Isn't that extraordinary?'

'Not really,' he said, with a gratified yawn.

10

The desert! I had longed to see it and now here we were, Alan and I, with sand, sand and more sand, all around us. It was smooth with small tufts of thorny scrub on occasional gently-sloping and often strangely-shaped dunes. The cold was bitter (we had brought sun-glasses and light clothing) but we kept the car windows open and breathed in deeply the clean, crisp air. We revelled in the stillness, the silence, and strangely, in this vast emptiness, I felt exhilarated.

We were invited down south to Douz for the annual camel festival. Camels fascinated me but so far I had only glimpsed them at a distance. This was our first trip south and now, driving alone through the desert, we felt free, unemcumbered. I longed to drive thus on and on.

Four hundred kilometres and we reached Gabes. All we made out in the dark were the thin silhouettes of spiky palm fronds nodding in the wind, black against the white walls of the little hotel. We bathed, changed and set off for a buffet supper with the local French commander, Colonel de Guillebon. He towered over his junior officers, his arrogant face held high, nose in the air. He was slim and straight, in a well-pressed and much-decorated uniform. The wife, short and plump, sat alone on a sofa, her lips curled in a half-smile as she watched the French officials' wives in the centre of the room. They greeted me formally, then continued, in the usual manner, gossiping among themselves, though the Americans and Italians were also present. They don't like foreigners, I thought, and I wondered at our hostess sitting by herself. I went over to her.

'Are you really Russian?' she asked, smiling, showing a row of perfect white teeth in a sun-tanned face. I nodded. 'I heard it, but I wasn't sure whether it was true. What do you think I am?' Black hair, dark eyes, high cheek bones. 'I'm Russian too,

Jewish-Russian, from Morocco.' She watched me, eyes half-closed – a warning – and I remembered; rumour had it that the Colonel picked up his bride in a notorious district of Tangiers. But, a refugee . . . who knows what she may have lived through? I sat down beside her and exclaimed,

'How extraordinary! We two Russians meeting in the desert!' We grinned at each other; she had a mischievous air about her.

'They snub me and ignore me . . . aristocrats!' She jerked her chin at the women. 'But I don't care. We live our own life and I am the commander's wife!' She sprang up and led me to the buffet. Politics and the troubles were far away in Tunis and only the camel festival was in everyone's mind.

At table, the talk was animated. But at one moment, I was left out of the conversation and, embarrassed, I pretended to be listening to those opposite me. I smiled and nodded though I could not hear a word. Mme de Guillebon, who missed nothing, leant across and asked,

'Do you know what we're talking about? How charming you are!' I felt extremely foolish while she rocked with laughter.

For the night we returned to the hotel.

At six next day, shivering in the early morning chill, we drove to the Colonel's for breakfast, and then we were off in a long convoy to Douz, two and a half hours' drive in the heart of the nomads' camel-breeding district. It began to rain, a sand-storm blew up, and soon we were driving inside a cloud of dust. We kept having to get out to clear sand off the wind-screen. We had all got separated and it felt very lonely. Soldiers were posted on the ridges, watching out for bandits, real bandits, the Colonel had warned us, for politically the country was calm. Tunisians were waiting, in a state of *détente* and *attente* as a French official put it. Occasionally army patrols passed with radios and sub-machine guns. I looked round nervously; we had not thought of bandits on our way down.

We had arrived. The locals, as dark as our Mahomet, squatted or stood around, motionless and silent, shrouded in burnouses, even their faces covered with only one eye showing. This single eye seemed to stare through us. It was unnerving. Did they think us Europeans strange creatures, unworthy of a greeting?

We got out of the car and stood fascinated. Douz was a tiny fort. In front a long line of Tunisian soldiers stood in formation on one side, turbans wound round their heads, under the chin

Troops at the camel festival at Douz.

The Camel Corps at Douz.

and falling over the shoulder. Cartridge belts, with leather shoulder-straps supporting them, gathered in their long, white gowns. The famous desert camel corps was drawn up on the other side. The soldiers perched straight-backed on great white mounts, clutching rifles, white gowns bunched up around them. The camels arched their long necks, and tossed the red tassels on their reins, flat noses high in the air.

'Alan, look! They're as haughty as their commander, Colonel de Guillebon,' I whispered. French officers, in white tunics and black Turkish trousers, sat astride their camels bare-footed like the men. The cavalry was drawn up opposite the fort on short, sturdy horses, the French officers in bright blue burnouses. Behind them stood the veterans, draped in blankets, their decorations pinned to the edge that hung over the shoulder. The local population, men only, stood behind them, wrapped in brown burnouses, faces covered against the dust that hovered inches above the ground.

I was hailed enthusiastically by the French ladies seated on a carpet spread out against the wall of the fort. The wind was freezing and I was carrying a car rug. We huddled under it. The soldiers on foot, on camels and on horseback were still and made no sound. Just occasionally hoarse shouting and cursing broke out as someone moved out of place. Then once more silence. We waited in this Beau Geste setting.

Drums and squeaky pipes shattered it; orders were barked out, the troops came to attention and in a cloud of dust an immense, black car drew up before us. The Resident-General's slight figure in dark blue, gold-braided diplomatic uniform, climbed out, his face paler than ever among the dark ones surrounding him. I remembered that his Minister, de Boisseson, had just had a heart attack. His Zouave bodyguard galloped up on white horses, scarlet cloaks billowing out over white tunics, and sabres glistening wickedly across their shoulders. Monsieur Voizard inspected the troops, then, to the sound of drums, the infantry marched, the horses trotted and the camels loped past him – a picturesque, enthralling sight. But why enthralling? I wondered. These soldiers are killers, trained to kill or be killed and I hate war, as I hate all violence, yet I continued to gaze entranced, trapped by the poetry of the scene.

The Caïd (Tunisian governor) stepped forward and speaking partly in French, partly in Arabic, poured out local grievances: the dates had not sold, the road was not tarred and more water was needed. Justifiable, I thought, for with all the troubles, the economy was almost in a state of collapse. The ladies, incapable of taking anything seriously, could not stop talking but in whispers since, they told me, last year the Resident-General had complained that the speeches were inaudible owing to their chatter.

Some thirty shifty-looking, ragged individuals shuffled up before the Resident-General. Bandits, my neighbour

Zouave bodyguard at the Camel Festival, Douz 1954.

whispered, who had surrendered to justice. They listened with sullen faces as Monsieur Voizard granted them pardon, then shuffled off again, a tough, frightening lot; I hoped we would not meet them on our way back.

A French officer and an ancient Tunisian received the Légion d'Honneur and at that moment, one of the ladies fell sideways in a faint. I sprang up to cover her with my rug, but there were loud protests of '*Non! Non!*' and the ladies under it held on tight. One of them jumped up and removed a burnouse off an officer's back instead. Mentchuri, the Tunisian Minister for Agriculture delivered one of those long, flowery speeches that Frenchmen there indulged in, stressing how much money the government was spending on agricultural development.

At last we drove to a hillock where prizes were to be presented to the best camel breeders and we were faced by an amazing sight. All round us, as we were later informed, were four thousand camels, big camels, young camels, baby camels, munching scrub, bellowing, grunting, suckling. Grouped round their breeders, their yellowish coats mingled in the distance with the sand – a sea of camels. I turned to Alan with delight.

'Well, you've got your fill of camels,' he exclaimed. Camels were rearing, hissing while their owners struck out at them, making them even more excited. Then the terrifying thought came to me – we're surrounded by these powerful monsters; they might stampede. With so few men, we might be overwhelmed, trampled under their hoofs. I kept close to Alan's solid bulk.

For lunch we were led into an enclosure containing several large, black tents of wool and goat hair, supported by wooden poles. Each had a small table about six inches high, with a two-inch ledge around it, covered with a carpet and cushions on which we settled. My neighbours were the Resident-General and Admiral Josan, both incongruous, sitting, cross-legged in their smart uniforms.

The Admiral greeted me with, 'Shall we continue arguing now, here, in the desert?'

'No! No!' I protested, 'You overwhelm me with your gesturing and you talk so fast I can't reply.'

'Yes, it's true. You English think slowly, and speak slowly.'

Monsieur Voizard, anxious lest I should be offended, quickly put in, 'Churchill was a great orator.' Frenchmen are witty, I thought, but few have a real sense of humour. Josan, who had, laughed.

Lunch started with shashlyks, followed by brics – thin, flaky pastry shaped in a triangle with a bulge in the middle containing a soft-boiled egg nestling in spinach. Mentchuri turned to me,

'Pick it up in your fingers, bite into the middle and suck quickly and hard. The egg will land whole in your mouth.' I sucked but the egg fell messily onto my plate. when Mentchuri finished eating there was not a crumb on his plate. The Caïd, who kept talking, breathed out and the egg trickled down his chin.

Colonel de Guillebon, ever tactful, exclaimed, 'Thank you, Monsieur Le Caïd, for putting us clumsy ones at our ease.'

Next came méchoui. We left the tents and were shown clay ovens, like round-topped bee-hives, covered with sand.

'The sheep are baked in them head down,' the Caïd told me. Their hind legs stuck out obscenely. I looked away. He went on, 'When the ovens are opened, if the sheep are properly cooked, they come out whole.' The first three broke and the head and shoulders – the best parts – the Caïd complained, remained in the oven. The hot carcasses were laid out on trays.

Guests pulled off juicy bits, eating them, tradition dictated, only with the right hand. I hesitated. They looked just like dead sheep, which was of course what they were . . . but then the Caïd tore off a few morsels, handed them to me and I had to eat. We washed our sticky fingers under water poured by servants from brass jugs, and returned to our cushions for couscous. We each dug ourselves a little excavation in a huge earthenware bowl of semolina with vegetables and chicken, filled it with hot sauce and spooned the food out round it. We finished with sweetmeats and fruit. For drink we were offered camel milk with a strange cheesy but pleasant taste, wine and finally green tea.

We left the tents to watch the races but I needed a toilet. I looked round but saw no arrangements. The fort was a barracks guarded by armed sentries. Soldiers were everywhere, even stationed round our cars; locals huddled under every palm tree while camels swarmed over the hillock. There were no thick shrubs or clusters of trees. I was desperate. What about the other women? I wondered. Then I remembered, none of them had touched the wine, or milk, or tea. So that was the reason.

A young official's wife hurried up to me, 'Are you looking for the same as me?'

'Yes, but there's nothing,' I whispered. We searched everywhere. Our only hope was a small outgrowth of camelthorn with a lone palm tree behind it. I stood beside the camelthorn, and spread my coat out while my companion squeezed in between it and the palm tree and squatted. She did the same for me. Then we hurried away, our faces red. What a comedown for two VIPs! We were too civilized, too far removed from nature, for the desert! We joined the other women. They were seated on carpets on top of a hillock, protected from the fierce wind by a palm fence. Too embarrassed to look at them, I stared ahead.

The races began. First a fantasia – horsemen on red, green and blue striped rugs with sparkling accoutrements galloped past, waving and firing rifles, screaming in frenzied delight. I hoped they were loyal, and I felt relieved when these warriors departed. Then the races. Little horses thundered past in clouds of dust and sand. They clustered dangerously close together at the far end of the course, almost out of sight.

'There's dirty business going on there,' Alan, standing behind me, whispered as we strained to watch them galloping back. The winner came up for his prize, white-robed, his dark face swathed in white too and closely followed by another contestant who jostled him and tried to get his horse in front. An officer waved him away. He retreated, protesting hoarsely and shaking his fist.

Next the camel races. The riders sat perched on flat seats in front of the hump, legs round a wooden pillar. They banged one foot on the camel's neck to make it go and waved the other in the air. The ungainly creatures set off at a good pace. Their heavy feet on spindly legs swung rapidly back and forth, but they made no sound. It was uncanny. The horses thundered by, the camels glided soundlessly past. Only the strident cries of the riders and the smack of the whip broke the stillness. At the far end of the course, the camels also bunched suspiciously together.

I had to present the prize, an envelope presumably containing money. I approached the winning camel that drew up before me, wafting a musty smell at me. Its thigh muscles quivered, froth covered its thick lips and uneven yellow teeth, not at all like the placid animals we see in zoos. The Romans, I remembered, were defeated by just such racing camels and with the same nomadic Berbers on their backs. Another rider whipped up his animal, pushed the winner aside, and the next moment the two men struck out at each other with hardened fists. The camels swayed and stamped the ground. I backed rapidly well away. An officer ran up, barked out orders and the men separated. He remained at my side but was obviously used to such scenes for he did not apologize. I looked up at the scowling, frowning face above me and quickly stretched up and delivered the envelope into the man's grasping fingers, keeping well clear of the camel's head. Camels spit, I remembered. The man turned his camel quickly and rode off, his rival at his side, both shouting and jabbing at each other. I returned to my seat. It's not sport for them, I thought. They're desperate for money; we merely provide it and what an unbridgeable gulf lies between us, the rulers and the ruled.

The festivities were over. Good-bye to the camels and good-bye to the desert, both too tough for me, I realized sadly. The Resident-General drove off and we followed but no longer in convoy so, at the risk of meeting one of those bandits, I was able whenever necessary to duck behind a convenient sand dune.

The Camel Corps.

11

The camel festival had been exhausting but there was no chance to rest. We were expecting visitors. Libet started coughing. When I persuaded her to eat or drink, she was sick and gasped, 'I told you so!' Her temperature rose and all one night I kept creeping into her room, and with a cool hand on her hot forehead, I offered her orange juice. Next morning our Doctor Tabone pronounced – jaundice.

'She isn't yellow!' I tried to dismiss the illness.

Alan carried her into his dressing room which was light and sunny, gave on to the back terrace and had an adjoining door into our bedroom. Libet dozed, a sick little girl, books piled high around her, while I hovered over her, but when she woke, she beamed, for her Dad was constantly in and out of the room.

Our visitors arrived, Sir Alec Kirkbride, our Ambassador in Libya, and Lady Kirkbride. Leaving Libet in Mavis' care with Lawrence scurrying about with a basin and wet flannel, I tried to concentrate on our guests. We met them at the docks; Sir Alec was enormously tall, even Alan, a six-footer, looked short by comparison, while his wife was short and plump. Alan and I then hurried off to attend two cocktail parties, leaving them in the care of the Picards, French archaeologists in charge of the excavations at Carthage. The city was a reliable standby for entertaining visitors.

We left as soon as we decently could and returned to find Libet asleep and Lawrence showing Sir Alec round our estate. They walked hand in hand, Lawrence gazing up at Sir Alec's great height from about Sir Alec's knee.

Mahomet chose this moment to abscond. Alan was angry and muttered, 'I'll have to get rid of him.' But Sir Alec pleaded, 'Don't! He's very dark. He must come from the south, and Arabs there are at heart nomads. Periodically they need to feel free of the constraint of walls and at night to see the sky above them. He'll come back refreshed, so don't sack him. He can't help it.' Maybe not, but how are we going to manage?, I wondered as at meals Hassin had to carry all our plates and dishes back and forth by himself.

After dinner Sir Alec strode off to his room and returned carrying a small slab of chocolate. We watched him unwrap it and break off a square. He handed this to Lawrence, who, accustomed to receiving official-sized boxes of chocolate, stared at the tiny slab, then up into Sir Alec's beaming face. He hesitated, then took it between thumb and forefinger and gave a slight, formal bow. Weeks later a Libyan judge passing through Tunis told us how at the annual Queen's Birthday Party in the British Embassy in Tripoli, Sir Alec offered his hundreds of distinguished guests a cup of tea and one small cake each. The judge heaved with laughter but then he added, 'However when we visit him, we have to mind our language. His is the most perfect, the most elegant Arabic. He is a great scholar, a great man.'

Over coffee in the drawing-room Sir Alec held forth with Lawrence sitting cross-legged beside his long legs. He had spent thirty years in Jordan, Palestine and Libya and had known Lawrence of Arabia. All through dinner I kept listening in case Libet called and imagining her flushed, feverish face, but now Sir Alec transported us into the desert – a young man wandering, lost, alone, on horseback in the eerie mystery of the dark night, he had suddenly spied a light – a nomads' camp. There he spent the night, out in the open under an immense, black sky, crouched over a campfire, wrapped in a woollen cloak. A slim, Arab girl read his palm while flames lit up her big black eyes and played over her long gold earrings and the gold bangles on her bare arms. She spoke of 'a great future and great happiness . . . ' Sir Alec sighed, a contented sigh.

The Kirkbrides stayed an extra day to explore more of Carthage. At least they're enjoying themselves and on their own, I thought, as I stared at Libet's blood-shot eyes and yellowish, swollen face.

When they finally left, Lawrence started vomiting. His head was hot and Alan carried a tearful little boy into his dressing-room to join Libet. I hugged him, but then I had to leave.

'The Resident-General is entertaining the Consular Corps,' Alan announced. 'It's the first time so you mustn't miss it.' I tried to put the children out of my mind as I hurried into evening dress. I was trained and disciplined to be 'on the job', to concentrate on whatever had to be done, and I was young and resilient.

At the French Residency our French colleagues greeted us, then resumed their gossip and flattery, huddled round the Resident-General, leaving their consular guests milling about on the fringes. I put on the composed and relaxed diplomatic face, inhaled deeply on my cigarette and joined my friend Lina Touloupas. Monsieur Choiseul de Praslin, who was in charge of the diplomats, did a perfunctory round of the ladies, inclining his head over a hand, as he raised it slightly towards his lips, and moving on to the next hand while he was still dropping the first. Lina, with a mischievous glance my way, clasped his hand as he raised hers and held it so that when he moved on and his head was already inclined over the Turkish lady's hand, his own was left behind in Lina's. He turned back and scowled at Lina, but went on to kiss the Turkish lady's hand respectfully. The French have no time for us, I decided, stifling a laugh and generalizing from this small group of French aristocrats.

Lina and I strolled on to the terrace. The garden was a contrast of black shadow and silver where the moon lit up the shrubs. Beyond it lay a placid sea, while a slight breeze rustled the palms.

'The children will be all right,' Lina said softly. I felt calmer and ready to face the dinner.

I gazed into Monsieur Voizard's pale face and listened with interest to what he had to say. 'The present calm cannot last,' he told me. 'France has three options: she must decide either to negotiate some sort of co-government with the Tunisians, or we establish armed occupation of the country, or we leave Tunisia and that,' he glared at me, 'never!' Evidently his government was dithering, unable to come to any decision – an unenviable position for him! But I was beginning to feel overwhelmed too.

Back home Hassin waylaid us. He was mopping his brown. 'My wife, Zora, has had a baby boy! Terrible, Madame! So quick. I ran to the road and stopped a cart. I told the farmer that the British Consul-General needed it. I pushed him out, whipped up his horse and fetched the mid-wife. Monsieur, Madame forgive me. I didn't know what to do.' There was no avoiding it; we had to admire the baby straight away. It was a tiny, brown bundle in Zora's arms. At the door Hassin's little son, Rida, greeted me, 'Mummy! Mummy!' and when we were finally able to leave he shouted, 'Good-bye, Daddy!' I was glad there were no French around with their Rabelesian humour!

We hurried to the children. Lawrence was sweating, tossing about and muttering. I sat him up and gave him some orange juice. Then suddenly before my eyes the dreaded zig-zags started. That wretched dinner, I thought, and now a migraine! 'Alan!' I called and leaving Lawrence, I collapsed onto my bed and hid a miserable face in the pillow. All night I was barely conscious of Alan stealthily carrying basins back and forth from the children's room.

Next day was Mavis's day off. She had not left the house for a long time, so Alan insisted that she go out. Fortunately the children seemed much better. I lay in bed while next door they laid out their toy animals over their bedclothes. Libet whispered, 'My cow wants orange juice,' and Lawrence, 'I'll get a flannel; my horse is being sick.' Hassin brought them drinks and teased them, 'Ouch Libet! Your dog may be china but he's bitten me!' He made them laugh and kept an eye on them.

Alan came hurrying in that evening. 'Dizzy's had a slight heart attack.'

'Oh no!' I cried. 'I can't cope with any more!'

'He has to stop smoking and drinking. We'll have to help him as he'll find it difficult in the company he keeps.' He was smiling apologetically. 'I'm afraid there are more guests descending on us.' It's too much! Too much! I cried inside myself, but I lay silent, controlled.

They arrived, Selway, our Air Attaché in Paris and Mr Mayall, a First Secretary, ending their trip through French North Africa. Our Consulate in Tunis came under the Paris Embassy. We had to organize a buffet supper in their honour. Mahomet was back but, just to add another complication, Hassin had a painful boil on his thumb. The doctor came to lance it. He grasped Hassin's hand, murmured, 'Arabs don't feel pain' and struck. Hassin leapt into the air, his yell echoing through the house. The doctor grunted. Hassin was trembling.

I was still weak and queasy but Mavis, Winnie Dismore and Lina Touloupas rallied round, carrying platters of food and drink to spare Hassin and give me a chance to pull myself together. About forty guests arrived. Selway, very smart in his uniform, took the light-skinned Tunisian General Tahar Maoui for a Frenchman and asked how he managed to keep the Tunisians down. The General smiled. Obviously he had not understood a word of Selway's appalling French. Mayall, tall and handsome, had the ladies crowding round and the party went with a swing. I leant against the central table, sipped whisky and watched the clock while cheerful voices buzzed round me till well past midnight.

Selway told me, 'It's more elegant here than our Paris parties. You're lucky to be in Tunis; it's the best spot in North Africa.' Was it really? I wondered, as I hurried back to the children, my head throbbing.

Now another ordeal. The Resident-General wished to give a luncheon for our representatives from Paris – the first time he was honouring us British.

'Tunisia is on the agenda at the UN,' Alan commented. 'The French need our support.' The migraine had passed. I'm all right, I persuaded myself, I'll manage.

We set out Alan, Selway and Mayall and myself for the French HQ. I must do my bit, I thought. We must make it a resplendent occasion.

A Guard of Honour presented arms. All the senior French officials were present. Admiral Josan had driven down from Bizerta and the de Guillebons up from the south. The French were doing us proud. Over cocktails the French ladies kept telling me how ill they felt in this climate and Mme de Guillebon said she had fainted twice the previous day. My head still ached so I tried not to listen to their suggestive talk. I kept smiling and for courage I inhaled deeply on one cigarette after another.

At table as first lady I sat on Monsieur Voizard's right. The guests were elegant, the conversation animated, the meal sumptuous. All was going excellently. I started on the iced bouillon. Then I put my spoon down. I could not eat. The room seemed hot, airless. Objects in front of me began to blur. I grasped my glass and gulped down iced water. I tried to listen to Monsieur Voizard. His drawn, ashen face began to recede, then to advance towards me. What was happening? I went cold, fearful. I clutched the table and gulped down more iced water. I mustn't give in; I must keep control.

Monsieur Voizard was holding forth. 'If we could only override the *colon* lobby in Paris we might reach an agreement with the Tunisians and all might yet be saved.' His face grew bigger and bigger. 'But with Nationalism on the increase and . . . ' Suddenly it was on top of me! I grabbed the edge of the table, struggled to my feet. Monsieur Voizard seized my arm. I was surrounded, led out and up into a bedroom, where I collapsed onto a bed, and lay there in the care of a French lady, wretched and sick at heart. I stared up at the ceiling, I had ruined everything!

My companion was sitting bolt-upright, smiling dutifully. She's longing to get back down. She's missing all the fun, I thought. My head had cleared, objects in the room had settled down. Perhaps there was time to put things right – 'Let's go down,' I said, getting up.

Coffee was being served. I accepted a cup from Madame Voizard whose plump arm was round my shoulders, as she whispered, 'We'll all start knitting!' I shook my head but she smiled knowingly. I inhaled a cigarette and everything whirled round again. Madame de Guillebon was beside me.

'Come. It's no good. We'll go upstairs and you can lie down again.'

She sat down on my bed and burst out laughing. 'You would faint just as the Resident-General lays it all on for you British!' I had to laugh too. She went on, 'But don't worry. Madame Voizard asked me to tell you that it does not matter a bit. They're used to it. Last year I was invited to lunch and stayed three days. The climate does strange things to us Europeans. We should rest more, like the Arabs. They move slowly. That's sensible.' Sensible but impossible, I thought, and it seems our rainy British climate is healthier than the sunshine here. I was touched by her kindness and grasped her hand. As we were chief guests we were able to leave as soon as I could walk.

The doctor prescribed vitamin injections. 'You're run down,' he said. 'Stay in bed for a few days and then take it easy.'

Hassin brought Ali. 'He wishes to express his sympathy.' Ali approached my bed roaring with laughter. 'All ill. Ha! Ha!' He shook my hand and departed.

That night Alan took our guests to a charity ball with Winnie and a lovely, blushing Mavis, in a full-skirted white evening dress – it was her twenty-third birthday. They danced all night.

I lay tossing miserably in bed. I was a failure! and Alan, a natural dancer was among those slim, elegant, entrancing, seductive French females! I sprang up and opened the garden doors wide. I needed cool air and the soothing, hypnotic buzz of insects.

Suddenly there was a whirring sound. A bat! It fluttered from wall to wall, and swept low over my bed. It might touch me! I could not bear the thought. I pressed hard on the bell and ducked under the bed-clothes. Hassin would be in his own house and Mahomet who slept at the other end of the house, would be unlikely to hear. But I heard footsteps and Mahomet came running in. I could hear him rushing round, hitting out at the bat till at last it flew out. Was he making up for his disappearance? He could easily have pretended not to hear. I felt grateful as I emerged, tousled and sweaty from under the bedclothes, but he was gone.

Our guests left next morning, saying Tunis had been a marvellous round-up of their trip. The French had been helpful and informative, though they had prevented them from meeting so-called 'unsafe' Tunisian notables. I received a bouquet of gladioli from them and roses from the Voizards.

There was no chance of resting in bed. I got up to receive the Astor family, Colonel the Honourable J.J. Astor of *The Times*, his wife, Lady Violet, her brother, Lord Minto and General and Lady Graham. The French guests, whom we invited to meet them, all titled too, were impressed by this galaxy of British aristocracy, even though in true-blue British style, they came in old sweaters and well-worn plimsolls. They in turn were impressed by the magnificence of our palace. Before their arrival Alan had checked on them in *Who's Who*; Lord Minto's recreations were 'hunting, shooting, fishing'; the General's were 'stalking, hunting, shooting, fishing' but they turned out to be easy conversationalists.

We were invited back for drinks on their yacht. It looked like a young liner as it lay in the Tunis docks. It was swaying as the Colonel showed us round and over a glass of sherry, to steady myself, I inhaled on a cigarette. The cabin swung round, I grabbed a table and gasped 'Alan!' We left.

Back home, once more in bed, I decided that was enough. Perhaps the climate was affecting me or perhaps we were doing too much. In any case I would cancel all engagements and take the doctor's advice seriously.

There was another decision I had to make, a difficult one – to give up smoking. On each occasion when I was about to faint, I had just inhaled deeply. I thought about it for several days as I lounged in the garden, picked flowers with Libet or cleaned out the rabbit hutch. The children, though still yellow, were up and about. We went to chose a father rabbit for their two female rabbits from among Hassin's and the children expected baby rabbits any moment.

Smoking, I realized, was a prop, left over from the war years when, working at Reuters Hadley Wood's radio station, I spent whole nights alone, listening to the radios droning on, hour after hour, tense, waiting for the air raids to stop and dawn to break. To last out till morning, I chain-smoked, drawing deeply on each cigarette. Later, any difficulty, and out came a cigarette. Now, I realized, I could not cope without this crutch. How shameful! How weak! What an example for the children.

'Alan! I'm giving up smoking.' The decision was made.

'Good. I'll keep you company and give it up too.' It did not seem to trouble him, while for weeks I faced a gnawing pull inside, a dreadful craving. I sucked barley sugar, a packet of cigarettes always in my pocket, to avoid a sudden panic and a rush to find some.

On the morning after we chose the father rabbit, Lawrence came running up. 'Mummy quick! Baby rabbits!'

'Nonsense. It takes time.'

'But yes, Mummy. Come!' He dragged me to the rabbit enclosure where the rabbits had dug themselves warrens. We crouched in silence and waited. A pair of tiny, pink and white ears appeared out of a hole, then another pair of ears and another, and a stream of white baby rabbits, tiny noses twitching, came bouncing out, an enchanting sight.

'One of your mother rabbits must be father,' I exclaimed.

12

'I'm really going to do nothing, absolutely nothing,' I told Alan. 'I'm going to lie in the garden in the sunshine and I'm determined to get well.' I had grown skinny and in the mirror I saw dark shadows under my eyes. My sister, Vava, was coming to stay with us; I wanted to get fit for her visit.

'Go ahead,' Alan agreed. Then he laid down his *Times* – he usually spoke from behind it – 'The Resident-General has flown to Paris. He's expected to return with reforms of the country's Constitution.' One of Alan's usual curt remarks but I understood – Tunisia's fate was hanging in the balance. I might have known . . . by all means rest, but if need be . . . He doesn't understand, I thought. For him, if you're in bed, you're ill – if you're up, you're well. But Alan's normal placid expression had gone; he was anxious so I kept my thoughts to myself. That chaise-longue beside the hibiscus shrub remained empty; the palms waving overhead, the children playing beside me . . . all melted away.

Then Mavis chose this moment to run a temperature of a hundred and four. I heard her vomiting. When I asked how she felt, she glanced coldly my way, her tall figure more aloof than ever and replied, 'I'm all right, thank you,' and she shut the door to her tiny bedroom. Obviously she had jaundice too. I took over the care of the children.

Mavis was young and healthy but that night I could not sleep. I crept up to her door. I did not dare go in so I peeped through the key-hole. She lay still, her breathing rapid but regular. She was asleep – that was good. Back in bed however I began to imagine that she might be delirious and I stole to the key-hole again. A disturbed night was followed by anxious days. The children, undeterred by Mavis's cold reserve, straightened her bed and puffed up her pillows. They picked flowers for her and talked in whispers near her room. They still

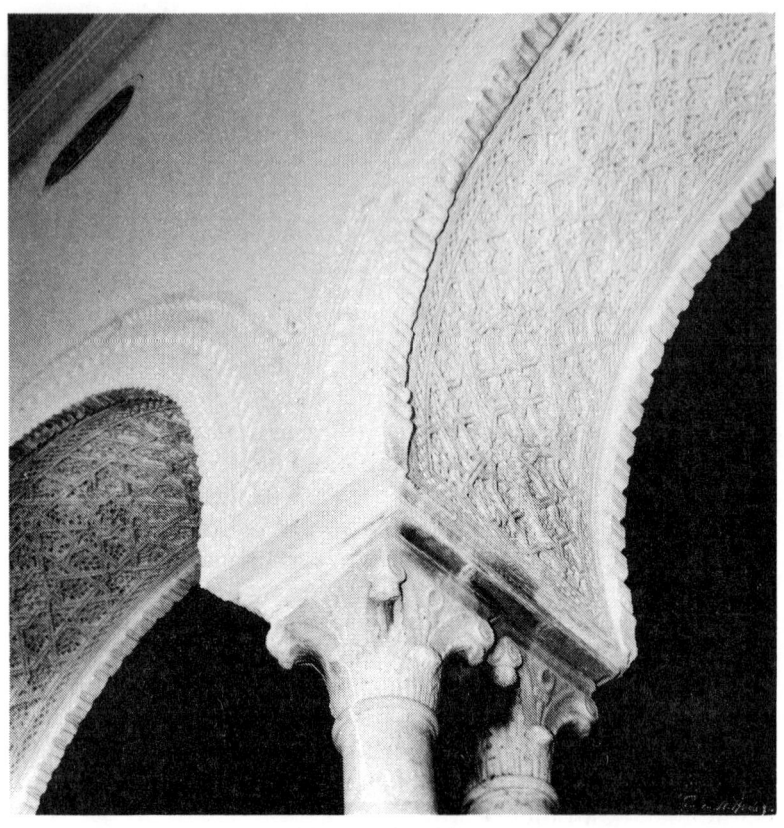

Column on front Terrace.

had yellow eyes and were on a strict diet. I had to watch that Hassin and Ali did not give them fried tit-bits in the kitchen. Libet, her usual smiling self again and her appetite restored, overate and had stomach pains. She complained,

'I do so love eating. What a shame we can't go on eating just as much as we want to!' There was still no rest or lying in the garden for me. If only we could all get well!

But in any case Lord Camrose, Chairman of *The Daily Telegraph and Morning Post,* brought his wife and a yachting party of newspaper magnates to Tunis – a rare opportunity for Alan to brief the press on what was going on, and since he never discussed his work with me, I would learn too.

Camrose climbed out of his car and walked slowly, with

dignity towards us, a large, imposing figure dressed in a symphony of light grey (Next morning Alan appeared in a light grey suit, grey tie, grey socks.) Lady Camrose struggled out of the car, a quaint, ample body, riddled with arthritis. She hauled herself up our grandiose stairway, clinging to the rail on one side and her husband's arm on the other, but though she could only shuffle along, once on the terrace, she dragged herself around, studying the tiles, chatting, laughing, missing nothing. That's courage, I thought, as I leant limply against a marble column. Their companions followed.

We gave them tea on the back terrace and then Camrose turned to Alan, 'Now tell us the position here.'

Alan stood against the parapet. He looks reliable, I thought. The newspaper magnates leant forward, the ladies leant back and Alan began,

'The Tunisians are holding their fire, I mean literally, violence has ceased. They're waiting, but they're impatient. Different French governments have time and again promised them sovereignty, or at least internal autonomy. But the *colons*, the French settlers, refuse even to consider it, and they have a strong lobby in Paris.'

Alan, I could see, was enjoying lecturing the press as he swayed from foot to foot. 'The government in Paris is divided; the die-hards say – don't give anything away; the liberal intellectuals repeat 'We've promised them sovereignty, we must grant it.' Now a decision has to be taken and the country is waiting for the Resident-General to return from Paris with reforms.' As Camrose questioned Alan further, he was able to stress the Néo-Destour's (The Nationalist Party's) deep, basic attachment to France and on the other hand the *colon's* additional fears that America was waiting for France to move out of North Africa in order to move in themselves.

The Camrose party sailed away just as Mavis insisted on getting up – too early, I thought. She crawled around the house, still weak, her delicate complexion yellow. She glared from yellowish-red eyes and kept snapping at us that she was quite all right, thank you. I had to watch her too as she kept forgetting her diet and eating eggs.

It was March 4th, a historic day for Tunisia. The Resident-General had returned. Would it mean peace and a quiet life for Hassin, Ali and Mahomet? I felt close to them and to the country itself. I forgot my own problems. We waited, tense, to hear what the reforms were.

The Resident-General had brought a new Constitution and plans for a new Administration, but based on parity of votes for Tunisians and *colons* alike, both in local affairs and in government.

'No independence.' I was disappointed.

'No. A step along that way though,' Alan thought.

The Bey was expected to place his seal on the new decrees. Would he? He had all along stood out firmly for internal autonomy.

The newspapers all denounced the reforms but from opposing positions. The Néo-destour condemned them outright, 'They mean co-sovereignty with France. Tunisia will become a mere extension of France; it spells the end of Tunisia as an independent state.' They called for a strike in the Medina, the Arab quarter of Tunis, and accused Monsieur Voizard of 'substituting for General de Hautecloque's brutality, cunning and corruption.' The *colons* condemned the decrees for giving away too much. Monsieur Voizard angered both. He lumped them together in a speech as 'opponents of reasonable progress'. Trouble ahead, I thought wearily. No one is happy. It was all a come down.

I had to start going out again. Alan had to mix and to be in the know. Nothing must stop him being invited out.

At a party at the Hugheses there was a conspicuous absence of Tunisians. The new Ministers had not been announced and 'They don't want to risk inviting the wrong ones,' Alan whispered. The conversation happened to turn to the insane. Someone maintained that not all were dangerous as, for instance, the man who recently rushed up and kissed the Archbishop in the Cathedral. Whereupon a young Frenchman announced that he had met a really dangerous lunatic.

'Why, I met a man who was actually satisfied with the reforms!'

There was silence, then titters and someone remarked, 'His diplomatic career won't last long!'

The Bey placed his seal on the new decrees. The Néo-Destour branded him 'a weak old man terrorized into submission just because the Sultan of Morocco was deposed for resisting,' and Bourguiba, their leader, from his exile, returned the Orders the Bey had bestowed on him. It was whispered that the Bey had been threatened with the arrest of his son, Prince Chedli, and the princesses, his daughters. Poor man!

Sir Keith Officer, the Australian ambassador in Paris,

arrived at this juncture. We never seemed to be free of visitors. Alan asked me to provide an informal meal for his first night. I told Ali to produce something simple. Hassin served a dish of boiled potatoes and a platter of cold meat. I looked round for a sauce, butter or some vegetables. There were none. I was annoyed and told Ali to do better next time.

When Sir Keith next dropped in with five French officials for an informal lunch, Ali produced five courses with numerous wines, capping them with champagne. Better, I realized, to let him do as he pleases and not to interfere. Our French visitors were keyed up. Sir Keith pretended not to know French and put on a 'dear old man' act and so was able to listen in to their excited exchanges in rapid French,

'How can the reforms work? The *colons* will never co-operate with Tunisians. It's asking too much.'

'I'm not sure the Tunisians will want to co-operate with the *colons*. I wish Paris would leave things alone.' The French officials were running down their own proposals!

We were invited to the French HQ for lunch. Officially Britain supported French policy in North Africa and our presence was to prove it. Privately, I gathered, we were urging the French to hasten reforms.

'I'm not going,' I told Alan.

'Why not? You're better now, aren't you?'

'I might faint, or start a migraine.'

'Oh come,' Alan put an arm round me, 'it doesn't matter if you do.'

'And Vava is coming today.' Telegrams had been flying back and forth and I had hardly dared hope that my sister would actually arrive, my family being highly unpredictable, but now she was on her way.

'The children can meet her. Please come!' I could not refuse and I did feel better. I went.

At the table, decorated with massive bowls of flowers, Monsieur Voizard beside me, plunged as usual straight into local affairs.

The Ministry of Finance will remain in French hands and of course the Resident-General will be French too, with control of the police and army . . . ' His white hands hovered over my plate, urging me to eat and drink. He was excited. He expected the reforms to pacify the country. But I remembered . . . This kindly, decent man had blackmailed the old Bey, had threatened to arrest those dearest to him, his daughters, Moslem women. All, as he thought, for his country's good. Then it occurred to me – in the name of patriotism, or on behalf of our countrymen, we all compromise with our consciences. 'Perfidious Albion', we British are called. But, would a Mr Smith of Hackney approve of an old man being blackmailed on his behalf? That is if he knew for it would be kept secret from him. No, it's wrong, I thought; I might be called an idealist, naïve, but deep down I know it's wrong and in the long run it doesn't benefit the country.

Monsieur Voizard was looking at me strangely. He pointed out the new Tunisian Prime Minister, a short man, Mzali, and his Minister for Arab Affairs. Weaklings and traitors, the Néo-Destour had branded them, but they looked pleasant, intelligent and civilized. Did Mzali really feel safe? Was he exceptionally brave collaborating with the French, or merely greedy? His ample figure exuded wealth. Were these men wearing masks? They appeared completely relaxed.

My thoughts strayed to the children and Mavis at the airport. The children had been excited; Lawrence had made up my sister's bed. As he said, 'Fatma doesn't tuck sheets up.' Fatma was now well enough for light housework. The children had arranged bunches of jasmine in Vava's room. If only the country remained calm! 'And that,' Alan said 'depends on whether the Néo-Destour or the *colons* have enough muscle to cause trouble.

13

As we sped home past the evil-smelling lagoon with its pink flamingos dozing, as usual, bunched up over a single leg, I imagined Vava's friendly, smiling face with the big blue eyes and red cheeks. As children we were always together, the last of five, a loving family, held close together by my mother. But during these past years as Alan and I were sent from post to post abroad, I had hardly seen her. Now, I thought, we could talk and talk and talk and become close again. I would tell her everything, my haunting fear of migraines and this fainting, still the result, I presumed, of stress from previous postings. I had had no time to recover. Despite the luxurious surroundings with swimming and servants, there was too much to cope with. Everything happened at one and the same time. Vava would help; she was practical; she ran her home and family efficiently. She would find a solution.

There she stood exactly as I had imagined, in a neat cotton skirt and blouse, beaming, eyes shining with excitement.

'I want to see everything,' she cried as I hugged her.

The children pranced ahead as we led her through our palace. We saw our home afresh as she admired the brightly painted ceilings, the intricate, fretted plasterwork. 'It's beautiful!' she exclaimed and rushed into the Grand Salon where she stopped and stared at the tiled walls bespeckled with rainbow colours from the stained-glass windows. 'It's fantastic!' she cried and we smiled at each other.

In the garden Libet led Hedia and Rida up to shake hands and she brought the baby Fathi in her arms to be admired. Vava was taken to the rabbit run and crouched down to be introduced to both parents and babies. The rabbits scrambled over the children.

That night we held a buffet supper for Sir Keith Officer. Vava's atrocious French rose above the hubbub as she chatted without embarrassment, slurring over difficult verb endings. 'We live in London. I've only just arrived. My plane was late. . .' She made immediate friends of our local dignitaries. They extended our invitations to her and she accepted 'Oh, I'd love to come. I love parties . . .' She's uninhibited by diplomatic restraints, I thought. She's even free to make a fool of herself. When diplomatic wives made fools of themselves, it is their country that suffers. But I had to admit that small talk did not come naturally to me as it did to her. I could not believe that people were interested in what plane I took and whether it was five or ten minutes late. It did not advance anyone's happiness or well-being, or solve any problem. But surely I wanted Vava to be a success and to enjoy herself. Of course I did! But there had been no chance so far of having her to myself, to talk.

Next morning Sir Keith left. Official visits were exhausting, however easy-going the visitor. Now I could concentrate on my sister.

We took her to Bizerta for a cocktail party on the French training ship for midshipmen, the *Jeanne d'Arc*. Vava was immediately swallowed up in the crowd of uniformed young men. After the long journey and several glasses of red wine, I needed the WC. There was none. Too late I remembered that the French did not provide such amenities and I should not have accepted any drinks. I searched from end to end of the ship and finally approached a French officer, and whispered, '*Toilette?*' He shrugged, raised his hands and hurried away.

'Don't you need to go?' I whispered to Vava.

'No. No, I don't,' she answered over her shoulder and went on gossiping. I stood by myself, tense, and waited for Alan to take his leave. I remembered being told that many diplomatic wives suffered from kidney trouble, because, though living in hot climates, they did not dare drink. What were we supposed to do? French wives avoided attending long ceremonies but we were expected to go. Another nightmare to cope with and Vava had not helped, I thought sadly. I longed for the sand dunes on the way home.

Next morning a young couple, Frank and Pat Maynard, arrived from our Lybian Embassy. We were a regular crowd as we walked to our nearest 'sight', the colossal Roman theatre in Carthage.

'They won't dig us up, will they, Mummy?' Lawrence tugged at my hand.

'No, darling, we're quite safe,' I reassured him.

The children ran up the great peach-coloured stone steps,

104

The ruins of Theburbo-Majus, a Roman city.

with us following, and sat us down on the uppermost tier of seats. Then they climbed down to the bottom and up on to the stage.

Libet spoke quietly, 'Aunt Vava, can you hear me?' They were two tiny figures far below but it was as though she stood beside us.

'Yes, I can. That's extraordinary!'

'It's the clever acoustics,' I explained.

'Mr Churchill spoke to thousands of soldiers here during the war,' Lawrence also spoke softly, 'and they could all hear him.'

Back home, 'I want to see more; I want to see all the sights!' Vava insisted. As Alan was free that weekend, the Archdeacon undertook to escort us. He arrived in his plus-fours and brogues, while Mrs Dunbar wore a long, grey suit and for once was hatless. We drove in two cars to Theburbo Majus, an ancient Roman city standing deserted among fields, too far from villages for its stone to be pillaged and used to build homes. Six of the temple's slender, Corinthian columns rose defiantly up against the blue sky from among scattered remnants of stone walls and broken columns. All goes to dust and ruin, they seemed to say, but we remain upright. In and among the ruins were poppies, daisies, irises, lilies, scabious and wild orchids.

Vava and I sat down on the warm temple steps, while the others dived under arches into the cool darkness of former residences. Mr Dunbar's voice resounded from within, 'These are luxury houses of rich Carthaginians. They lived well . . .' The sun was hot; crickets buzzed. It was peaceful and at last I was alone with my sister.

'Vava,' I began, 'you know, I haven't been at all well, and there's no one I can get advice from . . .'

'But all these friends . . .' she interrupted.

'They're not friends. They're people we have to entertain. They only come to meet other VIPs and to be seen in our palatial surroundings. I can't talk to them about myself and my troubles.'

'I don't see why not if you want to . . .' Vava began picking the flowers at her feet.

'I get migraines; they come unexpectedly . . .' I tried again.

'Lots of people get migraines . . .'

'But they're not officials. Look, I really am worried. The job is tough. I have to be fit. I've always been healthy but now it's all too much. I don't know how to cope.'

'Nonsense. You live in a palace. You have servants. If you don't feel well, then lie down.' She got up. 'Let's join the others,' and she was off.

I had not expressed myself clearly. She had not understood, or perhaps . . . I did not want to admit it . . . but perhaps . . . she did not care any more! As a child she had been so sensitive. She wept when my mother read aloud *Little Women* and she even wept when my brother and elder sisters quarrelled. I loved her for it but now it was almost as though I bored her! I sat on alone and told myself that probably Vava could not imagine our kind of life, so artificial, so isolated. No women's magazines, no radio doctor with useful hints, no way of knowing what was now available in the UK. Lina and Naida understood. We shared the same problems. We could not discuss them but we guessed. I got up. I would try again later.

'Come!' Alan teased Vava, 'since you want to see 'everything', on to the next!' We picnicked on the slopes of Mount Zaghouan.

'Reminds me of the bleaker parts of Wales,' Alan remarked. Springs gushed down all around us while below the rocky crags the fields and forests were spring-green. We sat around, a large, noisy crown eating sandwiches, Vava the centre of it all, but with no chance to talk privately. Then on along several miles of lofty arches – the remnants of the ubiquitous Hadrian's aqueduct.

'This supplied water to Carthage,' Mr Dunbar explained, turning to my sister, who gazed up with interest, her hair blowing in the wind, her cheeks touched by the sun. We visited the British War Graves cemetery at Enfidaville – straight, impersonal, endless, neatly tended rows of white crosses over graves. Nearly three thousand British soldiers died here. What agony they must have suffered! And the bereaved still mourning. In front of me, I read 'Sergeant Linsdale'. What did you die for, Sergeant? I asked him. Why don't we have the intelligence to avoid this useless, unnecessary slaughter? That's what we diplomats are for, but how to make people use their imagination, experience the suffering involved?

'Let's go on,' I cried, and turned away. The others seemed unmoved, yet young Frank Maynard had fought in Afghanistan and Vava had found the grave of a friend she had been asked to locate. They must, I decided, think wars inevitable and therefore acceptable.

Now we were driving beside the bright blue sea along the great empty beaches of Hammamet that sparkled cleanly in the sunlight. I loved the sea but my talk with Vava had left me uncomfortable. I had mismanaged it, but must I 'manage' talks with a sister? She seemed such an easy, accessible person. Was something wrong with me? Was I jealous? Forget it! I told myself. Stop analysing.

The sun beat down on the little town of Hammamet, its square flat-roofed houses squatted round the dumpy walls of the *kasbah* or fort. All was brilliantly white. I gazed with delight. But Alan chivied us along. 'Mustn't loiter or Vava won't see 'everything'!' Vava laughed. 'It's all so lovely, such fun!' She turned, smiling to the Dunbars and the young diplomats and they were quick to smile back. She really is enjoying herself, I thought gratefully.

Then across the ferry and back home. I was tired and ready for drinks. Vava wanted to plant the armfuls of wild flowers we had carefully uprooted, but when we peered over our garden wall, the field beyond was a mass of colour – the very flowers we were carrying. The rains and sun had forced them up in that one day. We had to laugh.

That night I asked Alan, 'Is there something wrong with me?'

'Yes, dear.'

'No, seriously. What's wrong?'

'Everything. I'm tired. Go to sleep.' Reassured, I fell asleep.

Sunday. Alan called, 'Quick! It's a lovely day and the Dunbars are waiting.' We were off to Dougga, another Roman city, sixty miles to the west. I knew little of architecture or Roman history, but I was as thrilled as Vava when high up on a mountain top, against the deep blue of the cloudless sky, we spied the slender pillars of the ancient city. The young curator, Monsieur Poinsset, ushered us along, pointing a long, thin arm and murmuring, 'The capitol . . . ornate pediment . . . acanthus-leaved capitals . . . ' So much elegance! So well-preserved! The sun caressed us, birds chirruped in the eucalyptus trees, and cicadas screeched an incessant chorus. I felt at ease.

We strolled into the forum, gazed up at the huge triumphal arch, and wandered through remnants of private villas, some with coloured mosaic flooring. It was all empty, dead, but I felt no sadness. The site was too beautiful. We sat in the theatre which, Monsieur Poinsset told us, had seated three thousand five hundred spectators. Wild flowers sprouted from among its stone crevices and from chinks in the walls, while far below olive and fig trees formed a green carpet dotted with minute white houses.

Then Monsieur Poinsset smiled, 'I suppose I must show you the Baths of Cyclops.' He led us to a horseshoe-shaped public convenience, backing on to a wall and seating a dozen people, knee to knee. The Romans were more considerate than the French today, I thought, but I kept the thought to myself.

Monsieur Poinsset motioned us towards a mausoleum some seventy feet high. He stood before it in silence, his face suddenly stern. We waited, wondering.

'This is a memorial to a Punic prince,' he stated at last and turned to Alan, 'Look, *Monsieur le Consul-Général*!' He pointed to its top. 'Up there, there used to be an inscription, bilingual, in Punic and Lybian script.' He paused, then, 'Your predecessor, Sir Thomas Reade stole it. Yes, he stole it!' He glared at Alan. 'It is now in your British Museum. He mutilated, he destroyed the monument.' He strode away. We stood around, embarrassed. I knew that Sir Thomas Reade had also removed much of Carthage.

Next day Alan and the Dunbars were back at work but Vava was eager to see more. I did not try to keep her at home. I took her and the Maynards into the Medina, the Arab quarter of Tunis. We stepped into the bustle of the souk, pushing

Alan visiting the Punic Mausoleum.

Tunis from the Dar El Bey.

through crowds of veiled ladies and dark, long-faced Tunisians arguing around stalls of bright red burnouses and patterned carpets. We landed at the Dar el Bey (the Bey's House). To rest our feet, smarting from the cobblestone, we climbed up on to the roof and sat in the sunshine staring down at the mass of little shining white domes and square minarets, honey-combed with narrow black tunnels.

'We'd better make our way back,' I said finally. The passage we had taken ran almost straight; all we had to do was follow it back but I got distracted by mounds of sheshias, and stopped to buy one for Lawrence. When we went on, suddenly instead of the dark covered passageways, we found ourselves hemmed in by thick high walls, that wound in and out and stretched on and on. I had never been here before. I hurried on searching for a familiar passage.

'Look at this doorway,' Vava exclaimed. It stood out against the general whiteness – bright blue with great black studs forming geometrical patterns and a huge 'Hand of Fatma' serving as a black knocker. We trudged on, such doors the only breaks in the endless high walls. It felt claustrophobic.

'Behind them you'll find sumptuous houses,' Frank remarked. 'But the silence! It's uncanny.'

'We didn't come this way,' and I glanced nervously round. 'Better turn back.' But passages forked and there was no one to guide us.

Frank said suddenly, 'Where's everyone?' I wondered too. Were people hiding and if so, from what? We were alone with no police to protect us, but I kept my fears to myself. We turned this way and that, our footsteps echoing in the stillness. At last an archway – an entrance into the souk. But that was empty too and the stalls were shuttered – a sign of trouble. At last we found a solitary stall-keeper who showed us the way out.

'Come on, quick!' I urged and to distract the others I added, 'We're already late for the Spanish Consul-General's party.' We were late.

'Ah, Madame! are you all right?' The Consul-General seized my hands, as guests crowded round. 'What did you see? You were at the Dar el Bey, were you not?'

'Yes, but why . . .? I lost my way; we've been wandering around.'

'Thank God!' the Spaniard exclaimed. 'Ah Madame, but how lucky you are! Shooting! People killed! More injured! It's begun. The troubles again! And the mob, some say two thousand strong, in the alleyway you should have followed. If you had met them . . . Ah, *Monsieur le Consul-Général*, she is safe!' Alan stood, hands in his pockets, smiling, unmoved by the general consternation. She's all right, he seemed to be saying, so why fuss?

'We missed it all!' Vava turned on me. 'You would lose the way!' I laughed. I had, though inadvertently, possibly saved all our lives and she was angry!

Monsieur Barron, the *Contrôleur Civile*, arrived, apologizing for being late. There were shouts of 'What's happening?' as guests surrounded him. I caught snatches of his explanations. 'It was students. They clashed with the police. One man was killed – a political agitator.'

Someone asked, 'Anyone else killed?'

'An Algerian, a vagabond. The police held their fire till their own lives were threatened. But it's only students and well, the usual riff-raff. Nothing serious.'

'Were others hurt?' the Spaniard asked.

'A few. Two, I think. It has no political significance.' In the silence that followed Alan and I exchanged glances. He was playing it down. He went on, 'We'll let the students go their

length. People will soon get tired of them.' There were murmurs of 'Students killed . . . there'll be more trouble . . .'

Was this the beginning of something serious? Was the calm
over and now assassinations . . . civil war? I went cold inside.
Now Vava would understand what we faced, but she was
chatting away.

There was so little time left. I hoped we could have it to
ourselves but Alan had once said, 'You expect too much. Like
your mother, you want to cling to the family.' And Vava was
keen to see more. She did so enjoy a crowd. Mr Dunbar
suggested a tour of the synagogues. Synagogues in an Arab
country – yes – that would be interesting for her, I thought.
Children, but only children, had been throwing stones at trains
and even at the police, but we decided to risk going.

It was the Sabbath. We picked up Mr Dunbar, now clothed
in his clerical garb and Archdeacon's gaiters, and Eli, his
assistant, rumoured to be the Archdeacon's only convert. Eli
led us into the first synagogue, a big square room, a raised dais
in the centre with a pulpit where the rabbi was reading the
Tora in a nasal sing-song. With a little silver pointer he
followed the lines of the scroll. Elderly men, in long black
kaftans, white scarves over their shoulders and caps on their
heads, followed in their texts. The rabbi shouted, 'I'm busy
now but I'll come and speak to you in a minute.' Whenever he
stumbled over his words others shouted out corrections. They
evidently had no difficulty with the Hebrew. Vava and I were
the only women present; the Jewish women remained in an
anteroom at the entrance.

The rabbi came down to shake hands. Eli introduced Mr
Dunbar and Alan, then added with a wave of the hand 'and
the two women.' The rabbi ignored us. Mr Dunbar whispered,
'I think we're intruding. Let's go.'

The next synagogue, in a basement, was crowded with men,
chatting among themselves. The rabbi could hardly be heard.
The prayers over, he came down, shook hands with Eli, Mr
Dunbar and Alan and led them to the dais. Vava and I
hovered half-way. The other women remained at the back. A
cantor wandered around chanting. The rabbi called out names
and people promised sums of money. Suddenly he called,
'Isaac Dunbar'. Mr Dunbar quickly shouted, 'Five dinars.' His
round face seemed even rounder as he beamed at his children,
as he considered all Jews.

The rabbi asked whether there was a Levi or a Cohen among us. There wasn't, but Alan found himself holding two ornate silver candlesticks without their bases, festooned with bells and wilted wild flowers. Vava and I did not dare look at each other. I was getting hysterical; he looked ridiculous. The crowd surged towards a wall-cupboard in which the six scrolls of the Law were uncovered. Each scroll was in a barrel-like wooden container that opened longitudinally down the middle. A scroll was extracted and Alan fixed his 'candle-sticks' on to the protruding ends of the rollers to which the scroll was attached. Women flung themselves to the floor, face down. They broke into a chorus of ululation. The clamour grew. It became deafening. The scroll was taken from Alan and was borne into the centre of the synagogue. It was held up at arms' length and displayed to the four corners of the room. I was excited, caught up in the fervour. Suddenly the scroll was facing Vava and me. The man carrying it advanced towards us. He was coming straight at me. It was right in front of my face. What was expected of me? I leant forward and, accustomed to kissing ikons, I kissed the edge of the scroll. Vava did the same. Had we done something wrong, defiled it, I wondered? But people surged round us, struggled to reach the scroll and they touched my arms and clothes.

Then Mr Dunbar took us off to the last synagogue, a tiny room in an old house built round a small courtyard with a well. The women there nodded as we passed. Inside twenty men bowed their heads, raised their prayer shawls and with an edge each covered the head of his neighbour. I was not wearing a hat, so I just bowed my head. An old beggar, in what had once been white robes with a grubby white prayer-shawl over his scraggy head, stood next to me. He smiled, raised his shawl, drew close and extended it over my head. We stood together under the shawl, heads touching and I could feel the warmth of his body. The rabbi, as I understood it, was blessing us. I was included in the prayers of these strangers. I felt humbled, grateful and calmer.

Vava's visit had ended. Next morning we saw her off. Even her departure delighted her for she left in a huge, bulbous, two-storeyed plane – something she had never seen before.

The children were quiet. 'I wish she wasn't going, Mummy!' Libet said as we watched Vava smiling and waving at the window. We waved back and went on waving till her plane was a dot in the sky.

'We're going to miss her,' Alan said. 'She's a cheerful companion.'

A sudden sob burst from me. Quickly I turned it into a sneeze. I had lost a sister.

14

'*Monsieur*, Mahomet has disappeared.' Hassin put the coffee pot down on the table. What again? I thought. He keeps letting us down.

'Damn it!' Alan banged his fist and set the pot trembling. 'I warned him I'd fire him last time he was late. Now he's done it again. He'll have to go. And just as we've another naval visit.'

'You did not tell me! When?' I was annoyed.

'Tomorrow.' Silence. 'I'm sorry. I forgot. It's only one submarine but we have to go through all the official rigmarole. I'll get help from the Consulate for our party. That has to be tomorrow evening.' He looked away embarrassed, then turned to Hassin. 'Do your best, Hassin.' Again silence, then, 'The Cresswells are arriving from Egypt.' Seeing my face, he added quickly, 'Only for a couple of nights.' Alan hurried off to work. Now I was really angry. Getting information out of him was like extracting a twin-rooted molar!

As I hurried to consult with Ali, Mavis called, 'We'll help,' and as soon as lessons were over, decked in a frilly apron, she retired into the kitchen.

Hassin pointed out of the window. 'Look, Madame. They're helping too.' In the garden Libet had settled on the roots of our big tree with baby Fathi in her arms, while Lawrence was pushing little Rida back and forth on the swing. Hassin smiled, 'Hedia is away, but now Zora, my wife, is free to help too.'

Next morning the phone rang. Lawrence rushed to it, shouting, 'The sailors!' Mavis started up from her chair, face flushing. The submarine, the *Trenchant* was in the Tunis docks. Alan set off to greet it and do the round of official calls with the Captain. Mahomet was still absent. What was he up to? All together we prepared for the party for a hundred guests.

Alan returned wafting champagne over us so I had to march him on to the tennis court to work the alcohol out of his system. He smashed the balls out of the court, up through the eucalyptus trees and all over the garden. After an hour's play he was his normal self again.

Still no Mahomet. I agreed with Alan that this was not good enough but then Mahomet, I thought, is part of our household. Shouldn't we put up with him? And what were we like at his age? I did not know about Alan but as head girl in my convent school I once went rowing with a friend's brother when I should have taken the school on a picnic. The Sister Superior, on my return, looked sadly at me and remarked, 'The least said, I think, dear, the better.' I did not care to remember other misdemeanours.

As a result of our communal effort, all was ready for the party. The Grand Salon was alight with vivid branches of mimosa and the central table was bright with red, pink and yellow poppies. The garden was full of spring flowers.

'I've seen Mahomet's father,' Hassin told us. 'He has no idea where Mahomet is.'

'He hasn't gone south then?' I asked, hoping that he had. Otherwise it was worrying. Where could he be?

'No. His father would know if he had. And I've spoken to some of his friends. They don't know anything either,' but Hassin smiled reassuringly.

'Hassin is so calm, so reliable.' I said to Alan. 'He copes with every kind of situation. He's a real treasure!' But I missed Mahomet, his sturdy figure, muscular arms swinging heavy pails, spilling water all over the floor, his long face solemn usually but when he grinned, he showed perfect white teeth. I smiled as I remembered how he escaped into the garden, glancing guiltily over his shoulder, thinking I was out of the way, resting. He kicked a football around the tennis court with Lawrence. It was their secret or so they thought. But now – he may have met with an accident . . . he might be dead and there was nothing I could do.

The party was in full swing. I had to concentrate. It seemed to be going well though, with only four officers there was stiff competition among the girls. Mavis, with her cheerful smile and 'don't approach me' act, won easily. The party over, still looking aloof, she disappeared into the Captain's car.

A French escort vessel, the *Lancier*, which had arrived simultaneously with the *Trenchant*, was tied up beside it. Alan had also invited the French Captain Laboucher. Six feet tall and almost as broad, he kept snatching glasses of whisky off Hassin's tray till, with glassy eyes and stiff back, he drew himself up before the Dismores, mistaking them for us, thanked them for the party and invited them back on to his boat.

As soon as the guests left, I called Hassin. 'Thank you, Hassin. All went very well. Any news?'

'Yes, Madame. Mahomet's father says he found him in prison. He quarrelled with a waiter in a café. Over a glass of water, I gather. That's all he knows.' Mahomet in prison! With criminals . . . in that filth . . . probably beaten up! We had to wait for further news.

We were recovering next day over morning tea in our dressing gowns, when Libet pranced up with three sailors in tow. Mavis and the children had already been down to the submarine and were now on their way to the Dismores with most of the crew for a day on the beach. The Dismores held open house with beer for all sailors. I caught Lawrence as they went off.

'How did you get on to the submarine.' I too would be expected there.

'There's a plank. You walk over it.'

'With a hand-rail?'

'No, of course not, Mummy. Just a plank.'

'And then what?' I whispered.

'You go down a ladder backwards inside and, Mummy, you won't find any pretty things there; just machinery and machinery and machinery.'

'Alan . . .,' I began, holding tight to the edge of the table.

He laughed. 'I got down there in full uniform, sword and feathered headgear and all so you'll manage, don't worry.'

At a luncheon given by the French for the two captains, Laboucher came up to Alan, murmuring, 'My mistake last night, *Monsieur le Consul-Général*. So sorry . . . Please have drinks with me this evening.' We had to accept the invitation.

On the docks I spotted the plank straight away. We had to cross it to reach the *Lancier* tied up on the further side of the submarine. It was narrow: the waters below were deep and dark, heaving under green oily slime. I did not dare cling to Alan. Do it quickly, I told myself, get it over with! Holding my breath, eyes fixed straight ahead, as I had learnt to cross the bar at school, I marched up; I was on the plank; I was over it! The *Lancier* felt solid under my feet and I rushed laughing with relief into the crowd squashed into the wardroom.

There was no room for the Captain's huge bulk. He stood outside, fat and joyful, a bottle in one hand, a glass in the other. When it was time to leave, buoyed up with drink, I rushed at the plank and got successfully over it.

Back home Hassin was waiting with more news. Ali and Cutajah hurried to join us and Hassin began, 'I've seen more of Mahomet's friends. He is accused of using threats while armed and in a drunken state. He struck a waiter who refused to bring him water with his coffee and gave him a black eye.' Armed, drunk . . . it did not sound like Mahomet. What would happen to him? Drunk . . . I thought of the French Captain so drunk he did not know who he was talking to.

' "Armed" might mean he had a penknife,' Alan remarked. 'But being drunk is a serious crime for Moslems. Their religion forbids alcohol. He'll be tried by Moslem religious law. I'll get our consular lawyer on to this. We must find out when he comes up for trial.'

'His friends all drink,' Hassin added, 'but Mahomet is not used to it. They should not encourage him.'

'Poor lad,' Cutajah exclaimed, 'so young and kind-hearted but he had no discipline as a boy.'

Ali burst out laughing, 'Ha! Ha! That'll show him! That'll teach him! But anyway Monsieur can get him off.'

Alan was not so optimistic. It was only a boy's scrape, I thought, but Hassin talked of one or two years in prison. Alan was silent about Tunisian prisons – a bad sign. I had heard stories and I shivered at the thought.

It was difficult to be merry on the submarine's last evening party. And then that plank had to be crossed again but I've done it, I thought, I know I can do it! I rushed at it and managed the ladder too, though, with the sailors standing below, it would have been more decent had we women worn trousers. Tights were not on the market yet. Below deck we dodged in and out of all sorts and sizes of nobbly machinery, rubbing shoulders in the confined space with massive Tunisian officials in voluminous gowns, excited at being on a submarine. None of us had imagined one could hold a cocktail party aboard! and make it a jovial farewell. Politics and bandits were forgotten. The Captain, when saying goodbye, presented us with a replica of the ship's badge, an upright sword cutting through blue and white waves.

Next morning Mavis, Anna Dismore and our children stood on the mole at La Goulette, the port guarding Tunis, and waved good-bye as the *Trenchant* glided past, the sailors waving from the deck, and headed out to sea.

Alan returned from the office with the news, 'Our lawyer has discovered that Mahomet's case has been dealt with by the Moslem court and he was given sixteen days. That's good news. Evidently the court didn't consider his case serious.' He would be out in about a week. With a great surge of relief I gave the children a fierce hug.

'Daddy, you won't send him away?' Libet pleaded.

'If he wants to continue working here, he's got to pull himself together and behave. Think of all the work landing on Hassin. Mahomet's unreliable.' The household was quiet, as we waited.

The Cresswells arrived, our new Minister to Finland, on his way from Cairo with his wife. More work for Hassin, and Alan kept threatening, 'That Mahomet! I'll ...' I did not grudge help to Foreign Service colleagues. They were invariably exhausted, especially the wives. Mrs Cresswell was coughing badly and looked feverish. I would have liked to tuck her up in bed but, conscious of the trouble involved, stoically she ignored it.

Mouchi came with them, a massive, old alsatian, who drove all fears for Mahomet out of our heads. He delighted the children, who stroked and cuddled this wolf-like beast with large, pointed ears and sharp, prominent fangs, something they were not allowed to do with local dogs for fear of rabies. With the mean look in his eye, he terrorized us and I kept well out of his way. Poor Fatma, more or less recovered again, shrank against the nursery wall when the children brought Mouchi in to show her. Libet whispered, 'It's all right, Fatma. He is Anglais and kind.' At dinner Cresswell threw him a bone; he crunched it savagely. It was quite a sight to watch Hassin politely lowering a plateful of raw meat and bones on a plate to the floor and then springing smartly away.

Hassin told us, 'He padded into the kitchen. Ali and I froze at attention while he sniffed us over in turn and I kept my weight on one foot, the other ready to kick, then he went off into Monsieur Cresswell's bedroom. He's there now at the foot of the bed and I dare not turn the bed down or put out his night things!' I sympathized.

Next morning out of the window I saw Ahmed, the old gardener, tearing round the central flower bed, arms held out in front like a praying-mantis. Mouchi came after him, yellow teeth snapping at the old man's flapping garments and Lawrence trying to seize the dog. All three ran round and round the flower-bed and not one of them jumped across it. I was too terrified to help but I rushed to Cresswell's room. He hurried out and caught the dog. Ahmed never stopped running till he was through the kitchen door.

'The dog didn't sniff the gardener last night so he didn't know he was part of the household,' Cresswell apologized. What if guests walked in? I wondered but said nothing.

When the Cresswells left, Hassin, as usual, stood at attention and saluted. He never skimps on his duties, I thought, however pressed for time. A tearful Lawrence stood saluting at his side: Mouchi, the horror, was leaving. I watched as Hassin lowered his arm and clasped Lawrence's shoulder. Lawrence immediately wiped his tears with the back of his hand and smiled up at him. Hassin, I thought, has what I value most in our peripatetic life and that is kindness.

Now we waited for Mahomet's return.

A few days later Hassin came up. 'Please Madame, all go in and stay inside. Mahomet is coming back.'

'Coming back! I want to welcome him, make sure he's all right.'

'No, please Madame, leave it to me.' Hassin's face was serious. I told Mavis and the children to stay indoors and we settled down in the drawing-room. Hassin reappeared.

'He's back. He's locked himself in the bathroom and he's scrubbing himself. I'm burning his clothes and all his other things. He wasn't allowed to wash or leave the cell.' Hassin shook his head. Poor Mahomet! The children stared up at me, their faces drawn.

'It's over now and he's home,' I comforted them.

At lunch Hassin was followed in by a sombre Mahomet clutching a bowl of rice, his squat figure in a clean khaki shirt and trousers. We watched as he hesitated to approach Alan. His dark, glistening head bent, his fingers tight on the bowl, at last he peered up at him. Alan was fiddling with his napkin rink, staring at his plate. Then he looked up at Mahomet. We waited. Alan nodded and Mahomet offered him the rice.

15

'Alan, you're crazy!' Every spare moment he bent over a spade digging deep into the clammy earth. After work or after a party he hurried into khaki shorts and sandals and headed for the garden.

'I want to make a large, flat space here where the old cactus hedge stood, under the juniper tree,' he told me and went on digging the rough ground, his broad, bare back covered in sweat and grime.

Was it a need to leave something of himself here? Was that why I kept planting geranium cuttings in odd spots of the garden? Did he need to create and get the feel that this magnificent palace was a permanent home? It was so beautiful, especially now in the spring, with splashes of brilliant red and mauve bougainvilia and the bright blue of plumbago against its startling whiteness. Our garden had burst out in white and purple irises, arum lilies, mysembruanthenum – an incredibly rich collection of flowers – sweet peas, nasturtiums, poppies, freesias, and roses everywhere. All would die in the summer heat but at present the garden was ablaze with colour. It was good, I decided, that Alan could spend his time here, in his comfortable old clothes and wipe politics out of his mind.

The weather was sunny and warm. I urged Mavis to keep the children out of doors. It had been an exceptionally cold, wet winter and they had had so many colds, developing into 'flu with frightening temperatures. The body needs time, I supposed, to adapt to change of climate, water, food, environment. Sickness is inevitable at first. Why doesn't the Foreign Office take this into account? The houses here, I thought, are built against heat; it's difficult to warm them in winter and it's difficult to train the household to put warm clothes on indoors and take them off outside. Lawrence is only five but he has already been to four postings, Baghdad, London, New York, Tunisia. It's a mental as well as a physical strain on all of us. If only we could stay here for a long period! My migraines might disappear. Were we achieving anything by hurtling from post to post, making only superficial friendships and possibly gaining only superficial views of the country?

After reading aloud under the juniper tree, the children acted out characters from their story-books. Mavis exclaimed, 'It's amazing the hours they spend happily play-acting' but as she spoke 'father' kicked 'mother' who wailed, 'fathers don't kick!' and 'father' sulked off into the house. But he was soon back again.

Hassin suddenly started creeping round a palm tree, his large body bent double. He clutched a heavy stick at the ready. The children gazed spellbound as with a savage growl, he hurled the stick into a bush. I called, 'What have you killed?' and he roared back, 'A tiger!' Then realizing what he had said, he burst out laughing.

Spring fever had seized him. He hid Libet's big china doll among Joseph's cabbages. Stumbling over it, Joseph yelled and sped back to his farm. Someone had dumped her baby on him! Next Hassin hid behind the roof door and waited for Mahomet to come up to lower the flag. As the heavy steps climbed up, he darted out and cried 'Boo!' But it was Alan! 'Ah, pardon, *Monsieur*!' and he fled.

The Sunday school children came to play in the garden and I warned them, 'The sun brings out snakes. If I shout 'Hanesh!' women and children must run indoors while the men come out with sticks.' The children promised to do so. I was nervous with so many of them around. I strolled down our main alley, golden with mimosa still in flower. Halfway down a log lay across its whole width. Strange . . . How did it get there? I stopped, then advanced cautiously. It writhed! A snake! Its black skin glinted wickedly, as it rippled slowly along. A huge snake!

'Hanesh! Hanesh!' I shrieked, backing away. 'Hanesh!' There was a stampede of little feet as the children came running up, Mavis and Fatma in their midst and Libet shouting in her best French, 'Look Hedia. Look zhere! Zhat over zhere!'

'Keep back! Keep away! Into the house, all of you!' I spread my arms wide to hold the children back as they strained to look. I knew nothing about snakes. Was it a constrictor? Would it strike? Bite? Squirt poison?

'Gee, it's beautiful!' Martin Dismore exclaimed.

'It's very dangerous! Back! Mavis, Martin get the little ones indoors. Quick!' They bustled the children away. No sign of any men. If anyone came along . . . Hedia, bare-foot . . .

'Joseph!' I shouted. Joseph came out of his farm clasping a shovel and sickle, so he must have heard my 'hanesh'. I left him to it, my only thought – the children's safety, and I ran to Alan.

'Alan, didn't you hear me? There's a snake . . .'

'Oh, sorry dear. There's such a hullabaloo I didn't realize you wanted help. Snakes are fascinating,' and he dropped a huge boulder into place.

On the back porch Hassin and Mahomet were laying tea.

'I suppose you didn't hear me.' I could not help the sarcasm. They continued to arrange the cups, saying nothing.

I spotted Hassin rummaging with a stick among the oleanders beside the alley. He pulled out the dead snake, and slung it across an overhanging branch. He saw me, put a finger to his lips and whispered 'Mahomet!' Then he hid behind a palm tree and we waited. It was Alan who came along from the swimming pool. He stopped, saw the snake, seized a stick and ran forward, hitting it, striking again and again, as it swung back at him, his bath robe flapping wildly. Hassin slunk away through the shrubs. Mahomet came alone and exclaimed, '*Monsieur*, it's dead!' Alan stopped hitting. The snake hung motionless. I did not dare explain that Hassin had the spring fever.

Alan had become ambitious, He wanted a bigger space so, putting on a shirt out of consideration for their modesty, he mobilized Ahmed and Joseph to help dig. He worked between the two men to stop the Christian Joseph from glaring down on Ahmed, the Moslem. They grunted and sweated till Joseph suggested, 'Why not get a gang in to clear the earth?'

'Good idea,' Alan agreed. A troop of Arabs arrived and set to digging. Every day Lawrence met them, his sheshia covering his head. He shook hands and was hoisted onto their scrawny white horse' back. He travelled back and forth carting the earth away. Alan urged them on and the 'Folly', as we called it, grew rapidly and was soon big enough, half a tennis court in length and several feet deep, for us to bring tables into it and two army camp beds with cushions.

Lina Touloupas, the Greek Consul-General's wife, came to rest on one of them. She was pale with great smudges under her dark eyes. Lawrence ran and gave her a great hug and kiss while she held him tight. Lina had been very ill. I had visited her in the nursing-home. Her face below the thick mop of dark hair was lined and grey against the white pillows. Women swathed in black, from the Greek colony, black scarves over their heads, sat round the room, hands folded, whispering, making the Sign of the Cross and shaking their heads. They're burying her, I thought, and then quickly stifled the fear rising in me. I sat down beside her. I knew what it was like to be ill in a foreign country, far from the family and, however ill, still having to act the part of the Consul-General's wife.

'Lina, here's a present.' She had turned her head slightly, her eyes dull. I handed her the bottom of a date box with a paper sail and a rusty nail for mast. 'From Lawrence. It's a boat and here's his note: 'With my best love, Lawrence'.'

'Oh the darling! Thank him. Please thank him!' She rummaged in a drawer and brought out two chocolate eggs. 'Give him these with my love. But wait.' She brought out two more eggs. 'For Libet.'

She'll be all right, she must be all right, I had told myself, inspite of those ghouls sitting here.

Lina had now recovered and we lay gossiping on our camp beds (I had had a shattering migraine). We gazed up at the clear blue sky between the branches above, their thick foliage buzzing with bees; Lawrence, on the ground beside us, played with a white baby rabbit while Libet picked sweet-peas for Lina. This was our kind of life. When Lina left, Lawrence gave her another hug and kiss.

'My husband's jealous,' she told us. 'He says I talk more about Lawrence than about him!'

It was my birthday. Alan gave me a little female, year-old donkey, with a huge head, an innocently-appealing face, long impertinent ears and a shaggy, ginger fur. The children wound their arms round her neck and clambered on to her back. 'Shaggy' stood beside them during lesson time, her nose skimming over the table surface and carrying everything off it on to the ground. She followed them about, nibbling their hair and Libet calling, 'Come on *bébé hi-on!*' Then one day suddenly Shaggy kicked her heels and, tossing her head, galloped off like a demented creature up and down the paths, jumping over our camp beds. The children scrambled to the safety of the table. Then as suddenly Shaggy calmed down, trotted up, lifted her nose to be patted and snuggled up to the children as they climbed down.

Ali, Hassin and Joseph gathered round.

Hassin, so kind to the children, advised, 'You should tie her

Lawrence riding Shaggy.

back legs and force her to obey.'

'No! Never!' Ali, usually so quiet, shouted, 'Never force an animal. Kindness is what she needs. Persuade her gently, slowly. She'll learn.'

'She may be getting thorns in her nose from the cactus,' the practical Joseph suggested. We consulted a vet, who thought Shaggy suffered from rheumatism. When it pained her, she went wild.

'Be careful,' I advised the children. They got used to scrambling up on to the table.

The children acquired two tortoises. We watched as one lifted the other's shell with its claws and landed it on its back, where it waved its legs frantically in the air. Then the first tortoise once more lifted the second one up and dropped it on to its feet. They must be playing, I thought, but Alan would not believe me; I had to drag him from the Folly to see for himself. But Shaggy remained the favourite.

Libet asked me, 'Mummy, do you love Shaggy more than me?'

'Of course not, darling.'

'But I love Shaggy more than you.' And then, beaming she added, 'Hedia loves animals now. She isn't cruel any more. She says she even loves ants.' Libet invariably took Hedia seriously.

Alan had another idea: to move a big marble column (presumably pilfered from Carthage) into a place of honour in the centre of his Folly. 'It weighs a ton!' he told us. 'It must be Lawrence's height and at least twenty-four inches square.' He brought a team of six Arabs who, with planks, crowbars, and three rollers borrowed from the War Graves' people, grasped the column and Alan shouted, 'Lift'. They heaved, their lean faces screwed up with the effort, long gowns trailing in the dust. They raised it up, up. 'Now stop! stop!' Alan was excited. 'Now onto the rollers. Here! Careful!' It lay on the planks. 'Now push! and the men shouted 'Dizz! Dizz!' 'Stop!' Alan cried as the planks pitched sideways. 'Zizz!' they shouted and so with loud shouting of 'Dizz' and 'Zizz' the column was rolled into the Folly and with more puffing and pushing it was righted. The solid, white marble looked good. The men stood back, grinning, their faces glistening with sweat. But we could not offer them a cool drink since it was Ramadan and Moslems were not allowed to touch food or drink between sunrise and sunset. To salve his conscience Alan doubled their pay.

To crown the general spring feeling – the *Gambia* arrived, a cruiser with enough officers and sailors to gladden all the local girls. At our cocktail party for two hundred and fifty guests, the French, grateful that Kirkbride had cleared up the rumours of Lybian support for the *Fellaghas*, the guerilla fighters, were ready to set aside their fears – several had received threatening letters – and enjoy themselves. They crowded round the Captain and crew.

I heard a group of officers discussing the Maltese. 'You can't trust them with anything.'

'No, I've yet to meet one with any intelligence.'

'What nonsense!' I joined in. 'They're neither better nor worse than us, just different and few have had your advantages in education.' When the officers drifted away, one came up to me.

'Thank you for what you said. I'm the doctor and you see, I'm Maltese.'

'Do they know that?' He nodded. 'And they make those kind of remarks in front of you?'

'They forget,' and he shrugged, smiling. He was more broad-minded than the others.

Mavis, surrounded by officers, forgot our children's bedtime. I glimpsed Libet dodging in and out among the blue uniforms. Because of Ramadan the Tunisians did not attend but suddenly I spied Lawrence's small figure at the top of our front stairway shaking hands with a short man in flowing robes.

'Alan, it's the Prime Minister, Mzali!' Alan hurried out to greet him. Mzali stayed a short while chatting to the Captain, then left for his prayers before sunset. It was a gracious gesture towards the *Gambia*. After the party Hassin told me, 'Guests do strange things, Madame. One man placed his glass on the air beside the table. Of course it fell and broke. Another leant his elbow near the mantlepiece and almost fell into the fire! Is it the wine, Madame?' I nodded. Hassin shook his head, then strolled off, laughing. The French wined and dined us, the officers and the sailors, while Mavis and the children either disappeared on board or entertained numerous officers at tennis in the garden.

On the last morning we drove to Bizerta to see the *Gambia* off. We watched her long, sleek, grey, elegant form gliding away, the Captain and officers waving. Two little figures, Libet clutching her doll, and Lawrence, stood at the water's edge, gazing wistfully after her.

Suddenly a voice boomed out across the waters '*HMS*

H.M.S. Gambia sailing from Bizerta, saying 'goodbye' to Libet and Lawrence.

Gambia says good-bye to Libet and Lawrence Williams.'
French officers must have smiled at the words as the voice
carried across Bizerta. Libet blushed; Lawrence dug his hands
deep into his pockets. Then both children waved and waved till
only two puffs of smoke remained on the horizon. What an
experience for the children! I hoped they would always
remember it.

Excuse me, Sir,' a hoarse voice broke in, 'I've a mutiny on
board my tug.'

Alan turned, 'A mutiny?'

'Yes, Sir. Three of my men beat up the engineer. They were
drunk. Would you hold a naval court on the men for mutiny?'

'And you wait till the navy has left to tell me this?'

'I did not want to disturb you. The engineer refuses to sail
with the men who attacked him.'

'If you want to go in for the expense and delay of recourse to
law you'd better do it at a British port or at Valletta or
Gibraltar. Otherwise I suggest you sack the ringleader and
send him home. If there's any more trouble let me know,' and
Alan strolled off. 'Silly fool,' he muttered as we got into the car.
'But he's tough; he'll manage them.'

128

Alan was silent. Was he mulling over the mutiny, or the *Gambia's* farewell gesture? I longed to share thoughts and feelings and relive experiences – Russian style. He had no such desire but as I watched his thoughtful face, a deep feeling of tenderness swept over me.

At that moment Alan murmured 'We need grass.'

'Grass?' The only other mutiny I had heard of was on *The Bounty* and I did not remember grass coming into the story.

'Grass for the captain?'

'No, no. I want grass beside the Folly. There's too much space for just flowers. Half will have to be grassed over.'

16

I wrapped a cloak tighter round me and tried to listen to Gluck's Alceste agonizing on the stage.

"Where am I? Oh, wretched Alceste!" Specks of flame encircled this Roman theatre, lighting up the gendarmes' peak caps as they drew on their cigarettes. Soldiers guarded every entrance, rifles in hand, while others kept watch over the dark Carthaginian countryside. We were seated conspicuously in the Roman Pro-Consul's box, isolated from the few opera enthusiasts scattered throughout the immense theatre. The usual audience had not dared venture out after dark. We had, Alan explained, to show our faith in French ability to enforce law and order. I had no such faith, but if Alan chose to risk his life, I was going to be there too. It was a beautiful, starry night. The Roman columns were illuminated, the acoustics perfect and the Italian voices melodious, but I could not concentrate; my thoughts flew over the events of the past few days. Everything had happened so fast.

The Resident-General, in a grand gesture of reconciliation, released four hundred Tunisian political prisoners. He did not release Bourguiba, that elusive leader of the Néo-Destour. 'Bourguiba is nothing,' a Frenchman told me. 'He scribbles his articles. He's been in prison so long, he's out of touch, a figurehead.' So Bourguiba was merely transferred from exile on an island off Bizerta to better quarters on the Ile de Croix off Lorient in France. A grave mistake as we immediately realized. The Néo-Destour reacted with violence. They first demanded Bourguiba's release, then declared a general strike and their *Fellaghas*, those merciless guerillas, burnt down several French farms, murdered several *colons* – the first Frenchmen to be killed – and attacked a train. These were no longer isolated assaults on empty highways. This was war on the *colons*. Three to four thousand *Fellaghas* formed an 'Army of Liberation' scattered over the countryside. The *colons* fled in panic from their country farms, demanding, 'Where is law and order?'

They accused M Voizard of yielding too much power to Tunisians. They mobbed his plane as it came in from Paris and when he tried to speak they shouted, 'Traitor! Betrayal! Resign!'

'A humiliating spectacle,' Alan called it. 'A public onslaught on their own country's representative.' When I called on Madame Voizard she sighed saying, 'We're caught between fanatical reactionary *colons* here and left-wing politicians in Paris, and whatever goes wrong, everyone blames us.' Monsieur Voizard promised to send troops to protect the *colons* but they marched in protest down the main thoroughfare of Tunis. Ignoring the ban on open-air meetings, they demonstratively laid a wreath on the Unknown Soldier's grave.

'Since he is unknown,' Alan remarked, 'he might well be Tunisian!' The grave was outside the French HQ, a tempting target but there were too many police and troops massed in front. The *colons* restrained themselves and stood instead in mournful silence. Thousands of irate people in one spot – tempting for the *Fellaghas*.

What now? I wondered, as I leant closer up against Alan's firm 1shoulder. More violence? Would the *Fellaghas* distinguish us from the French? It was so dark. On the stage Alceste was at last dead, then resurrected and soon the performance was over.

We drove home through the starless, menacing countryside. Useless to hurry Cutajah. He was slow in thought and in action, but we reached home safely.

The French Residency cancelled all entertainment so, to gather information, Alan attended every ceremony and every party, 'ears flapping' as he put it. At a Consular Mass he sat through a long Papal *Pronunciamento* in Latin, without learning anything. At the races he learnt nothing either, but the Spanish Consul-General's farewell party seethed with rumour. I was laid up with the usual migraine, but Alan reported, 'Someone took a pot-shot at the Prime Minister and hit his guard in the leg. The French officials are very nervous, and the *colons* refuse to return to their farms though the harvest is about to begin and troops are there to guard them.'

That night we listened as M Voizard pleaded over the radio. 'Both sides must give up violence,' he kept repeating.

'He sounds very angry,' Alan remarked, and added, 'the *colons* call him 'Mohamed Voizard'! I felt for him, cornered between the Tunisians struggling for the dignity of independence and the *colons*, deeply attached to the land their ancestors

131

had lovingly nurtured. We had made friends among them, hard-working, hospitable folk. They did not invite and then ignore us like the Residency clique. I felt for all of them. But when I once tried to suggest that there were elements in Tunisia who wished for friendship with France, one lady exclaimed, 'You can't make friends with Arabs!'

'People don't know whether to give up entertainment,' Alan said, 'as the situation is not really serious enough for 'making the best of things!''

At home Alan and Joseph hurried to fill up the holes in our cactus hedge with barbed wire. 'It's only a precaution,' Alan told me. 'A nasty, prickly business, but with children around. . .' We were all tense.

A welcome distraction was a young British jet pilot who collided with another jet, managed to eject and was pulled out of the sea near Bizerta. The other pilot also ejected and was safe in Malta. Dizzie drove there to fetch him. We started worrying when it got late and dark, and they had not returned. Finally when they arrive, Dizzie explained, 'We missed the ferry and the French wouldn't let us drive round by Ferryville. Said it wasn't safe. They've had a lot of trouble with 'terrorists'. They're no longer bandits or *Fellaghas*.'

The children gazed admiringly at the pilot's red eye where a blast of air had caught it as he ejected. On the beach they watched with interest as Anna and Leo, in the briefest bathing suits, spread themselves out on the sand, pretending to ignore the pilot, who kept turning somersaults. As they would not pay attention he drenched them with water till they squealed in unnaturally high-pitched voices. The young were fortunately not troubled by political crises.

Hassin was not his usual, smiling self. I spotted a massive shoulder behind an open cupboard door. 'What are you doing?' I asked him.

He stepped out, one hand behind his back.

'What is it, Hassin? Something wrong?'

'I'm smoking,' and he showed me the cigarette he was concealing.

'So I see, but why hide?'

'I'll get beaten up if anyone finds out.'

'Why?'

'Cairo radio says Moslems are forbidden to smoke, drink alcohol or enter cafés. Those who do will be punished.'

'But why worry what Cairo says? And anyway who's to know what you do here?'

He glanced towards the kitchen. 'Young men in the streets are stopping people and beating up smokers. They force people to tell on their neighbours and friends. They could seize Mahomet, threaten him and force him to tell. Everybody's frightened. Ahmed only just got away on his bicycle.'

One morning Hassin told me, 'These young men beat up a Tunisian who works for the French. Frenchmen were drinking coffee in the street. They watched and did nothing to help.'

'And you, Hassin?' He shook his head.

Next day Hassin looked very pale as he reported, 'Madame, today I tried to help. Two men were attacked. I ran to them, but a young man was holding a razor.'

'I'm sorry, Hassin! I shouldn't have said anything. It was not fair. It's too much for any of us. No, keep away from it all.' We sighed together.

I could hear Cairo radio blaring forth in the kitchen. Cairo, so far away yet with the power to terrify Hassin. Alan confirmed what Hassin had told me and added, 'The French are delighted. They say Tunisians are getting a taste of Arab ideas of government.'

I felt safe in our own household but one morning Libet came running in, tears on her plump cheeks, 'Mummy! My rabbits have gone, and the door is closed. Someone's stolen them!' Sure enough, they could not have escaped. How did anyone know where they were kept? The rabbit run was concealed from the entrance by thick shrubs. The thief must be acquainted with our household, an alarming thought.

My arms round Libet, we hurried to the kitchen. Hassin, Mahomet and Ali jumped up and Hassin asked, 'What's happened, Madame?'

'My rabbits have been stolen,' Libet wailed.

Lawrence came running in, '*Arabes méchants!*' he spat the words out like Joseph. The three Arabs stood transfixed, staring at the floor, the guilt of the whole Arab world on their shoulders.

'Darling, don't say that,' I spoke in English. 'Hassin is an Arab and you love him.' Lawrence choked back his sobs.

Hassin looked up and spoke urgently, 'Madame, Arabs are not thieves, but times are troubled and people have become so strange.'

Mahomet murmured, 'Ahmed?' Could it be Ahmed? He was so poor. We were instructed to pay the minimum customary wages and that was not enough to feed a family. The Foreign Office invariably repeated that they or rather the Treasury had the tax payers' interests in view. Would the taxpayers approve if they saw Ahmed's hungry family? I could not put out of my mind an old Bedouin woman collecting chaff after a field had been gleaned. Her wasted flesh showed through holes in her dress.

Hassin ignored Mahomet. 'I'll find out who's taken the rabbits,' he promised.

'Perhaps someone's eating them at this very moment,' and sobbing Lawrence ran out, and hid his face in Shaggy's furry neck.

That night we locked the main gates and padlocked the rabbit run. Shaggy was transferred to the farm.

Hassin insisted, 'I shall stay up and watch the rabbits tonight.'

Next morning Hassin had a black eye. 'Ah Madame, what an adventure! It was so dark. No moon. I stayed close to the rabbits. Suddenly I heard something stirring. Bent double I sprang forward and crashed head-on with the thief's forehead. We were both knocked out. I heard him gasp and I passed out. When I came to the thief had gone!'

I laughed. 'You had better go to the village and see who has a black eye.' Ahmed was cleared.

In the midst of these events Alan announced, 'Another naval visit, in four days's time. *The Cumberland*. Not an opportune moment; the French have now despatched Moroccan *goums*, their toughest Arab troops, to chase the *Fellaghas*. A dirty business. Let's hope our chaps don't get involved.' Alan was already pale with late night reporting and now this naval visit! I burst out, 'Every time there's a crisis we have a naval visit!'

Alan was called to the French Residency. I did not expect to be told anything; Foreign Service officials were not allowed to confide in their wives but on his return Alan exclaimed, 'The government is collapsing. One Minister has resigned and others are expected to follow suit.' More trouble, more uncertainty.

The Cumberland's arrival was proclaimed by a telephone call. 'Is Mavis there? This is *The Cumberland*.' So Mavis's attractions had spread throughout the Malta naval base! Libet answered the call and shouted, 'Mavis! The Navy!'

Alan drove off to Bizerta resplendent in white summer diplomatic uniform with a high gold-braided collar, gold buttons and, to the children's delight, with a silver spike on his white helmet.

I had to drive up alone for lunch on board. Cutajah and I chatted but as we neared Bizerta, I remembered the cutting in the cliffs where Alan had joked, 'It's ideal for highwaymen!' The *Fellaghas*! Without Alan's flag there was nothing to show we were not French. Our Spanish colleagues had been held up by *Fellaghas* and panicking they had claimed to be British. 'It's not right!' I had exclaimed. 'They've put us in danger. The *Fellaghas* will never believe we're British too!' Alan had merely shrugged.

As we drew nearer Cutajah's voice died away and I fell silent. The countryside looked desolate. Nothing moved on the stony, reddish earth with its deep gullies. Pitted, cruel rocks loomed up on either side of the road. Cutajah crawled up to them.

'No, Cutajah, please fast!' He gripped the wheel and for the first and probably only time, he stamped on the accelerator. We shot in among the rocks, and into the cutting. I held my breath, staring ahead. Then we were through. Cutajah slowed down and wiped his brow.

On board *The Cumberland* I grasped a glass of wine and was glad of the chatter. In an argument with my friend M Le Mire, he concluded by saying, 'You are right, but I also am not wrong.' Typical French reasoning!

Many guests did not turn up, sensibly so, I thought. Admiral Josan grumbled, 'It's all this fuss over Bourguiba. He has a telephone, the postal service, visitors, not much to complain of.' Then he went on, 'Tomorrow, after my dinner party, please stay the night. I will feel happier, but now please go, before the sun sets.' He was insistent though his second-in-command remarked cheerfully, 'It's quite safe. I chased the bandits away.'

'Let's not prove him wrong,' Alan remarked and we left. Only one car passed us on that normally busy road. We were silent all the way.

I was arranging the place-names for our lunch party the next day when I heard Mavis shouting, 'Mrs Williams! Mrs Williams!' I rushed out. She was carrying Lawrence, his face and shirt covered in blood. 'Shaggy bucked,' she gasped, 'caught his hoof on Lawrence's face.' Lawrence was murmuring, 'I can't see! I can't see!'

Hands shaking I laid him on his bed. Was he badly hurt? His brain damaged? His eyes? Stifling my fears into frozen calm, I clamped a thick wad of cotton-wool over his face. I sat beside him, holding his hand and we waited for the doctor. At last he arrived. Lawrence had a deep cut between his eyebrows. The doctor put a clip to hold the edges of the wound together. Lawrence did not cry or struggle. He lay still. He realizes this is serious, I thought. The doctor washed, disinfected and finally bound his head up. My mouth was trembling; I could not speak.

'He's all right,' the doctor said. 'There'll be no scar, but no riding the donkey for a while.' Then he turned to Lawrence, 'You were a good boy,' and he gave him a kiss. Lawrence jumped up, gave us a mischievous grin from under the bandages and ran to the kitchen to show off his bandages. Then he obediently got back into bed. Later I saw him in the garden, arms round Shaggy and I felt reassured.

Our guests included Tunisian Ministers, though now they were no longer Ministers for that morning the whole government had resigned.

'Such a waste of invitations!' Alan exclaimed.

I was able to sit quietly and recover as the officers tucked into Ali's succulent dishes, the Tunisians dispensed charm and the French wit as though nothing untoward had occurred. Not a word was spoken about the troubles. The navy would consider it bad form. But after the champagne and liqueurs, and over coffee, I could not resist asking my neighbour, an elegantly dressed Tunisian doctor, what Tunisians hoped for from the French.

He chose his words carefully and formally. 'In an interview with *Paris Match*, a magazine banned here,' and he glanced round the room but no one was paying us any attention, 'Bourguiba explains that he wants close co-operation with the French on strategic, economic and cultural matters. We both need it, he said. We are geographically close. But this can only arise when we have freedom and sovereignty. Colonialism and freedom do not go together; they clash.' So Bourguiba was prepared to concede much to the French and was ready to collaborate with them.

'But this violence?' I asked.

'It's the result of despair, Bourguiba says. We've been

promised sovereignty over and over again and every time it has come to nothing. We are a peaceful nation, unarmed. The French are militarily strong. It's the French who by their arrests, deportations, exiles have provoked the violence. Naturally we deplore it but . . .' he shrugged. I understood. Without violence they could never achieve sovereignty. We sat silent, saddened by the thought. He had been careful not to indicate his own views. I could well believe that he wanted close co-operation with France. French came naturally to him. But for his dark hair and olive complexion I would have taken him for a Frenchman. It seemed that as for so many Tunisians, France was his cultural *Alma Mater*.

He lent towards me and lowered his voice. 'Bourguiba says the French must act before the trench of tears and blood which is being dug becomes insurmountable.' He turned quickly away. He was what the Nationalists called a 'French stoodge', yet he evidently agreed with Bourguiba.

When the other guests left, the officers fussed over Lawrence. He was on the swing, playing the hero and shouting, 'Higher! Higher!' and the officers pretended to push him higher while I watched anxiously. The usual functions then took place and soon the naval visit was over.

So many frightening things had happened. I had braced myself to cope, but now I collapsed into an armchair on the terrace.

'Alan,' I said, 'I've never known such a post for guests, official visitors and the navy.

He was silent at the door. Then half-way out, he said, 'I'm afraid we've another naval visit straight away and it's Mountbatten.'

'Mountbatten!' I exclaimed.

'With Lady Mountbatten, their daughters Lady Brabourne and Lady Pamela Mountbatten and Sir Malcolm Sargent. He's musical director for the navy. They hope to have a good rest here informally. Some hope!'

'But Alan . . .' He grinned, spread his arms wide, palms up, Arab-fashion, and as usual escaped to the office.

Royalty! Rest . . . here . . . My head in a whirl, my heart beating unnaturally fast, I ran into the garden and headed for the rabbit run. There was something soothing about Shaggy trotting around, rubbing up against me, the rabbits scurrying about, the tortoises climbing over my sandalled toes. A small round object lay on the gravel. A tiny tortoise egg! I picked it up; it was intact. Carefully I laid it back on the warm gravel. I placed four bricks round it, two on top to cover it and a heavy stone to keep them in place. The egg should be safe. A tortoise egg of our own!

17

Lawrence and I clutched hands and gaped! Handsome as a Grecian god, Mountbatten stood at the top of our sweep of steps, tall, straight, uniform startling white against his sun-tanned face. The red ribbon of the Legion of Honour stretched across a chest, covered with decorations; a diamond star glittered in the brilliant sunshine. From his shoulder hung a golden lanyard and at his side a sword. His blue eyes in classical, strong features, gazed down at us. Police vans and motor-cyclists circled around in the court-yard below. We stood rooted.

'Aren't you going to let him in?' A voice brought me down to earth. Sir Malcolm Sargent was prancing up the wide steps, his long legs taking two at a time.

I pulled myself together. 'Yes, do come in,' and I led this magnificent figure into the Grand Salon, followed by a grinning Flag-lieutenant, resplendent in gold braid.

All morning I had prepared for the moment. Remain calm. Nervous? Why be nervous? I should be used to VIPs. I was rated one myself! Ridiculous! But my insides were all fluttering wildly.

Sir Malcolm gave Lawrence a hug and whispered, 'Now away with you, there's a good boy.' Lawrence ran off.

Slowly, with the deliberate gestures of an actor, the Admiral unbuckled his sword, laid it on a side-table and stood waiting.

'He's roasting! He wants to get out of all that paraphernalia,' Sir Malcolm commented, his monkey-face beaming.

'Yes, would you like to change?' Alan also in uniform, had joined us and he led him and his adjutant off to the bedroom set aside one for the men, the other next to it was for the women. Sir Malcolm was already in an open-necked shirt.

Another car swept into the driveway. The famous Lady Mountbatten! 'Infamous', she had been called. Gossipers maintained that she was frivolous, spoilt by too much money and, worst of all, her name was linked with several famous men.

Here she was, slim, in a simple cotton dress, with a sun-tanned face, a broad brow and large, friendly eyes – a very attractive woman. She came towards me, arms outstretched, followed by her two daughters. I took to her immediately.

As we shook hands, I told myself, no getting flustered or overawed . . . concentrate, do the right thing. My only contact with British Royalty had been at a Buckingham Palace Garden party when a gust of wind burst the elastic on my wide-brimmed straw hat and sent it spinning across the lawns. Nothing like that mush happen now. I showed the women to their room. Arab-style, the rooms led into each other so that they had to pass through the mens' room to reach the bathroom. That's local colour, I decided, and can't be helped. The valet went off with Hassin to iron the clothes to be worn later.

Mountbatten had made it a rule to accept only one meal or one party in any consular household. He had asked for a cocktail party that afternoon. But evidently the family would be hungry after leaving *HMS Surprise* in Bizerta early that morning; we had to feed them. We had discussed what to do.

'Rules are made to be broken,' Alan had decided. 'Prepare a sumptuous buffet – he is royal – but call it a snack.'

While he was changing Alan told me, 'A policeman's been shot by the *Fellaghas*. This morning. The French immediately said the whole family must stay aboard the *Surprise*. They're scared stiff something might happen to them. But the kudos of entertaining such a famous personage was too much! They've relented. Now police vans are all over the place. It will be like that all the time. The Admiral gave me a dirty look when he saw them. Bang went his hopes of being left alone.' Alan sighed. 'Yes, the French are scared stiff and so am I! I'll be glad when it's all over.' Then he added, 'if he wants me around all the time, I shall collapse, but if he doesn't, I shall fell slighted!' and he grinned.

'Surely,' I protested, 'the *Fellaghas* wouldn't touch the Mountbattens! He led India to independence!'

'You never know,' and Alan sighed again.

We found Lady Mountbatten chatting to our guest, Janet, a secretary and a friend from my pre-marriage days. She had introduced herself saying, 'Oh Hullo! I'm Edwina Mountbatten.' Janet explained that she was on holiday here.

'Oh good!' Lady Mountbatten exclaimed. 'Then you can

join in all our festivities,' and she sat down beside Janet and wanted to know all about her.

'What a friendly person,' Janet later commented.

The others joined us. I said my piece, 'Shall we go in for a light snack?' and I led the whole party into the dining-room. Mavis refused to appear. 'I'll faint if he speaks to me!' she assured me.

'Dickie!' his wife whispered, 'it's a buffet. Pick up a plate and help yourself. Go on!' He did so, taking generous helpings of smoked salmon and cray-fish pâté with red caviar. The others followed suit. They all had healthy appetites.

'Some snack!' Sir Malcolm murmured as he helped himself to vol-au-vent stuffed with prunes and shrimps, and waved a hand at the pineapple stuffed with fruit salad and ice cream.

As he ate Mountbatten chatted to his daughters, 'The Beylical guard did a spirited but such an unusual rendering of 'God save the Queen' that I didn't recognize it till it was over.'

Lady Mountbatten turned to Janet. 'Dickie was calling on the Bey this morning.'

He went on, 'We were given sweetmeats – awkward things to manage if you are called on to talk at any moment.' Lady Mountbatten smiled at Janet, making sure she felt included. With her around, I thought gratefully, no one will feel left out.

The chocolate cream mousse sparkling on ice had disappeared. Lunch was over, 'Can we explore the palace?' the women asked.

'Of course. Do. Anywhere you like.' They strolled off, examining and exclaiming over the patterned and coloured wall tiles. I admired all three, so elegant in their simple, cotton frocks.

The Admiral headed for Alan's study and his books, and I saw Sir Malcolm's tall figure in the garden, Libet and Lawrence clinging to his hands, prancing along, leading him to the rabbit run. All had made themselves at home and I dived into the kitchen which was seething with preparations for the cocktail party.

Later I sat waiting for our guests on the back terrace when Sir Malcolm joined me. We started discussing music. He maintained, 'Whatever is good should be left to express itself, even if it has been said a hundred times. Everyone is taught nowadays to be original and that makes one false and the result worthless.' Then he suddenly asked,

'Are we overwhelming you?'

'No, not at all,' and I smiled politely.

'I don't believe that.' He sat down beside me. 'How do you cope, and with this enormous place to run?'

'Nothing's difficult in itself.' And then I found myself speaking frankly, 'It's just that we wives never know what to expect. We can't plan in advance or arrange things our own way. We have no control over our lives.'

'I couldn't live like that!' His eyes, in a darkly-tanned face with the thinning hair swept back off a high forehead, were kindly, sympathetic. Suddenly I was saying,

'Silly things. For instance, we have to attend functions involving long journeys and well, it's ridiculous, but people don't provide ladies' rooms or even if they do, you can't be certain they will so you're a nervous wreck worrying about it.'

He laughed, then was serious again, 'Can't you tell all this to the Foreign Office? Tell them what's needed?'

'As far as the Foreign Office is concerned, wives don't exist.' I had never talked so frankly before, nor did I feel embarrassed. I looked at Sir Malcolm closely – a sensitive face.

We foregathered on the back terrace over tea. Lawrence showed off Billy, his chameleon, that our Irish friend Miss Bourke had given him, a grotesque, frog-like, speckled creature with a long tail.

Mountbatten exclaimed, 'A chameleon! I brought two for my nieces, Elizabeth and Margaret, the Queen, you know.' The children nodded solemnly. His references to 'My cousin, the King of Sweden,' or 'My nephew, Prince Philip,' plunged us into an awed silence but his natural manner put us immediately back at ease. 'I'll show you how it eats.' We had spent whole evenings catching flies for Billy and watching his tongue, twice his own length, whip out, seize a fly and in a flash whip back in again. But politely we crowded round as Mountbatten placed Billy along his index finger and Billy, as was his nature, took on its pink hue. He clutched the finger with his long-nailed, five-toed claws. The front ones had three toes on the outside and two on the inside; the back claws the reverse. Flies buzzed around.

'Come on old boy! Eat.' The Admiral encouraged him. We willed Billy to perform but he only hissed; his eyes, flat on either side of his head, swivelled individually round at us but he refused to catch a single fly.

'Come on! Come on!' Mountbatten was getting impatient, and we embarrassed.

'Showing off never pays,' Sir Malcolm remarked. The Admiral laughed and handed the obstinate Billy back to Lawrence.

☆   ☆   ☆

We separated to change for the cocktail party. Tunis had seethed all day with excitement. The telephone rang every few minutes: 'Do we curtsey? Are hats compulsory?'

We lined up with the Admiral and Lady Mountbatten to receive the guests. The officers from the *Surprise* came early, ready to entertain the guests, who started arriving, elegant in garden-party clothes. (The husbands must have ruined themselves over the dresses). They filed past, bowing and curtseying, then darting away, too overawed to stop and talk, though the Admiral tried to restrain them. Once the Grand Salon had filled up, we moved to the terrace. It was a warm evening, not too hot, with a gentle, refreshing breeze. The sun was setting and shone straight into our eyes. The Mountbattens could not see whom they were greeting.

'Better change over to the other side,' the Admiral suggested and we hurried across only to find that the guests were now squinting at us.

'It's no good. They can't see anything,' Lady Mountbatten murmured. 'Back we go!' They stood all evening, the sun in their eyes and hot on their faces, smiling and shaking every hand. Mrs Leland-Smith was a magnificent sight – a symphony in white. She nearly tripped as she curtseyed low, her long, gown billowing out and her colossal straw hat inclined gracefully over her long neck. 'He's even handsomer than I thought,' she whispered later and the women standing nearby nodded. Sir Malcolm had been entertaining the prettiest girls but now he loomed up at her side, twirling a monocle attached to a black ribbon round his neck. Mavis and the Dismore girls had been swallowed up among the white uniforms.

Later Sir Malcolm was whispering behind me, 'We locked up the animals and I've given Libet and Lawrence a bath, I've read them a story and they're tucked up in bed.' Before I had time to thank him, he had disappeared. Mavis must have forgotten the children. Afterwards they told me Sir Malcolm had taught them 'a lovely game. You jump on one leg and try to push each other into the bath water!'

☆   ☆   ☆

143

We retreated to change for the dinner-dance at the Resident-General's. No one mentioned the inconvenience of going through each other's rooms. Would I get at least a waltz with Alan? I wondered, as I dressed quickly into my best evening dress – white organdie with a tight bodice and full skirt, over a stiff petticoat. Once dressed I hurried to the drawing-room to await the others. I heard Sir Malcolm's voice, 'I'm exhausted' and laughter. He was in evening dress and sprawling on a couch, an arm round each of the Dismore girls, with Mavis at his feet. A group of officers were scowling at the far end of the room listening as he went on, 'Darlings, I was telling a story to my guests one lunch-time and I heard my daughter, aged eight, ask her brother 'What are you laughing at?' 'Dad's joke, It's a new one on me.' To which my daughter replied 'You're lucky'.'

What a flirt, I thought. Then remembering our conversation before tea, he's like Billy, the chameleon, I decided, and responds with sympathy to the personalities around him. He enjoys animals, children and pretty girls equally.

The Mountbattens were ready and looking more glamorous than ever, including the daughters, the elder with dark hair, big dark eyes and a lively face and the younger – 'a golden goddess' an officer later called her, after he had watched her water-skiing. We carried Sir Malcolm off, to the relief of the officers who could now crowd round the girls. So far all had gone well and was under control.

Police cars prodded us forward. The huge white mass of the French Residency rose up from behind graceful, arched fronds of palm trees. We sat down, forty guests, long menus before us – *Foie Gras, Langouste, Escalope de Veau* . . . The Mountbattens, cheerful and friendly, entertained at either end of the table. The rest of us talked in subdued tones. The whole table was electrified by Mountbatten's powerful presence. My neighbour whispered, 'Such charm, so much warmth and both natural to him!' and then he added, 'He's so masculine, virile; makes us look like sissies!'

Dancing followed on the patio under the wide, star-lit sky. The Mountbatten daughters danced and chatted with their French hosts with the confidence I envied but I suddenly realized that, just like myself, they remained backstage, on the sidelines, forming a background for their parents just as I played a supporting rôle for any visiting VIPs and always for Alan.

I did not enjoy dancing with these relative strangers whose clammy hands were on my bare back, their hot breath in my face, and their bodies too close to mine. But when an old-fashioned Viennese waltz started up Alan hurried over and we floated off together. He was a superb dancer, so light on his feet. We whirled round and round, my wide skirt billowing out, then reversed round and round again. I was myself, happy, relaxed, unworried, no longer a background.

The music stopped too soon. The Mountbattens were off to Bizerta and Alan and I left soon after. It had been great fun and I was enjoying basking in the Mountbattens' glory!

☆　　☆　　☆

Next day we drove to Bizerta for lunch on the *Surprise*. We were well on time so as to arrive before the French guests were piped on board – the Resident-General, Admiral Josan and his wife, and two other Admirals, Sala and Barrière who had managed to be on hand. General de Latour, C-in-C Tunisia, was missing. M Voizard sat frowning; Admiral Josan kept looking out of the portholes but the Mountbattens remained unperturbed and supplied us with cocktails. A quarter of an hour passed, then half and still no General. M Voizard refused further drinks and stared glumly at the floor. At last piping announced the General's arrival, three quarters of an hour late.

'My most humble apologies.' The General bent low and kissed Lady Mountbatten's hand. 'My car broke down twice and then I missed the ferry. I am desolated.' M Voizard did not return his greeting but Lady Mountbatten, welcoming as ever, led the way into the dining-room.

The first course was a cheese soufflé, well risen and firm. I turned to the officer beside me 'How could the chef produce such a soufflé just at this moment? It's incredible!'

'It's his third!' he laughed.

As one delicious dish followed another the French thawed and soon the room was filled with laughter and loud voices, all hoping to be heard by Mountbatten.

'Mrs Williams thinks we should free Tunisia and receive her into a French alliance,' Admiral Josan said. 'As you did with India.'

'I never said anything of the sort!' Alan had warned me repeatedly never to discuss French policy.

'But that's what you think! I know.' Josan could never resist teasing me, but what he had guessed was true. The Resident-General frowned. The French rarely laugh at themselves, I thought, but when he saw me smiling, he relaxed.

Lunch over, we took coffee in deck chairs on the quarter deck where it was pleasantly cool. We could see the square minarets and the line of flat-roofed, white houses along the sea-front whose reflections in the still waters formed a kind of water-patio.

Mountbatten turned to the Resident-General beside him, 'How many of these difficult *colons* do you have in Tunisia, Monsieur Voizard?'

'Fifty thousand.' M Voizard sighed. 'And all they can think about is repression. As for reform . . .' he made a hopeless gesture with his hands. 'And if Mendés-France comes to power. . .'

'Yes? What do you expect then?' Alan raised his voice for the Admiral's eyes had closed and his mouth opened slightly.

'I dread to think . . . Could he command the respect of all parties? I doubt it.'

'Has Mendés-France the courage to carry through reforms?' Mountbatten was awake again but only for a moment. As Voizard began, 'He'll be unpopular with almost everyone . . .' Mountbatten was dozing once more.

The Resident-General smiled. His host was too handsome, too intelligent, too kindly to offend. He rose to take his leave. The Admirals followed.

'It's good, this place,' Mountbatten remarked. 'The navy should come here more often.' Alan and I did not dare laugh. More often! We went ashore. Arrangements had been made for us to take a siesta in Admiral Josan's house.

☆   ☆   ☆

We were back on the *Surprise* for the cocktail party. The deck was surrounded by little iron-work lanterns, whose reflections danced on the water. An orchestra played light music. I climbed eagerly aboard, no longer shy. I was wearing a brooch Lady Mountbatten had given me, fashioned in the shape of the *Surprise*. The whole of Bizerta turned up and most of official Tunis, in spite of the bandits. The Admiral concentrated on each guest equally, from the most arrogant to the most humble, and when M Le Mire, the Governor of Bizerta, poured his

146

troubles out and the next guest was waiting, Lady Mountbatten intervened, 'You were explaining about the troubles here?' She provided M Le Mire with an opportunity to finish what he was saying. I was impressed. The officers took care of people standing alone and no one was overlooked. I'm learning, I thought. Lady Mountbatten even glanced round to make sure her daughters were enjoying themselves. If all hostesses were as considerate, I thought, cocktail parties could be fun!

A piercing 'Hi-on'. A donkey cart had driven up to the gangway. It was Miss Bourke, our Irish friend, in her best flowered, straw hat, who lived in a Moorish residence, Ben Negro, overlooking Bizerta, once owned by her father, a British Vice-Consul. He sold it to the French when they decided to build the naval base. Miss Bourke lived alone with a few old retainers, surrounded by donkeys, sheep, dogs and cats.

Miss Bourke's ancient Tunisian driver helped her as she stepped with great dignity out of the cart. Mountbatten turned, laughing to Alan, 'Who is the lady?' Alan explained, adding, 'Usually she's on the donkey itself.'

We left with the setting sun. M Le Mire was anxious. 'Does your husband carry a gun?'

'No, he doesn't believe fire-arms are any protection. A gun gives an assailant an excuse to shoot. The flag should protect us.'

'In the dark? Guests from Tunis did not dare drive up. In fact, people won't go out at all after dark.' He made me nervous as we left the lights of Bizerta and plunged into the dark countryside.

'Well, thank goodness, no one's been shot so far,' Alan remarked.

18

It was the Mountbattens' last day. They arrived in time for a late breakfast, the Admiral in an open-necked, short-sleeved shirt, with a panama hat set at a jaunty angle. Colonel Mas-Latrie, who was conducting the day's tour to the holy city of Kairouan, hurried to the telephone to inform everyone that the Admiral was *en tourist*. Nevertheless, the officials turned up in white suits, and Alan too was formally dressed in a white suit and black tie.

During the night Fatma had been taken seriously ill and had been carted off to her mother's. Later, eyes flashing and waving her arms, she told me she had fainted. Ali decided she was dead, wrapped her in a sheet, laid her on the floor, climbed back into bed and fell asleep. She came to, imprisoned in the sheet. She struggled and cried out, but Ali thought she was a ghost and hid under the bedclothes. It took him some time to realize she was alive. I laughed, to Fatma's disgust. Hassin's Zora was also down with influenza. Nevertheless, both servants carried on as though nothing had occurred.

We all sat down with our guests; I did not consider sending the children away. Lawrence stood at the Admiral's elbow, and watched each morsel of poached egg as it went into his mouth.

Mountbatten turned to him. 'Do you speak Arabic?

'A little.'

'What's father in Arabic?'

'Bou.'

'Daughter?'

'Bint.'

'What's 'Imshi'?'

'Go away.'

'Well then, 'Imshi'!' Lawrence stared at the ground but did not move. Alan and I looked at him imploringly. He could be so stubborn and Mountbatten was not someone to be disobeyed. But the Admiral laughed and ruffled Lawrence's

From left to right, Sir Malcolm Sargent, the author, Admiral Mountbatten, Lady Brabourne, Libet, Lady Mountbatten, Lawrence, Alan, Lady Pamela Mountbatten. Taken by Mavis.

unruly fair hair.

As we were getting ready to depart, I glanced out of the window; men in dirty jackets and faded trousers with berets and red scarves were climbing out of a car!

'Alan! Quick! Come here! Suspicious characters!'

He was with me in no time and put a finger to his lips. 'French Secret Service! They're coming with us.' I did not like the look of them.

We foregathered in the courtyard. The children pranced round Sir Malcolm.

'No! No! Best behaviour,' he whispered. They immediately stood still and held his hands. Mavis plucked up immense courage and asked for a group photograph. The Mountbattens lined up. Then the convoy moved off – a police car, Mountbatten driving himself and Sir Malcolm in an open Austin, Alan and I with the French Colonel, the three Mountbatten women and another police car. The 'rogues', as I labelled them, followed at a distance. Lawrence, a tiny figure, stood at attention beside Hassin and saluted the Admiral as he drove past.

The Colonel apologized. 'Madame, I'm sorry my wife is not coming. She does not feel up to it.' I understood. My stomach was a-flutter. A whole day . . . so many pitfalls . . . and would they be safe even with the police and the 'rogues'?

'Is everything quiet?' Alan asked.

'Not exactly' the Colonel answered. 'They've started machine-gunning cafés in the Arab quarter. One lot machine-gunned people in the street as they ran away.'

'So, it's the French now, the *colons*?'

The Colonel nodded. 'The Resident-General is furious. He's bringing in parachutists and *goumiers* from Morocco. We've already got a thousand Tunisian suspects in detention. We're rounding up anyone without identity cards but the *colons* are never satisfied. In fact, they don't want any dialogue with the Tunisians. They want the *status quo* and nothing else.' He sighed and stared out of the window at the troops stationed at turnings and on hilltops, who kept saluting not the big man in an open-necked shirt driving himself but Cutajah in the back of our car – Alan was driving – in his smart white cap and white uniform. Not much of a family outing for the Mountbattens, I thought!

It was a dreary but peaceful scene, the land scorched dry. Donkeys ambled along, boys perched on their loads, legs hanging limply, and horses with heads lowered under the blazing sun, pulled carts filled with bundles of snoozing Arabs.

An occasional driver, awake, leant on an elbow, and stared into the distance while his horse went its own way. Everything moved slowly, sensibly and ignored us as we sped past in a continual storm of dust. Why couldn't we drive slowly too? We overtook camels, their inquisitive noses held high as they advanced at a dignified pace, pulling carts or carrying great weights. One, on the very edge of the road, did not even turn its head as we whizzed past.

At Enfidaville we were unexpectedly met by the French *Contrôleur Civile*, in uniform, and the Tunisian Caïd, in long, flowing robes and headcloth with a twisted coil holding it in place: together the source of power. They made their bows and led us to the War Graves' Cemetery, where Mountbatten inspected rows of white tombstones. As a hero of the last war, even on holiday, he could not ignore our casualties in Tunisia. But, I wondered, had it occurred to him that by honouring the armed forces above all other institutions, we were sanctifying the use of force, sanctifying war? We venerate war, I thought. His face, always composed, told me nothing.

Then down into the heat below. Slithers of shimmering

water under the trembling air, retreated before us – mirages. An eagle soared away above us into the blue, broad wings spread wide.

A line of lorries approached. The police car motioned them to the side of the road but one lorry drove straight down the middle. Sir Malcolm jumped up and 'conducted' him away, waving long, slim arms. The astonished driver swerved and nearly came off the road. Sir Malcolm sat down, satisfied.

Suddenly on the horizon, out of the heat haze, a magic city appeared. Behind white crenellated ramparts rose a multitude of minarets, domes and golden globes on slender spikes. This was no mirage. It was the ancient city of Kairouan. Mountbatten put on a tie, the ladies tore the scarves off their heads, put combs through their hair and looked fresh and calm. Cavalry was lined up to greet them.

We swept in, escorted by motor-cyclists, and up to the house of the *Contrôleur Civile*. Madame led us into clean, neat rooms where we could wash and brush up. I asked, 'Madame, please, where is the toilet?' She looked embarrassed, then reluctantly led me down a dark passage where children's dolls, toy cars, discarded clothing and heaps of magazines littered the floor.

She murmured, 'I'm sorry. I wasn't expecting . . .' And she glanced back towards the Mountbattens.

'It's all right. They won't mind,' I assured her. 'It happens to us all.'

We came down for lunch. We had asked for something light but we got what the French consider a light lunch – three courses with three wines and there would be no siesta to sleep it off.

We were ready to go. At the front door stood a Tunisian with a large camel and a young one beside it.

'The little one is a present for Lady Pamela,' the Caïd explained. 'Only it isn't yet weaned.' The baby camel muzzled up against her as Lady Pamela, so fair beside the Tunisians, stroked its velvety nose, and whispered, 'What shall I do?'

'Just thank him,' her mother said. 'Ask him to keep it for you.' The camels were led away.

The *Contrôleur* took us sight-seeing through rows of soldiers lining the streets. Lady Mountbatten rushed ahead while her husband followed, dozing on his feet. We visited the so-called Mosque of the Barber. It contained, our host explained, the tomb of a companion of Mahomet's, who always carried on his person three hairs from the Prophet's beard. These were buried with him and hence the name of the Mosque.

The minaret was pink with a gilded crescent. A horseshoe archway, a blue tiled hall, and open passages led into a quiet inner courtyard. Then we passed multi-coloured tiles depicting stylised cyprus trees and flowers, and polished marble pillars decorated with delicately pierced plaster work.

Inside, the shrine was cool and dark. Stepping from brilliant sunlight, we could see nothing. Then we made out people kneeling in prayer all round the walls, men in silken robes, and Berber peasants side by side. It was quiet. The tomb stood in a domed alcove lined with tiles and decorated with stylised quotations from the Koran. Clusters of small votive lamps hung from a crystal chandelier while candlelight flickered over the gold draperies covering the tomb. Below the gold was the green of Islam. We stopped in the entrance. This was a holy place and for the first time I felt Mahomet as a real person, a religious leader, and this the tomb of a real man, who loved him deeply. We stood in silence, then withdrew quietly. So peaceful here, I thought, and all those soldiers outside.

We came out once more into the scorching sunlight and entered an enormous open courtyard surrounded by massive walls leading into the Grand Mosque, the oldest in North Africa. 'Built in 695 by Oqba ibn Nafi,' the Caïd told us. Arab leaders had such intriguing names! It had been desecrated by French troops and therefore we infidels were allowed to enter it.

The Prayer Room was one mass of pillars,. 'Collected from Carthage, Sousse . . . almost everywhere,' the Caïd explained. They were of every colour, of marble, porphyry, onyx, alabaster, granite. The columns were Byzantine, Roman, Agladite, their capitals Roman, Byzantine with crosses on them and Arab too. An amazing scene, lit by numerous golden-glassed chandeliers. But beneath them, we suddenly realized, was a multitude of Tunisians, in robes and head-cloths, kneeling on their prayer mats, awaiting the call to prayer. They stared at us Europeans and unveiled women in silence.

'This seems the wrong moment . . .' Mountbatten began.

'Oh no, it's all right,' our host assured him. 'We have permission, have we not?' and he turned to the Caïd. The Caïd agreed. It was embarrassing being stared at and not knowing whether these men really approved of us being there or not.

Our host continued, speaking too loudly, I felt. 'There are seventeen aisles of columns here and eight larger ones crossing them.' He pointed to two pillars close together. 'If you can slip through between these two, you will go straight to Heaven.' Lady Mountbatten passed through easily and so did her two daughters.

'Sir Keith Officer couldn't squeeze through,' Alan murmured. I refused to try.

'I think we had better go,' Mountbatten decided.

'Right. Then let's go up the minaret,' Lady Mountbatten suggested. Our host and the Caïd exchanged glances. That was not part of the programme, but Lady Mountbatten was already crossing the courtyard. She was kind, dutiful and considerate but if she wanted something she was evidently used to getting it. Husband and daughters followed without protest.

We trudged up three storeys past walls pierced by narrow slits at least ten feet thick, and steps like ancient gravestones. We came out on to a domed pavilion opening on to a terrace on all four sides. The city sprawled out below us – flat square houses with green inner courtyards and winding black alleyways, surrounded by massive walls. The view stretched across flat, open country far away to the sea some forty miles to the east and in the west as far as the mountains, also some forty miles away. Ancient Kairouan was built safe both from the Byzantines along the coast and the Berbers in the mountains. Lady Mountbatten had been right to bring us up here, but the Caïd hurried us down again. The *muezzin* was waiting to call the faithful to prayer.

'The souk! Let's go to the souk.' Lady Mountbatten was climbing into the car. The *Contrôleur* and the Caïd started arguing in rapid French. I caught the words 'not safe . . . can't refuse . . . just at the edge . . .' The 'rogues' sped ahead. We followed. The police cars stationed themselves on either side of the souk entrance. The colonel went ahead, we followed. Black berets and red scarves mingled with brown burnouses and white abas in the dark recesses and alleyways.

'Do you think it's all right?' I whispered to Alan.

'They're worried. There's no room to prevent an incident or to cope with one.' We tried to admire the famous Kairouan carpets, beige and brown with geometrical designs, but were too conscious of dark corners around us.

'Where's your mother?' Mountbatten suddenly turned to the daughters. Lady Mountbatten was not among us. The 'rogues' rushed down the dim passages and dived into black recesses. There were so many. They darted in and out. We all stood still and listened. The Caïd glared at the *Contrôleur*. He had allowed us to come here. The Caïd was wiping his brow. If anything had happened to her Alan would be blamed. Could she have been kidnapped? Attacked? No sound, no cry. Where was she? Mountbatten's face was expressionless and the girls were watching him. No one moved. I felt cold. All those precautions, police, army, 'rogues' and she had disappeared.

Then suddenly Lady Mountbatten was among us. 'I was only looking at the silver,' she explained.

'She doesn't know what fear is,' Alan whispered and I remembered that as wife of the Viceroy of India she had cared for the sick in the slums in Delhi during the civil strife. No one could stop her and she always came out safely. We were bustled out of the souk, and climbed back into the cars.

We followed the Caïd's car to a little square. There our two guides got out and started shouting and waving their arms. Both wished to offer the Mountbattens a drink in their house. We were thirsty in that heat and after the wines. We climbed out of our car, but Mountbatten drove slowly round the square, and round and round again, and waited for them to calm down and to tell him where to go. Kairouan was an Arab city and the Caïd won. We traipsed into his house. His wife offered us coca-colas but the *Contrôleur's* wife refused to join us and the *Contrôleur* stood in a corner by himself. Then we left Kairouan.

El Djem was our next stop. We were behind schedule and the police car in front roared ahead at ninety miles an hour. I sat very still, holding my breath, staring at Cutajah's red neck. I'm always speeding, I thought, speeding through life ... Mountbatten's car, which Lady Pamela was now driving, got overheated and, to my relief, we had to slow down.

The Colosseum rose up suddenly out of the featureless plain, enormous with three tiers of high arcades – El Djem, the colossus of the desert.

'It is the largest Roman monument in Tunisia,' the Colonel told us. 'Nearly as big as the Colosseum in Rome.' It looked warm and glowed like honey in the sunlight. The *Contrôleur* and the Caïd met us and vied with each other to supply us with information. The Caïd began, 'It was built in 230 AD, the breach in the walls was made by a Bey to capture insurgents inside, since then . . .' Here the Caïd fell silent and the *Contrôleur* continued, 'Locals have stolen its marble and stone to build their own houses.' An old Tunisian, the official guide, hovered behind us. We were led down into the dark dungeons, gloomy and chilling, where 'Christians, and wild beasts were kept waiting sometimes for weeks for the games to start.' Waiting close together, the humans listening to the animal noises. Strange, this lust for horror that people feel. I imagined lions tearing at the sensitive flesh of men and women, crowds watching avidly right to the last agonizing cries . . . Quickly I led the way back up into the sunshine and the brilliant blue sky.

A policemen came running up and the Caïd informed us, 'A man has been shot. A Tunisian, by the *colons*! I must go, I'm sorry. The guide will take you round,' and he and the *Contrôleur* hurried away. Danger was close to us too and I was glad of the 'rogues' hovering around.

The guide, delighted to be back on his job, led the company up the high stone steps, along the vaulted galleries and out into the seating area. Birds flew out of nests in the broken capitals and in and out of the arches. He told us, 'The beautiful Queen Kanera, with her Berber tribes, held out for a whole year here against the Arabs. That was in 703 AD.' He spoke with pride. He must be a Berber, I thought. 'What a woman! When a more powerful prince insisted on marrying her she stabbed him to death in his sleep. When the Arabs defeated her, she plunged her sword into her own breast. Hassan, the Arab general cut off her head and sent it in a jewelled casket to his master, the Caliph of Baghdad.'

A typical gruesome Arab story, I thought. That severed head haunted me as I stumbled over large slabs of fallen marble, slipped dangerously close to the edge of what remained of the flooring. We were high up. There was no balustrade. I kept close to the wall, my hand touching it, and stepped slowly, gingerly forward. A wide gap! I looked down. It drew me! I felt sick and giddy. I could never step over it. The others were well ahead. I stopped and stood shivering. I can't go on! No! I clung to the wall, then slowly, I turned and started back. I groped along the wall, eyes straight ahead, down the steep steps, and finally, at last, I reached firm ground. I leant against a block of marble and felt humiliated.

'You don't like heights?' Sir Malcolm was beside me. 'Don't let it worry you. They're all athletes.' He glanced up at the Mountbattens near the top of the Colosseum. 'Like goats on a mountain. Let them enjoy themselves while we sit down in the shade and relax.' He looked in excellent shape, slim and muscular. He must have come down specially to reassure me. I smiled back at him.

We were off again, now to Sousse where the *Surprise* was awaiting the Mountbattens. The Admiral had again put on his tie and jacket and the ladies had combed their hair, though they always looked as though they had just stepped out of a glossy magazine. Just outside Sousse a large-sized motor-cycle escort surrounded us, swept us through the city walls and up to the docks. We arrived, a dusty bunch of tourists, to find an imposing guard of the Fourth Tunisian *Tirailleurs* drawn up with Colours and a band playing. Mountbatten smoothed his hair down, jumped out of the driving seat of his car and took the salute with the local Caïd, *Contrôleur* and Mayor.

'They expected him to turn up in a huge car and in spotless uniform,' Alan whispered. But the Mountbattens could cope with any crisis. They swept the officials on board and in no time an impromptu cocktail party was in full swing as the officers offered food and drink to the delighted guests.

The Colonel had been jittery. 'Better get back to Tunis before dark. The police cars are waiting to escort us.' But Lady Mountbatten insisted on a light supper first. Alan was about to decline; the Mountbattens had their official guests on board but the Colonel, glass in hand, and now red in the face, announced, 'Oh, never mind, it's not that late.' So, as the party proceeded without them, the Mountbattens kept us company in the dining-room while we ate an omelette, salad and bread and cheese with fruit, already prepared and laid out for us. As we were finishing, an officer rushed in and turned to Lady Pamela, 'There's a wagon outside with a couple of camels in a cage. What am I to do with them?'

'Good gracious! What shall we do? What shall I say? Perhaps just the baby?' Lady Pamela was on her feet. Alan got up too, for once looking distraught.

'We can't have camels on board. Certainly not! Out of the question!' The Admiral was firm. Lady Pamela hurried out with a worried Captain. Mountbatten grinned. She was back in no time, 'Really!' and she glared at her father.

'You believed me! Camels!' and he rocked with laughter. We joined in and so did Lady Pamela. 'You had me worried,' she admitted.

As we were saying good-bye, Sir Malcolm reminded me, 'Remember, I'll help with the children when they go to boarding school. I'll meet them as they fly back and forth to wherever you are. I mean it. Don't forget!' He did mean it, I felt sure.

We waved for a long time as we drove off. The police cars in front and behind us, with the 'rogues' bringing up the rear, gathered speed and were soon racing along, a terrified Cutajah jammed between them. We'll be killed, I thought. They can't see where they're going. An animal . . . another car . . . and Alan does nothing. This mad racing . . . those treacherous heights . . . he knows I'm afraid. But then what can he do? The police are frightened of the *Fellaghas*. I clung to the car seat.

'There's safety in speed,' the Colonel remarked. I did not agree but at last we roared to a halt in our courtyard.

19

Outside it was ominously dark. 'Must we go? You said we shouldn't go out at night. No one else does.'

'If we're invited, we go.' Alan was firm. 'If the French go out then we must too.'

'What's the point of getting killed just for a party?'

'Nonsense, we won't get killed.' We might well, I thought, with the nationalists out to get any Frenchman, and who can distinguish a Britisher from a Frenchman in the dark?

We set out for Salammbô, just beyond Carthage, where a French lawyer was defying the assassins and giving a party. It was unbearably hot, with the sirocco blowing and I felt particularly vulnerable in my cotton evening dress with bare arms and shoulders. To be stopped by guerillas in what might seem to them almost a state of undress! I stared fearfully into the night.

The party was in full swing; couples swayed over the terrace tiles to a slow fox-trot played on a gramophone. The local French, unlike their aristocratic officials, were friendly and welcoming. They still exclaimed about Mountbatten's handsomeness and we basked in his shadow. Alan and I had received charming thank-you letters from the Admiral and from Lady Mountbatten, who wrote: 'You gave us such a happy and interesting time.' Cutajah was beaming. He said, 'Now I can hold my head up again. Everyone was saying that England is partly to blame for the troubles and I felt miserable, but now when I mention Mountbatten, everyone smiles and praises Britain!' Our host took my hand and we waltzed slowly round under the coloured fairylights – a tempting target.

It was an elegant scene, the men in white dinner suits, the women in low-cut gowns, displaying soft glowing pearls and brilliant diamonds, their perfumes mingling on the warm air. They're determined to preserve this kind of life, I thought, especially after the tremendous effort to achieve it. But somewhere below in the moon-lit countryside, I imagined a young man in a dark shift, crouching in the shadows under a palm tree, rifle in hand, his lean face determined, driven to ruthlessness, to murder. Get the French out . . . only way . . . and then freedom! I shivered. My host was staring into the darkness too and he gripped my hand painfully.

'It's so hot,' I said, 'I'd like a drink.' We joined a group arguing heatedly.

'Booing you own Resident-General! It should never have happened. And at a funeral! Someone even threw stones. In front of Tunisians too.' It was the legal adviser to the Residency speaking.

'Four Frenchmen were killed. Did he protect them?' a young man shouted.

'You forget the two Tunisians killed.' At that they all turned on him.

'Strike them hard! Force is all they understand.'

'Restore order. Make life safe, then talk of concessions.'

Eric da Rin, the Italian Consul asked quietly, 'And what sort of concessions?' They fell silent, long faces all round. The music stopped, the dancers crowded round and listened.

'We'll see what happens on July 20th,' and the official smiled at the faces glaring at him.

The Da Rins, the Touloupases and Alan and I settled at a small table. I felt comforted among these consular friends. The moon shone down on us, lights twinkled below along the coastline but the darkness threatened. We leant forward and spoke in whispers.

'July 20th?' Eric began 'Of course the elections in France. The magic date. To be or not to be for Mendés-France! And for Tunisia.' From the group of arguing Frenchmen we heard 'Mendés-France, a socialist! A Jew!'

Eric, invariably calm, frowned and went on, 'But even if he is re-elected Prime Minister will he have the courage to restart negotiations?'

'With the Nationalists?' Alan whispered the question. 'He'll have to. There's no one else left. And what a rumpus that'll cause here! Negotiating with murderers, they'll say.' I thought of my young man crouching over his rifle. 'But if he's not re-elected, then more arrests, shooting, assassinations.'

Johannis Touloupas joined in, his voice harsh, 'It's tragic. No leader whom all parties respect. No strong political party to take unpopular steps.' His thick eyebrows and his hands shot up. I couldn't help smiling; he looked like a conspirator himself.

'And they'll blame the Libyans, the Arab League, us British, the Americans or perhaps just the communists,' and Alan sighed.

There was a commotion as an officer rushed in. 'Dr Mami has been shot, getting out of his car, in front of his house, and a cousin with him too.'

In the silence someone murmured, 'Good riddance,' and someone else, 'Shut up.'

'The Bey's physician. He lives in La Marsa,' Alan spoke quietly. 'Better go home. We're not wanted here.'

On the way I asked, 'But who shot him? French *colons*?' Alan shrugged.

Next morning we heard over the radio that Colonel de la Paillonne had been shot. 'Nice man,' Alan remarked, 'but he stood for a tougher policy towards the Nationalists. A useful target – he was both French and close to the Bey.'

'Don't be cynical, Alan. They mustn't go on killing each other like this. It's horrible! But who is right, the French or the Tunisians?'

'Neither or both. There is no right or wrong: it's a matter of finding a solution that satisfies both parties. But we'd better put off any excursions into the countryside and keep the children at home. I notice the servants are keeping to the house and in any case the cafés are all closed.

'They're so quiet. There's no shouting. They're terrified.' I was too.

The Dismores sadly had been posted to Macao so we agreed to take their two dogs. 'They'll keep any undesirables away,' Alan decided, 'and we'll feel safer with them in the garden.' Blanco was a small brown and white terrier, an old dog, whose white streak across the forehead gave him a worried and, at the same time, a menacing look. He snapped at visitors, but allowed the children to hug him and followed them around. When he grew tired he settled at Alan's feet under his desk. We heard continual cursing as Alan inadvertently kicked him but did not like to dislodge him.

Herta was terrifying. Half alsatian, half St Bernard, a heavy, handsome creature. He had a fiercesome growl that rose to crescendo inside his massive neck and burst forth in a blood-curdling roar. I felt sorry for the undesirables and I kept well away from him too, though I hoped the children would not notice. Herta allowed the French in without protest, but rushed barking wildly at all Arabs. We did not know how he would treat our Maltese British – he chased Joseph up a tree – so I constantly shouted to the children, 'Who is he barking at now?' The servants kept out of his way, but when cornered, they turned and threatened him. To our surprise, Herta backed away. He was a coward! Alan killed a mosquito in front of his nose and now he was scared of Alan. I felt braver and felt affection for him as I watched the children marching him to the juniper tree where they liked to play, with two empty whisky cases full of their toys slung across his back. He was gentle with them.

Admiral Josan was leaving his command. Alan decided against taking me to his farewell party in Bizerta and I did not insist for I was recovering from a migraine. I was sorry not to say good-bye to the Admiral – a distinguished gentleman in the true sense of the word. I admired his love of France, his pride in her history, her 'greatness', but, I agonized, could he not sympathize with Tunisian pride too? Tunisians suffered banishment, imprisonment; they hid in the desert and in the mountains, all for the love of their country. Bourguiba, even from his prison, extended friendship to the French. I had read his appeals – keep defence and Foreign Affairs but give us home rule, a generous offer, besides being practical. And he spoke of the strong cultural, economic and political ties between France and Tunisia. Why didn't Josan see a patriot in Bourguiba? He called him – assassin! As a result Alan's in danger. We're all in danger. The children too.

Alan returned safely. I hugged him.

'I bet you were the only guest from Tunis,' I cried.

He grinned. 'I was stopped by a French patrol once and stones were thrown at the car, possibly by children. That's all that happened.' Then he told me, 'Mendés-France has scraped through. Now, if he chooses to, he can turn to the problem here. The French are horrified and I'm told the shootings are still going on.'

We had had numerous French children to play in the garden. Now I invited Mme Tahar Maoui to tea with her children. She brought six and beamed happily as she introduced them, the stalwart youth Raouf, then Hamel, Nela, Yussuf, and the twins Zoza and Mundjiya, all with big dark eyes and great mops of black hair. We sat on the back terrace as the children rushed for the swing, up the rope ladder, scuttled off on the tricycles and disappeared up the trees.

The Tahai Maoui Twins.

Children were everywhere. Ours gaped at the boys and girls laughing and calling out in French.

'Only the twins don't speak French,' Mme Maoui told me. She only knew a little herself.

At table the children were too excited to eat much, and rushed back into the garden, to Libet's disappointment. She hesitated, then had to leave Ali's chocolate cake to join her guests.

'You have lovely children,' I told their mother, 'and they all look so healthy.'

She beamed. 'Libet is pretty too and Lawrence is such a sturdy little man.' We continued to admire our children.

I taught them to play 'Palochka Postukalochka', a Russian game. They all hid, then they had to reach a certain tree and strike it three times with a stick while the child guarding the tree tried to catch them. Lawrence was the first guard. The others hid, then they came rushing in from all sides. He missed most but managed to catch the youngest boy.

'My little one!' his mother cried ecstatically and we looked down on the plump little fellow with his black curls and large, heavy-lidded eyes. He and Lawrence clutched each other, laughing hysterically.

When the car arrived to take them home, Mme Maoui invited Alan and me to a cous-cous lunch and a bathe the next day. 'And bring the children,' she added. 'They behave so well and do not trouble the grown-ups.' She climbed into the car, leaving the chauffeur to collect the children. As soon as he thrust several into the car, others scrambled up the banyan tree. Mme Maoui took no notice and continued talking to me. The chauffeur kept calling, 'Children please! Come! Children!' At last all were inside.

At that moment Alan drove in from the office. 'Monsieur Voizard is leaving,' he announced. 'Apparently he's lost his nerve. He's unpopular on all sides.'

Mme Maoui leant out of the car, 'And who's replacing him? Such terrible times!'

'General de la Tour.' The General had commanded the French forces in Tunis. 'He's nearing the end of his career; he won't be inhibited by thoughts of the future. Six thousand additional troops are arriving in Tunisia.'

I told Alan of the morrow's invitation and added, 'Perhaps, Mme Maoui, you would rather postpone our visit?'

'No, no you must come,' she cried, and they drove off.

'I'm sorry the Voizards are leaving,' Alan said. 'He's conservative, like the French here, but they undermined his every effort to calm things down. I like them both. Troops are now pouring into Tunis. They're all over the place, presumably because of the General's appointment. That should at least stop all these assassinations, and no one will dare throw tomatoes at a general nor boo him! He's a strict disciplinarian but he's no fool.'

'Mummy, were we all right?' Libet was pulling at my sleeve.

'Yes, darling, you were both very good.' I assured her. So they had both made an effort to behave well. I wanted to tell them how Mme Maoui had praised them but I decided it would be unwise. We all looked forward to the morrow's lunch.

That evening, when the children were in bed, Lawrence asked, 'Please Mummy read us our new history book. I want to find the two bad kings I learnt about in Sunday School.' I began reading.

He interrupted, 'It's mostly fighting so it should be my book and not for Libet at all.'

Libet exclaimed, 'People were always fighting each other; I'm glad I'm alive now.' I kissed her earnest little face.

Next morning the phone rang. An excited Mme Maoui breathed heavily down it, 'Please Mrs Williams the lunch is off. I can't tell you why but you will hear this afternoon.'

'Alan, it looks as though something's happening!' I shouted. He rushed off to the office. I switched on the radio and carried it around with me. Soon the announcement came. 'Prime Minister Mendés-France has arrived in Tunis. With him are Monsieur Fouchet, Minister for Moroccan and Tunisian Affairs and Marshal Juin . . .' Hassin, Mahomet and Ali rushed in, all grinning.

'Madame, it'll be all right now!' Hassin exclaimed. 'Monsieur Mendés-France will settle everything, and no more shootings!' and Ali, 'Ah, Madame, isn't it good news!' We shook hands all round and they hurried to the nursery to shake hands with Mavis and the children.

Alan was home for lunch. 'It's marvellous news! It's taken everyone by surprise. And to come here straight away! It'll give real hope to the Tunisians. And what a stroke of genius to bring Marshal Juin, the very embodiment of strong-arm methods. That'll reassure the French.'

☆   ☆   ☆

After lunch we listened to Mendés-France over the radio addressing the Bey and at the same time speaking to both the French and Tunsians. 'It is urgent to avoid further division between Frenchmen menaced by terrorism and Tunisians deprived of the very rights which France has taught them to value . . .' He pledged internal sovereignty for Tunisia and promised to safeguard the interests of the local French. For a politician, a generous, brave gesture. I was so delighted I could hardly listen.

In moments of deep emotion, Alan and I escaped into the garden. Now the sky was ablaze with colour. The horizon was bright orange melting into bands of yellow and grey while above the deep purple merged with fiery scarlet. The children stood transfixed, Libet lifted a plump finger. 'Listen, Mummy! The evening noises!' I became aware of a bird, cricket and bee chorus all round us and at that moment the Mullah's call to evening prayer rang out from Sidi Bou Said. I said, 'We've been here just one year!'

'Oh let's have a cake with one candle,' Libet cried, 'to show what a nice year it's been!' Ali made us one of his delicious sponge cakes.

20

In cafés the owners were raising the shutters, bringing out tables and chairs on to the pavements, cars poured into the streets. Tunis was alive once more. In our palace everyone was smiling.

It was Sunday, a hot day and the sirocco was blowing. Alan drove us to the beach. Soldiers were everywhere, even patrolling the sands; the new Resident-General was determined to forestall terrorism. The Consular Corps had foregathered there with the local French, ostensibly to cool off in the sea, but really all were eager to pick up information. The children and Mavis plunged into the water.

'What a day!' a French official exclaimed as Alan and I joined the others on the sand around him. 'It was a complete surprise! I had to hurry everyone to the airport. Then I realized General Tahar Maoui was still with the Bey while his uniform was back at his home. It had to be rushed to the airport while he drove straight there. Mendès-France was forced to circle above us till we were lined up and ready to receive him. And from then on all was chaos.'

'Whom did he see?' Alan asked. 'He was only here a day.'

'Literally everyone! He listened to everyone's views but he's promised Tunisian sovereignty and on that he won't give way.'

'But wait,' a local farmer interrupted. 'The plans must still go through parliament. There's a chance they won't get through.' He was pale, his face strained, and I realized the French were staring with drawn, anxious expressions at the official.

'Marshal Juin's presence here will win over the conservative vote and the press back home have generally welcomed Mendès-France's plan.' There was silence. Gloom settled over the group. I felt sorry for them as I felt happy for the Tunisians. The sun shone, little sparkling waves broke at our feet and the sea was as blue as ever, but how difficult life was!

Johannis whispered to Alan, 'Bourguiba has approved the

plans and he's called for an all-round cease-fire.' Bourguiba had been released from house-arrest but was still under police surveillance in France, to the fury of the Tunisian press, but among the local French his name was anathema. 'He says the French minority will enjoy special privileges and protection, and will take part in municipal government.' That's fair, I thought. Alan whispered back, 'It won't be easy. The Tunisians trust Mendés-France, but the French and Tunisian officials don't trust each other. There'll be hard bargaining ahead.' I listened avidly; Alan never discussed politics with me. That was work.

☆   ☆   ☆

Parties started up again and rooms buzzed with excited talk. We were able to give a farewell cocktail party for the Dismores – a sad occasion. They had become almost family – Dizzie so welcoming with open house for all Britishers, Winnie plying sailors on the beach with beer and sandwiches. She did not speak French so at parties her plump figure surged through the crowd, large trays of drink balanced on one hand above her shoulder; the children in and out of our palace, a crowd of lively youngsters, inventing games in the garden, and in the midday heat, playing Happy Families indoors. Martin, aged eight, the only boy, walked around arm in arm with Libet. She ignored his stammer. She had asked him to marry her and Alan overheard him say, 'I've already got the younger Mrosovsky girl on my hands; not the elder one, she's too skinny.' The girls' father worked for Shell. Mavis spent all her free time at the Dismores.

On their last evening of busy packing, we were entertaining guests and were about to go in to dinner, when Dizzie dropped in unexpectedly. I motioned Hassin to wait and Alan offered him a drink. He downed two large, neat whiskies, launched into a monologue and gave no sign of leaving, while our guests fidgeted and Hassin and Mahomet waited at the door. Finally Alan had to lead him out.

'He's worried,' Alan apologized to the guests. 'Transporting a wife suffering from epilepsy and five children to Macao . . .' They all love adventure, I thought, but for Dizzie what a responsibility!

At the Leland-Smiths I listened eagerly to Eric da Rin, his long face serious, speaking quietly, privately to Alan,

'The *colons* realize that the talks will take place inevitably,'

Left to right. Alan, Mrs Russel, M. de Boisesou, and Lipkowski.

he hesitated, 'unless there's violence. If there is, the authorities will refuse to talk so it's just possible the *colons* might be tempted . . .'

'They might,' Alan agreed, 'if it means losing their land, their crops, their everything. But I suspect they have a sneaking hope that Mendés-France, Jew though he is, might find a solution, that will save both their honour and their wealth.'

'The Tunisians must get a government together immediately, in the next day or two.' Eric concluded. 'That's their only hope.'

The only Tunisians present were the Belhodgas. He had been Minister in a previous government. We only met Tunisians who worked with the French – 'collaborators' according to the Nationalists. The French would not countenance us associating with other Tunisians – 'natives' – as they referred to them, with whom they themselves had as few dealings as possible. Though officially we supported the French, they did not trust us too far. They imagined we had 'Lawrences of Arabia' lurking everywhere. Belhodga, slim and elegant, could be taken for a Frenchman any time. How quickly Tunisians assimilated a foreign culture. Would we be able to assimilate their culture as quickly? I did not think so.

☆　　☆　　☆

We kept the radio switched on and heard the Bey appealing for calm. Then the Prime Minister, Tahar Ben Amar, who had agreed to form a government, called on both Tunisians and French to give him their support. Rumours spread that the French were refusing to accept Néo-Destourians into the government. We waited impatiently, praying that fanatics would hold their hand while the government was forming and that nothing would prevent the talks starting.

Most French families had left for France to avoid the heat and those that remained became friendlier. They invited us, consular families, to bathe on the beach reserved for French officials. Lina and Naida joined us. We lay floating in the water. Libet dived off Mavis's back and both were more under than above the waves. Lawrence, ashamed of his fear, screwed up his eyes and thrust his head under water.

'You don't have to dive if you don't want to, darling,' I told him. 'Just enjoy yourself. Bathing's fun. Do whatever you want to.' I did not add that I had been secretly practising diving in our pool, ashamed of my own fears.

Naida had brought her little, red-haired son, Danny. The tiny fellow rushed at Lawrence and struck him on the chest. Lawrence hit back, they rolled in the sand, punching and kicking while Naida and I hovered over them shouting, 'Stop it!' Suddenly Danny laughed, and Lawrence burst out laughing. They hugged each other and ran off into the sea.

'I'm sorry,' Naida exclaimed. 'Danny's so rough, no one will play with him.'

I pointed to the two boys jumping hand in hand in the waves. 'Danny's welcome to play with Lawrence. They're both toughs.'

We left them and sat down with Lina and the French ladies. One of them got up and went away.

'You know why she always tries to be so witty?' another asked looking after her. 'Her husband's secretary is beautiful while she's . . .'

'Dowdy and plain!' they laughed.

'And he's not exactly faithful . . .'

'Dowdy and plain'. Must one be beautiful to be loved, I wondered. Is Alan handsome? He's no film star and that's not why I love him. Clever? No, not that either. Sensitive? I sighed. I don't know. It's just that, well, because he's Alan.

The Spanish Consul's wife joined us, saying, 'I'm on my way to a lunch party.' I admired her straw hat with a colourful mass of spring flowers round the rim. She had first worn it at a party the day before.

'What, still the same hat?' someone exclaimed.

Lina sprang up. 'Let's join the children. It's too hot in the sun.' In the water she whispered, 'They're so spiteful! One tries not to listen and not to believe what they say but then after a time one begins to wonder . . . Only ugly French women are nice!'

'I hope our diplomatic wives don't get so cynical.' I remembered with a stab of pain overhearing a remark about myself. 'Madame Williams is so good!' I could still feel the sting in it. I did not repeat it to Lina.

☆　　☆　　☆

The new government was formed under the Prime Minister, Tahar Ben Amar. It included Néo-Destourians and the ceremony of investiture was held in the Bey's Palace. A few days later for the festival of Aid el Kebir, Bourguiba sent a telegram of congratulations to the Bey, a gesture of reconciliation. Bourguiba still had the status of 'prisoner'; the French were determined to keep him away from Tunis as long as possible, but from Cairo Radio we learnt that Tahar Ben Amar was in constant touch with Bourguiba and that he was in fact directing the government. Negotiations on the new treaty were to start in September.

At home Fatma was in hospital again. Ali came to me with a long, gloomy face. He spoke so softly that I could hardly hear. 'She needs a blood transfusion. Now, or they say she will die. But I can't do it. I can't!'

'Do you have to? Don't they have blood?'

'No. Someone has to give it.' Tears streamed down his face. He was trembling and kept murmuring, 'I can't! I can't!' Ali looked pathetically thin. I glanced at Hassin, who, big and strong, was staring at the floor.

'Hassin?' I asked.

'Oh, Madame. I can't bear to think of it.'

'But she'll die! Please, Hassin. There's no pain, you won't feel anything.'

He sighed, shook his head, shuffled his feet, then '*Bien, Madame.*' With clenched fists he strode out. We watched him disappearing down the alleyway, shoulders hunched, a tragic figure. Ali shrugged and went back to the kitchen.

Hassin returned grinning, 'That's it, Madame.'

'Thank you, Hassin.' The remark seemed inadequate, but he would know what I felt.

It was hot, the sky was clear. Now was the time to take advantage of the calm to attend to household affairs. I decided to give our carpets a dip in the sea, the best way to preserve them Lina had told me. Hassin, Mahomet and Ali between them rolled up two big carpets and lifted them into the station-wagon. They were not too heavy. We collected the little ones and all drove to the beach. The men slipped out of their sandals, rolled up their trouser legs and dragged the biggest carpet into the water. Little waves splashed over them, the children pranced round them.

'I've never been in the sea,' Hassin exclaimed as all three beamed.

The carpet soaked up the water and began to sink. 'Better bring it out now,' I suggested. They pulled and strained but it was heavy with water and they could not move it.

'Come Mavis, children, let's all pull.' We seized the carpet edge and tugged. Mahomet started giggling, slipped and next moment he was sprawling in the water. As he struggled up, water dripping off him, and his eyes wide with astonishment, Hassin and Ali started laughing hysterically and the carpet slipped from their hands. It sank to the bottom. We stood in the water doubled up with laughter.

'Please, now everyone, pull hard. We must get it out.' We tugged, waves washing over us as we bent to grasp the carpet. I was soaked through, but slowly the carpet scraped along the sea bed and on to the shore. We left the other carpets unwashed!

'Ah, Madame, that was good!' Mahomet exclaimed. 'I like the sea.' In the station-wagon we all continued grinning. When I recounted our adventure to Alan, he exclaimed, 'What a crazy thing to do!' 'But it was fun!' I protested.

That evening the zig-zags came back – one of my migraines. As I lay down on my bed, head throbbing, I thought, we have so much here and I am so lucky, it would be unfair if I were always well!

21

The sirocco blew, and Tunis held its breath, for the negotiations kept being postponed and the Tunisians were uneasy. The Resident-General toured the country, now in the grip of his military, and the populace turned out to greet him, but what they shouted was '*Vive Bourguiba!*' Bourguiba, that shadowy figure, dismissed by the French as a man of the past, with no future, of no interest, but whom they nevertheless held in France; there was no question of allowing him to return to Tunis or even to live in Paris, the political hub of the country.

As we tried to keep fit in the heat and I kept the children as much as possible in the sea, we watched events unfolding. The terrorists – 'martyrs' the Nationalists called them – were promised amnesty if they surrendered with their arms. Many did but as the negotiations, when they finally started, dragged on and in secret so that no one knew what was going on, *Fellaghas* ceased to come forward and some European cars were stoned. French residents began leaving the country and their young sought jobs in France.

'When Home Rule begins the deluge will start,' Alan remarked, for the French kept telling us, 'Tunisians are incapable of holding down responsible positions, let alone running a country. There'll be chaos. They're still in the Middle Ages; the world is flat and the sun whirls round it. They have nothing in common with Western thought.' We believed them and waited anxiously.

We heard rumours – Bourguiba was demanding that the state of siege should be lifted and political detainees freed and, sure enough, the Néo-Destour party was allowed to resume its activities openly. But the authorities were jittery. When a Nationalist leader returned from exile the police barred off the main road, afraid of a crowd gathering. Cutajah was held up and we were stranded on the beach, missing both lunch and tea. But still no news about the negotiations.

'If they don't speed things up Mendés-France might be

172

thrown out and his successor might go back on the agreements.' Alan was worried. 'It's happened before.' So long as they don't start murdering each other again, I prayed.

But with most of the French still away in France, to avoid the dust, mounting heat and resulting general irritation, we fled to the almost empty Residency beach. It was a lazy period. Lina and I stretched out on the soft white sand and gazed across the blue waters at Cap Bon with its twin-peaked Bou Cornine, pinky mauve in the morning haze. As the children and Mavis ran down into the clear, smooth water, we listened to our French colleagues pricing each others' bathing suits and deciding how much of themselves they could decently expose. We learned of the new 'bean' look (*la ligne haricot vert*) and of the cat-style hair-do. Lina worried about her health and as the sirocco continued to blow everyone felt depressed, irritated, and suffered from colic. I alone revelled in the heat. The outdoor life suited me. I was not haunted by fear of doing the wrong thing and I could stand anything, cold, heat, endless speeches, if only I was out-of-doors. The migraines were fewer too, though I was still having injections.

In the evenings we had to bestir ourselves; the Minister, Monsieur de Boissesson, was leaving. The daily farewell parties were held around small tables on terraces with a dance floor in the centre. The men looked cool in white evening dress, and the women in strapless cotton gowns. Monsieur de Boissesson, solid and plump, talked politics and chewed gum. He had been ordered to do so after a heart attack, to stop him smoking. One evening Lina was sitting, tense and frowning, when she half-rose from her chair. Yannis was dancing cheek to cheek with his French partner, held close in his arms. The music stopped and Yannis came over. One look at his wife's face and, hands spread out sideways, he blurted out,

'I couldn't help it.' And shrugging, 'anyway there's nothing to it.'

'Nothing to it!' Lina spluttered.

'The path of duty . . .' he tried to joke.

'What about paths of duty for me? Shall I dance like that? Shall I?'

'That's different.'

'Different, is it?' Conchita Casso, our Spanish colleague hissed. 'That's what my husband says. He says women snuggle up to him and he can't help himself.' I looked round quickly. Where was Alan? No, he was not dancing. He was safe. I left

173

Left to right. The Author, M. Martie (Swiss Consul-General) Alan, Mme Frahier and Dr Frahier at a cocktail party.

the two women still protesting as I went off to dance with a young French official.

Later Lina kept glancing my way and laughing.

'What is it?' I asked, nettled.

'You have complexes!' she grinned. 'That young man told me so.'

'I pushed him away. I refused to go on dancing with him. It was horrid!'

Lina put her arm through mine and we decided that we were too old-fashioned for this fast, smart French set.

The Consular Corps gave a luncheon for the Minister. The Turk was now our doyen and since his wife did not go out in hot weather, I acted hostess.

'I'm your second wife!' I joked. He turned his face quickly away, and pretended not to hear. I've shocked him, I thought and I guessed Alan must be looking at me reproachfully, but Lina was laughing into her table napkin. Neither of us could keep serious. The heat had gone to our heads.

Monsieur de Boissesson survived his farewell parties and we gathered at the airport to see him off. Troops were drawn up, a band played and, as the crowd milled around, Monsieur de Boissesson shook our hands in order of precedence.

Monsieur Seydoux, the new Minister, rushed into our midst and flung his arms round Alan's shoulders in greeting. We had known him in New York. Alan introduced the Turk and Seydoux clasped him by the shoulders. The Turk blushed, embarrassed and delighted at the same time.

'Seydoux thinks he's still dealing with American pressmen,' Alan whispered. Seydoux turned to me, '*Ah, chére amie!*' (My dear friend) he cried. Then seeing astonishment and disapproval on the faces of his colleagues and new staff members, he quickly changed back into the staid civil servant, bowed and murmured '*Bonjour, Madame!*' The official good-byes had been said and we left de Boissesson to await his plane.

We all suffered stomach troubles as the days became uncomfortably hot and heavy. Lawrence whined and even Mavis grew irritable. Our children had grown pale, but the French children looked even paler. However, their parents told us that as soon as summer was over they would pick up quickly; it was just a question of getting through to October. European children needed to get used to the climate, I presumed; the locals remained healthy.

Animals helped; they kept the children in a permanent state of excitement. We took Lina on our favourite walk, across fields to the ruined Rotunda. Both dogs were on leads as we avoided the usual bulls. In the last field we saw Bedouin tents on a distant hillock. There were shouts of '*Bara!*' (Go away). We hurried on. Behind us we heard noise and panting. Dogs were streaking towards us, large, scrawny dogs. I seized Lawrence's hand and Lina Libet's as we hurried on. The dogs burst into a volley of barking and next moment they were on to us. Mavis and I bent down and threw imaginary stones – there was nothing but grass. They sprang back a few paces. We advanced backwards, bending down, aiming at the dogs, staring into their eyes as I had learnt to do in Baghdad. The dogs leapt at us then fell back. Herta and Blanco barked furiously. Herta strained at the leash, ready to attack but with four dogs against him and Blanco too old to help, Mavis did not dare let him go.

'Let's go home,' Libet sobbed. 'I'm frightened.' We crept forward, Herta's jaws repeatedly at the dogs' throats as they sprang at us till at last we reached the road. The dogs stopped, left us and raced back to the tents. We had been crossing their territory, we then realized.

'I'm not coming here again,' Lawrence stated, but he was grinning. Too interested to be frightened, he had enjoyed it all. We made our way home by a round-about way, peering nervously ahead.

'You're trembling,' Lina exclaimed, as she grasped Libet's hand tighter. To distract her she started singing Greek songs till the children smiled and skipped to her singing. Back home we felt like heroes as Alan and Yannis listened to our adventure.

Next day Lawrence came running up white-faced. 'Herta took my rabbit off my shoulder and he's run away with it.' Libet followed, tears streaming down her cheeks.

I called, 'Hassin! Mavis!' and we rushed around, shouting 'Herta! Herta!' Finally Mavis found the rabbit lying under a bush, Herta beside it. The rabbit seemed unhurt.

'Oh Mummy!' Libet exclaimed, 'first those nasty dogs and now this!' Next morning the rabbit was dead. Alan buried it stealthily, as he had poor Billy, the chameleon, whom we found dead one boiling night.

Libet's rabbit escaped. We set the dogs to find it. They dashed at a hedge, barking and squealing madly. Under the hedge sat a big, fat toad. The rabbit had disappeared for good.

The children were tearful. Joseph brought Lawrence another tortoise and he joked, 'I'll chop their heads off and eat them!' but Lawrence was now used to his teasing. Stella, his sister, brought Libet a tiny, grey kitten.

'You'd better leave it with us at the farm till it's strong enough to cope with the dogs,' Stella advised. The children both had scratched necks and chests because, as Libet said, 'We like to carry the kitten under our chins; it's so soft and cuddly.'

Suddenly dust rose up in a massive sheet and whirled through the garden, blinding us.

'It's a tornado!' Hassin shouted. Thunder roared overhead, lightning flashed round us. Then rain lashed down. We stood stunned.

'Inside, quick!' Hassin called.

'The animals,' Mavis cried. The children rushed to shoo the rabbits into their hutches and the tortoises under cover. Libet clasped the terrified kitten in her arms. We heard agonized braying. Shaggy, eyes wide, nostrils flaring, came galloping down the central alley, Alan clinging to him, running at his side. We stopped, rain beating down on us, and stared as they

176

galloped into Shaggy's shed, where Alan stood stroking the trembling animal.

'Daddy said he didn't like donkeys.' Libet, dripping with rain, smiled up at me. 'I think he loves them!' With the animals all safe, we ran through the storm to the house. At that moment Jessie, Cutajah's wife, came running to meet us, in her hands two fluttering baby pigeons.

'For the children,' she shouted above the fracas. 'But they're babies. They still have to be hand-fed.'

I seized her arm and ran her up the terrace steps and into the house. What a time to bring more animals! However I thanked her and sat her down to wait while we changed into dry clothes. When I returned the children had already learnt to feed the young birds. They felt the pouches under their long, hooked beaks for food. There was none so they forced their beaks open and pushed grain down their throats, and then water. Pink flesh showed through their yellow and white down and the occasional blue feathers. Huge pink claws clutched the children's fingers as they squatted on their hands. We put them in a seven-foot high rabbit hutch to protect them from cats till they learnt to fly and could be transferred to the dovecote.

'The children are not frightened of lightning or thunder,' I told Alan that night.

'Why should they be?' I did not admit how frightened I had been.

'They're wonderful children!' I added. 'They really are, and Libet's such a good little girl.'

'Humph,' was all Alan said.

Next morning I was helping Libet to clean out a rabbit hutch when she went off to fetch food, slammed the door and locked it. I thought I was mistaken and shook it hard. It did not give. I called Libet. No answer. She had locked me in deliberately! Maltese and Tunisian workmen were repairing our roof. They heard me calling and could see me inside the rabbit hutch but they went on working. It was humiliating. The Consul-General's wife locked in a rabbit hutch! I was forced to shout loudly, 'Help!' The men stopped work, stared down at me and one of them climbed down his ladder, came across and unlocked the door. I hurried away and found Libet giggling in the nursery.

'That was very naughty,' I shouted at her. 'I shall never again help you with the animals,' and I marched out. That evening it grew very dark early and I ran out to bring the animals in, then remembered, and came back. I said good-night coldly to Libet. She had not said she was sorry, but she was red in the face and breathing rapidly. It was not like her to play silly tricks – more like Lawrence. I hugged her. 'Silly girl! I suppose it was too tempting!' and we clung to each other.

We had reached October. Still no news of the negotiations, but we had enjoyed a respite before normal diplomatic life resumed.

22

At last October and relief from the stifling heat but now we were overwhelmed by parties; parties for new officials and parties for those leaving. With all the coming and going in the Foreign Service there can be no lasting friendships. If we did not attend these parties Alan would not gather useful information and those honoured might consider themselves slighted by Great Britain. Everything we did had political implications. Also there was ominous news – the *Fellaghas* were striking out again; twenty-five were killed on one day and sixty-five the next. More deaths, more widows, more inconsolable grief, but I told myself sternly I must not think of that. The French were threatening to stop negotiating. At parties drink loosened the tongue and Alan could learn more.

The new Resident-General with the aristocratic name of General Pierre Boyer de Latour de Moulin opened the social season with a dinner for the Consular Corps and the new members of his Residency.

'It's embarrassing,' I grumbled to Alan. 'I liked the Voizards and this General had them chucked out without even a good-bye.'

'I know, but it's none of our business.'

I sat, according to protocol, next to the Turk. Like me, he enjoyed a good argument.

'My brother-in-law's family lived for generations in Turkey,' I told him. 'He praises everything Turkish.'

That remark and the champagne drew from him, 'Some things in Russia are good too.' He's guessed that I'm Russian, I thought. 'Things of the soul – literature, music, a compassionate philosophical strain . . .'

'Even today?'

'Today no! The cruelty, the concentration camps . . .'

'And your Armenian atrocities?' I hit back.

'Exaggeration! Atatürk had to modernize the country.'

'You can consider him a great man?'

Libet, Lawrence, Ping the puppy and Hedia.

Left to right. Faa di Bruno, Mr. Brook, Y. Oyeda and the Author.

'No! It is the Turkish people who are great and I am proud to be their representative.'

'Revolutions, civil wars bring out the worst in men but that soul you speak of is still there in modern Russia . . .' He denied it and got very excited. We were enjoying ourselves.

After dinner I tried to talk to our hostess, a small, shy woman who just sat, contributing nothing till I mentioned the *Fellagha* threat. Then she started indignantly 'The whole Tunisian government have publicly condemned individual acts of terrorism!' Later we went on to discuss existentialism in literature and finally she talked about her six daughters. Madame La Tour was not going to be as difficult to get along with as we had feared. It also crossed my mind that perhaps the French sometimes talked so loudly and rapidly because we made them nervous!

Next the Consular Corps gave a dinner for the new Resident-General and the Seydoux. As I was placed next to the General, all I had to do was listen. His tall figure stooped over the table, eyes fixed on it with just occasional glances my way, as he lectured me on how a French cavalry regiment saved the situation at Balaclava during the Charge of the Light Brigade. The French keep harping on France's glory, I thought. What an inferiority complex! All because they surrendered in the last war while we fought on and won.

Then followed a discourse on the Soviets and the 'grave threat they pose to the West'. I kept silent; I saw no threat to the West. Then he suddenly condemned all Slavs – 'an uncivilized, inferior race'. That's me, I thought, shaken and not knowing what to do. It was insulting! How could a man in his position be so ignorant, so prejudiced? Uncivilized! What about Tolstoy, Pushkin, Dostoevsky? I seethed. And inferior! The Soviet Union had won the war and France had lost it, so who was inferior? I looked round the table. The others were all nodding. I could hardly control myself. Alan, seated opposite me, winked. In a sudden reaction I nearly giggled. On my other side the Turk was asking whether I knew the delicious Russian dishes that his wife prepared, *pelmeni* and *pirozhki*? Was she Circassian? She knew some Russian and clung to me? I leant forward as a screen to stop either side overhearing the other. Lina was laughing into her table-napkin. I felt better.

The General announced as he rose from the table, 'The state of siege will not be raised till these communist *Fellaghas* surrender. As regards the negotiations, there is no news because the problems are complex and all have agreed not to negotiate in public.' We had at least learnt something but unless both sides compromised . . . I could hear Roger Seydoux repeating, '*Il faut trouver la formule! Il faut trouver la formule!*' (We must find the right formula). I hoped he would, and in time.

The Touloupases and the Da Rins were leaving, the Touloupases for Ethiopia, the Da Rins for Tripoli. I was devastated. Some people are self-sufficient but I'm not, I thought sadly. I need close friends. I need their affection.

So now they were wined and dined to exhaustion. Arriving and leaving are the greatest trials in diplomatic life. When the Touloupases came to break the news, I looked at Lina's sensitive, animated face with the generous smile and wondered miserably, would we ever meet again? I won't know where she is or what is happening to her and as relations between our countries were at rock bottom, we could not give a farewell party for them. We were not supposed to associate with them.

A Mr Silcock, a Ministry of Works' engineer had arrived from Cyprus to supervise repairs to our palace. As Cyprus was a British colony at the time, we accused Greece of inciting the Cypriots to murder our troops and to demand *enosis* – union with Greece. Silcock was hardly well-disposed towards Greeks but one glance at Lina and he whispered, 'Such a beauty and she probably came with a large dowry too!' When I whispered this to Lina, we both cheered up.

Lina invited the children to a farewell tea. They returned clutching large cacti, farewell presents, which they put in the place of honour – at the foot of each bed. Mavis and I kept tripping over their prickly leaves. Lina rang to say how much she had enjoyed the visit, adding, 'My last memory of this house will be one of laughter and affection. I want children just like yours!'

Marchiori, the Italian Consul-General next fêted the Da Rins. There we were, a consular crowd, leading similar lives and therefore at ease with each other, with no French or their troubles to dampen our spirits. Tunisians had started attacking collaborating compatriots but we brushed politics aside – we were young, we had to lead our own lives too and we enjoyed each other's company. Marchiori was a bachelor. We thought up suitable wives and at each name Yannis Touloupas raised a vertical sardonic eyebrow while Cassos, the Spaniard, lifted both palms in horror. We tried to make Yannis speak without using his eyebrows and Cassos his hands but it was useless. We were in fits of laughter, including Lina and Naida who had arrived looking very pale.

Alan asked Marchiori why Eric Da Rin was always working in the Italian consulate while the others were constantly away?

Marchiori shrugged. 'He works hard. He had a Dutch mother.' He did not understand why we laughed.

Naida's alsatian had had puppies and Naida arrived with the cuddliest bear-like creature for Libet, who rushed beaming round the house showing it off. His face solemn, Lawrence helped arrange the basket they had both slept in as babies for the puppy. He forced a smile for me but with tears in his eyes. I drove to Naida's. Did she have another puppy?

'Yes and I'm longing to find a home for him. I didn't dare land you with two!' The puppies, named Ping and Pong, rollicked over the floor, the children chasing after them with mops, for they had promised there would be no messes. Herta and Blanco slunk away, heads, ears and tails drooping till Mavis laughed, tore off into the garden and, tails wagging, they chased after her.

Mr Pell, our new consul arrived, a neat, slim figure, with Mrs Pell, also slim and neat, and a daughter of nine, Diana. On the quay AP Vella took one look at Pell and blurted out, 'Older men are always more difficult!' but Alan pointed out that he, AP was one month older than Pell. We drove to the

Mavis, Libet and Lawrence on the back terrace.

office and found it full of painters, electricians and carpenters. 'I must send off some telegrams to London,' Alan whispered, nodding at the Pells. 'For God's sake remove them.' It was a difficult and tense time for him. The French maintained that *Fellagha* activity impeded the negotiations, while Bourguiba, at the Néo-Destour conference, referred to the *Fellaghas* who had been killed as men who had 'died upon the field of honour' and he spoke of the 'sacred struggle until the final victory which God has promised the Faithful.' The *Fellaghas* could not, he asserted, surrender to the French whom they did not trust, but only to a Tunisian government: an impasse which worried our British government. We wanted the Tunisian problem settled quickly and North Africa made secure, with France retaining its defence.

I whisked the Pells away and we drove to La Marsa, to the Dismores' house. There was a significant silence as we drove past scruffy beggars and scrawny donkeys and then ran into the awful stench of the lake.

'Look! A camel!' Diana exclaimed. Thank goodness! I thought, if she enjoys the place, the parents may learn to like it. The house looked dilapidated. I had not noticed the peeling wallpaper and rotting window-frames. It had been filled with young voices, laughter and sunshine, with sea and sand outside. I could visualize Mrs Pell in a spotless small, modern bungalow with matching curtains and carpets back in the UK. The silence grew ever more noticeable as we walked through the dingy rooms. I left the parents with AP, who would help them settle in and promised to find them a servant. Meanwhile I took Diana home with me and handed her over to the children.

The parents came to lunch. 'It's all very foreign!' Pell exclaimed. They had arrived from Geneva, a clean and tidy city, but Pell had served in Mexico and Panama and Alan remarked, 'he ought not to worry about a spot of dust here and there.' The Dismores had mentioned a bath leaking, but they had taken it for granted. Mrs Pell sat silent; Diana was the only one to smile.

We gave a party for them to meet their colleagues and the French officials. They arrived harassed and frowning; they had already dismissed two servants and now they could not find another. I watched Mrs Pell. She kept in the background and stared at the floor, her lips twitching uncontrollably. She did not speak French. I felt irritated. Lina was watching her too.

'What delicate features she has and such a fresh complexion,' Lina whispered. 'She's so English with that spotless white collar and starched cuffs and every hair in place. So very . . . decent. She's lovely!'

What a lesson! I felt ashamed. Mrs Pell was thrust without preparation among strangers in a country almost in a state of war and she was understandably frightened. I too had migraines and Winnie had developed epilepsy; we were pushed too hard. We lived in an artificial cocoon, moulded into shapes that did not suit us. It undermined our self-confidence, our very identity. I kept Mrs Pell at my side.

The Da Rins left. Danny spent their last day with us. He and Lawrence stuck together, though they quarrelled all day long.

Then Alan and I had to fly first to Paris for a consular conference and then onto London for a few days. Mavis's parents arrived to keep her company. On our return we were met by Mr Pell with the words, 'I've had flu. What a climate!'

'Where are the children?' I interrupted him.

'I think they're ill but I don't know what's wrong with them.' I glared at him but Monsieur Choiseul saw us quickly through the customs and we hurried home to find the children in bed with high temperatures. Hassin had not thought to start the heating so the house was very cold. Mavis was distraught.

'The Pells haven't helped at all. All through my parents' visit they kept asking me to do this and then that. As though I didn't have enough on my hands and with all the workmen here too . . . and Diana was no help. She told the children it was silly to do what I say and she led them on to the roof. I had forbidden that; the balustrade is low. Fortunately Hassin found them. Lawrence finds it exciting to follow her and Libet, when I scold her, keeps saying, 'But I love Diana too!'

The Touloupases were off.

'Can we go to the airport?' I pleaded. 'We can't let them go without seeing them off!'

Alan shrugged. 'All right.' The children were now well enough to come too. We landed in the midst of what looked like the whole Greek colony, the black-robed, round-hatted, bearded priest, and black-robed women, heads covered by black shawls. They stared at us surprised and bowed politely. As Lina shook rows of extended hands, Libet clung to her coat, her eyes full of tears. We hugged each other and then they were gone.

'Mummy, we're always saying good-bye!' Libet wept in the

car, but back home she cuddled her puppy and cheered up. Lawrence was cuddling his. I wanted to cuddle someone too, but it was Sunday and Alan was already changing into shorts to dash to the pergola he had started building.

Later, back in a dark suit, he said, 'I've got to go to the synagogue. The Bey is laying a foundation stone for a Jewish community house.' The Bey, as a protest against the French, had not appeared in public for two whole years so his appearance would be a sensation and it also meant a reassurance for Tunisian Jews. Alan came back in high spirits.

'There was chaos in the synagogue, everyone trying to get out at once and I was right in the middle of it all. I had to fight my way out, literally.' He looked refreshed and was smiling – a frantic struggle was apparently the best cure for exhaustion and tension.

23

The navy again! Two destroyers on the way!

'It's too much!' I exclaimed 'A never-ending flow of ships! You'd think we'd been sent here specially to entertain the navy!'

Alan handed me a heavy parcel. 'This has just arrived.' I opened it – a beautifully fashioned replica of the ship's badge of *HMS Surprise*, a black sailing ship on a white background. Enclosed was a note from Mountbatten saying it was to be added to our 'small collection of badges of the ships which visited Bizerta and Tunis'. The 'small collection' was the *Trenchant* badge in the dining-room. We were 'surprised' and most touched. So much was expected of them, they had already written to us and now the ship's badge! I stopped grumbling about the coming naval visit.

'It's a good time to come,' Alan was smiling. 'The Resident-General says Mendés-France has promised the Tunisians control of the uniformed police. They had been pressing for it but the French resisted so the Tunisians are now delighted and the *Fellaghas* are surrendering in their hundreds. Things are moving and the crews should be safe.' It was indeed good news.

It was almost Christmas so we decided to put the Christmas tree up for the usual cocktail party for the destroyers. Hassin would not hear of us buying a tree so once again we drove down to his father-in-law's estate and were presented with a magnificent fir. When we put it up and Alan came home from the office, the children rushed him in to view it. 'It's swagger!' he exclaimed.

The destroyers arrived and our house was plunged into its usual state of chaos before a party. Once everything was ready I decided we must get some fresh air, especially as the children were pale after their influenza. I'd give Libet a tennis lesson. I stood on one side of the court, Lawrence lying on his stomach at my feet with the new gun he had bought himself, and old Blanco stretched out in the sun beside him. I threw the balls at

Lawrence.

Libet. She pirouetted, smiling broadly around the court, missed them and Mavis, standing behind her, caught them. When Libet did hit the ball it was with her head, the ball skidded sideways and the puppies fell over each other chasing it. This was family tennis.

Suddenly we froze. Herta! A terrible sight – blood all over his head, chest and legs, a gaping wound across his head and down over one eye.

'Don't touch him!' I cried, as the children rushed to him. Rabies! the constant fear . . . I called Herta, led him quickly inside and Hassin helped me arrange him on some straw in a room on the reception side that had a tiled floor and walls. We gave him water and bits of meat. I did not dare clean him up or touch him. There were no other marks beside that great wound, no bites. He probably got tangled up in barbed wire or someone may have thrown a brick at him. But the risk . . . and for the children . . . He lay quietly, his massive wounded head on his paws, his one eye watching me. Quickly I shut the door and locked it. Neither the doctor nor the vet had a telephone and Cutajah was unable to find the vet. Alan phoned Bizerta and asked that the naval doctor should be included among the guests coming to our party. He did not mention that the patient was a dog!

We heard on the radio (we listened constantly to news bulletins) that eight or nine bombs had exploded in Tunis, damaging Tunisian homes and injuring several children. The police were stopping all cars entering and leaving the city. Disappointed and thrusting away visions of children in pain and crying, I wondered, would our guests venture out?

The navy drew them. Three hundred crowded in, French, Maltese, diplomats, our own UK citizens and several Tunisian Ministers, the ladies in tight, black dresses, the autumn fashion, so unbecoming I thought, in this sunny climate. They mingled, even the Maltese greeting the Tunisians whom normally they despised and ignored. Strange that it should be the military, the navy, who brought people together in this way.

Guests were subdued; those bombs! Everyone wondered who had thrown them. A Belgian businessman whispered to me, 'The French are responsible. Those that wish to stop the negotiations.' A French official maintained, 'It was either the communists or the Old Destour to spite their rivals the *Néo-Destour*.' A *colon* insisted, 'It's the *Fellaghas*; they should be rounded up and shot, not allowed to surrender.' But his companion protested, 'No, they're not bandits. We can all see now – they're controlled by the Néo-Destour. They're told not to surrender, they don't. Now they've been ordered to do so and they do. They're a disciplined force to be reckoned with.' Another official stated, 'Whatever happens, we'll never surrender North Africa. Security in the Mediterranean depends on it.' All were anxious once more.

The officers arrived. I asked Mavis to find the doctor and take him to Herta. Guests smiled, forgot the bombs and the negotiations and the Grand Salon resounded with loud voices and the clink of glasses.

Suddenly there were loud exclamations. Squeals. Guests pushed and fought to reach the doors. Chaos. From among the fleeing guests came a bloody, repulsive – Herta!

'It's all right!' I shouted. 'He's had an accident. He hasn't been bitten. No need to be afraid.' I grabbed Herta's thick fur and, as I went on shouting, 'It's all right ... just an accident ... not a bite,' I led him through the crowd that parted rapidly, out of the Salon and to his room.

The door stood ajar. Mavis and the doctor, a blond, blue-eyed uniformed Adonis, faced each other, laughing and chatting.

'Mavis!' I cried. 'You let Herta out! The guests are terrified.' She turned startled. She had obviously forgotten Herta. I hurried back to reassure everyone and soon talk started up again and Herta was forgotten. When the guests had finally left I found Herta sewn up and clean, eating his food. With Mavis beside him the doctor had evidently been very willing to attend to Herta!

Herta's eye would not heal so we brought in the RSPCA vet.

'Make him lie down,' he told Mavis as Herta lumbered up, 'and hold him.' He stood over the dog but at a distance and never touched him. A gentle, dreamy-eyed man, he kept going into a trance.

'Dogs don't get their eyes torn like that in a fight' he announced at last. 'It must have been barbed-wire.' He sighed and we waited. After a long silence he started again 'A dog bitten by another dog that can't be traced and examined should by law be put down.' In the silence that followed Mavis's hand gripped the rough fur round Herta's neck. The children clutched my skirt. Then with another sigh the vet went on, 'But the law is more honoured in the breach. Rabies is brought up by dogs from the south who catch it from jackals.

The disease can lie dormant in a dog for a year and not all rabid dogs attack people. Most creep away to die.' He stared at Herta. 'There's no diagnosing the disease while the dog is alive.'

Was he going to put Herta down? He had gone into a trance again while we waited motionless, watching his face.

'Better bring the two dogs, and the puppies when they're older, and I'll give them anti-rabies injections.' Herta was safe! We did not mind waiting while, in another trance, he apparently debated which cream to recommend for Herta's eye.

We showed him Shaggy. 'That donkey has rickets,' he pronounced. 'The puppies too. Better give them all vitamins.'

Alarmed, Alan asked Dr Tabone whether perhaps the children too should have vitamins. He assured him it was most necessary. Was it really necessary or was he considering our peace of mind?

As the vet left he added, 'Watch that dog. If he doesn't drink and shuns the sun and light, then you'll know.'

For a few days I watched Herta lying down in dark corners under the back terrace. I had to make a decision. Were we right to take the risk? Those painful injections or an agonizing death. Miss Bourke, our Irish friend whose home was in Bizerta, lived surrounded by dogs. I had asked her, was she not afraid of rabies? She had smiled and answered, 'We were brought up among dogs. We never gave it a thought.' Blanco lay in the shade too and the puppies kept out of the sun curled up against Herta's stomach. I came to no conscious conclusion but made sure that Herta was drinking buckets of water.

A year later, back in the UK, Mavis told me how she was driving the children to her home in Leeds when, waiting at red lights, a sports car drew up beside her. She glanced at its driver. It was the naval doctor! They grinned; the lights turned. They waved and drove on.

24

Eight o'clock and no one at the breakfast table. They're late again! I was annoyed. Mavis has got slack. Lessons should have started by eight and they haven't done any of their chores. They were supposed to look after their animals themselves. The dogs hadn't been let out yet. I hurried to the nursery. I could hear an angry voice.

'You've got so slack. Can't you hurry? And look at the toys all over the floor.' Mavis had taken the words out of my mouth. I crept away.

Breakfast was a silent meal. The children ate their eggs without the usual chatter.

All morning I waited for an opportunity to speak to Mavis but the children were always with her and I could not reprove her in front of them. The rabbit hutches had not been cleaned and how could Hassin sweep with carpentry tools all over the nursery floor?

I was to be interviewed on the radio in French in the local 'We the Women' programme. I must be careful, I reminded myself. Just after the war a German friend had slipped up over just one unfortunate word and with tragic consequences. Her husband was German Minister in London. In a speech to the staff my friend had referred to Britain as 'enemy country'. She meant to advise them not to act ostentatiously or to attract attention since only recently they had been the 'enemy'. A disgruntled member of the staff leaked the word 'enemy' to the press who blew it up into the day's sensation. The husband lost his job. We wives had to watch every word we said.

I gripped my pen and tried to plan what to say, but I could not concentrate. It can't go on like this, I thought. I can't watch Mavis all the time; I have to get on with my own work. I must talk to her, get it over quickly. Some people are so good at this sort of thing.

I dreaded that broadcast. Calista had also been asked to speak. She was to be interviewed first. The French were awkwardly placed. We British were their oldest allies but they desperately wanted American approval for their North-African policies and they needed the American vote in the UN. Calista and I were embroiled in this too. Though I was her diplomatic senior, since I had arrived in Tunis first, we were treated as equals. I resented it. I must do better than Calista, I told myself, and this made me doubly nervous.

The children were on the swing in the garden! What about their lessons? At last Mavis called, 'Come on children! We must start.' I should hope so, I fumed.

When the children were resting after lunch I called Mavis and I blurted out,

'It's not good enough, Mavis. Every day you oversleep, the children don't do their lessons properly, the animals are not cared for. It can't go on like this.'

She stared ahead, the smile gone from her face, but her chin up. Then she said, 'You're being unfair.' And after a pause, 'Anyhow I want to go home. I'm leaving,' and she walked away.

'You can't do that,' I called after her. 'You agreed to stay two years,' but she had closed her bedroom door.

For the rest of the day the household was tense; the children kept glancing from Mavis to me. I did not look at Mavis and she ignored me.

Calista was on the radio. She read her text without any attempt at disguising the fact, and her French was only just recognizable, with a strong American accent. I can do better than that, I told myself, but a cold feeling spread through my stomach.

Days passed and Mavis said nothing more. Every day as I returned from different functions, I was met with an unsmiling face and a drooping mouth. Did she really mean to leave us or not? I knew I should ask her, but I could not bring myself to do it.

Alan kept saying, 'Have it out with her' but my feelings were mixed. I could not get that upturned chin out of my mind. That spelt courage! Anyway, I had to think first of the broadcast.

It was my turn. The engineers behind a glass partition stared at me as I stood in the studio and the presenter put the first question – 'What do the Royal children eat for breakfast?' I had no idea but I could not go far wrong. I read my prepared text pretending to be speaking it. 'Porridge, eggs and bacon, then toast with butter and marmalade and they drink milk.' That was no good. I was obviously reading, and I could hear my Russian-Swiss accent. I had attended the Swiss Montreux college for two years. The presenter hardly glanced at her text. I lowered mine.

'Do they leave England at all?'

'Oh yes, of course they do. The children have just been on a trip in the Mediterranean.' I had answered spontaneously and that was better. As I went on I ignored my prepared text.

Now the last question, 'What do the English think of France, Frenchmen and French women?'

'The French have good taste, in architecture, art generally, literature, in fashion. As for the people, they're intellectual and it's wiser to listen to them rather than argue with them. French women are brave and elegant, even those in humble circumstances, and above all they are very feminine.'

It was over and I felt pleased with myself. Alan vouchsafed a 'Not bad'.

Mavis was waiting for me. 'I've been thinking,' she started. 'I won't go home. I did promise to stay.' She blushed as she looked at me, 'And I'm sorry; I will try to do better.' What a relief! and, I thought, she's braver than me. She has spoken first and with that chin still up.

'Good, Mavis,' I smiled, 'Let's forget it and start afresh.' Then as she was turning to go, I added, 'I was nervous about that broadcast and perhaps I was unfair.' She smiled back.

Next morning I woke late, at 8 o'clock. On the back terrace two small figures were standing at the table in bright sunlight wearing long aprons and floppy white hats making clay pots, while Mavis, in a Chinese-style, wide-brimmed straw hat and dark glasses leant over them, instructing them. All three were intent on their work, all else forgotten. She must sometimes be lonely out here, I thought, with so few British families and the French ignored governesses, even such an attractive one. There's only the navy . . . and two years without family is a long time. I must be more patient, more considerate, and not take Mavis for granted.

☆   ☆   ☆

Mavis's tennis balls skimmed low and powerfully over the net, skidding across the opponents' court and no one could return them. She won her set and, beaming, came off the court. Mavis was an erratic player but at her best she was unbeatable. We had arranged this party with the local British specially for her. Now I took her place. I was an indifferent player but the sun was shining, our slender eucalyptus trees threw fanciful shadows over my opponent's white dress and I enjoyed the game. I lost my set and was walking off the court, swinging my racket when Mavis hurried up.

She could hardly speak. 'It's . . . Lawrence. He's had . . . an accident.'

I seized her arm. Panic welled up in me. 'Where is he? What happened?' I ran indoors.

The women were gathered round Lawrence's bed. He lay stretched out, grey-faced, unconscious, but he was breathing.

'The doctor . . . Has anyone called him?' Silence. 'Hassin!' He was always there. 'Quick! Phone *Monsieur* . . . the doctor immediately . . .' I felt Lawrence's forehead; it was burning. 'What happened?'

Mavis's voice faltered. 'Joseph found him lying in the alleyway, beside his bicycle. He'd seen him riding, hands in his pockets. He thinks he hit a stone.'

'When was this?'

'About ten minutes ago.'

'Ten minutes! and I was playing tennis! You didn't call me!'

'We didn't like to interrupt your game,' one woman said.

Incredible! But I said nothing. There was no sign of a wound. I willed the doctor to come quickly. The women stood around. 'Mavis, get them out. Give them tea and let them go home.' They left. I bathed Lawrence's head with cold water. 'You'll be all right, darling. The doctor's coming,' I whispered in case he could hear.

Minutes dragged on.; I did not dare undress him. I sat there watching him. He was breathing. Then suddenly his face twitched, his lips moved, his eyes opened and he was violently sick. He gasped, 'Mummy!' as I lowered him back on to his pillow. I could see the pain in his eyes. But he closed them and gave a little sob. I went on bathing his face and forehead and I talked on, 'It's all right, darling. You've hurt yourself but the doctor will make you better.' He kept being sick and gasped, 'My head! What's happened?'

'You fell off your bicycle.'

The doctor arrived with Alan. He examined Lawrence and peered into his eyes. I clung to Alan's arm. He asked how long Lawrence had been unconscious and shook his head.

'He's got concussion. Badly, I'm afraid. Keep him quiet. Hold ice to his head. I'll be back first thing in the morning.'

As Mavis and I undressed Lawrence I could hear Alan walking round and round the house. I put an ice-cube in a flat rubber bag and held it to Lawrence's head. Mavis put Libet to bed in the day nursery. Alan watched with me for a time then, sighing, he too went to his room. All was silent. I remained in an armchair beside Lawrence, a shaded lamp behind me.

He's strong, he's young. I tried to calm my terror as I studied his round, childish face, the sloping eyes, tight shut, the thin, sensitive lips, and that tuft of hair that shot straight up off the middle of his head. Oh God, please! Is there a god? He's so still. Is he sleeping? He's stopped breathing! No, he's vomiting again. My poor darling! The silence! The darkness! Time moves so slowly!

Suddenly, 'Mummy, I'm very ill, aren't I?' I mustn't lie. He remembers everything. When Marcel bathed his pigeon in the fish pond, Lawrence cried, 'The water washes oil off the feathers and it won't be able to fly!' He remembered Konrad Lorenz's book I read them weeks before. 'Sweetheart, you'll be better in the morning. Try and sleep.' He's closed his eyes but his little fists are clenched. Oh God! So little and so serious. Too serious? Too sensitive? No! When I took the pigeon from Marcel, he jumped on Hassin's back as he leant over the fish pond, with such an impish grin. No, he's mischievous too.

The night's so long. It's still dark. Alan was beside me, his eyes questioning. I shook my head and he slipped away again. His head's still burning . . . that ice-cube . . . I held it to his forehead. The doctor was so grave . . . This vomiting . . . he's weaker. What can I do? I can't think; I'm so confused. Oh, to blot it all out! Lawrence to wake up, prance around . . . I can't stand it!

At last the iron bars on the windows began to stand out against the grey outside and I watched as they threw shapely shadows over the floor. The table and chairs added their forms and I switched off the lamp. Dawn was breaking and the doctor would soon be here. Alan crept in and waited with me.

The doctor walked in. 'What's this?' and he lifted the ice bag. 'One ice cube? It must be filled completely, to cover the whole head. This is useless and his head is as hot as ever.' He stalked out of the room to the kitchen.

I turned miserably to Alan. I had sat there all night and had failed to do the right thing.

The doctor returned and placed the bag filled with ice cubes on Lawrence's head. He would be back in the afternoon. Alan gave him a lift home on his way to work.

Lawrence's eyes were closed. He dozed, then he slept. I leant back in the chair and fell asleep.

I woke suddenly. Lawrence was smiling up at me. His face was white, no longer grey. He sipped some orange juice. His head was cooler, I swallowed my tears and we both fell asleep again.

The doctor that afternoon smiled down at Lawrence. 'That's better.'

Lawrence began to toss and turn and to complain. 'It's hurting my head!' and he tried to push the ice-pack away. This was more normal behaviour and I felt a great surge of relief.

The next few days he grew stronger and began to sit up. He pretended to be an orchestra by scratching on a balloon and humming in half-tones, Arab-style. He kept asking 'How many more hours till I can get up?' And once up, 'Can I ride my bicycle, please, just very slowly?' 'No!' I was emphatic. Then he was back at his lessons and the household returned to normal.

I don't face crises squarely, I thought. I blot out feelings, put up a kind of shield around myself and hope for the best, instead of thinking clearly and doing the right thing. That shameful ice-cube!

25

We were off once more for the annual camel festival but this time to Sidi Touil, deeper in the desert, on the Lybian frontier. We left all worries behind and were out to have a peaceful and interesting holiday. Alan drove, Cutajah sat at the back.

Outside Tunis everything was grey and shrivelled. Groups of Bedouin hurried past, urging their scraggy cattle northwards, searching for water and fodder. There had been no rain since autumn. Crops had failed, people were starving. We had prayed for rain at a meeting at St George's. To add to the misery the sirocco swept over the parched earth, drying it further and bringing swarms of locusts that devastated the remnants of the crops. They made a revolting, crunchy noise under our tyres and several struck our windshield. But although they are a pest, their wings looked beautiful – silvery-pink against the sun.

It was a sad beginning to our trip but food, as usual, restored my spirits. It affected me like wine. We lunched in the shelter of a sand-ridged wadi while, with cries of '*Ah! le pique-nique anglais!*' French guests waved from their cars and swept past to the comfort of an hotel in Sfax.

We were to stay the night in Djerba, the legendary lotus island where Ulysses landed, and as we had decided it would be more interesting to cross by ferry rather than over the causeway, the usual method, we branched off the main road. The countryside became very deserted. Not a soul on the bleak sands, not a single urchin or stray camel. 'Typical bandit country,' Cutajah remarked. We stopped chattering and scanned the sand dunes shimmering in the heat. I wished I was brave and could stop thinking of sharp, curved knives, and of what bandits might do. Why had we risked coming this way? 'Too much imagination,' Alan was always telling me. There were no troops on guard here either, but we reached the sea safely and I gazed at the water with relief.

Little fishing boats were plying back and forth. One of these

Our Bedouin neighbours.

came alongside and with two planks athwart the deck became the ferry! Anxiously, we watched as fishermen, in spite of the long robes fluttering around their legs and the ends of their head-cloths waving across their faces, nevertheless guided a car on to the boat with astonishing speed, and it left.

Another boat drew up. A car and a jeep were driven on to its planks and then the fishermen beckoned us on too! Cutajah pleaded '*Monsieur!*' but Alan nodded for him to go ahead. As Cutajah drove our car on to the planks, to keep the boat in trim, the jeep was driven further over. Finally, the jeep was overhanging on one side of the boat and our car four or five feet on the other. The fishermen tied it down with old bits of rope and put large stones behind the wheels. We climbed into the stern but Cutajah remained balanced on a plank, his hand protectively on the car, the other clutching a rope. Why, I wondered, as I grabbed the edge of the boat, must everything we do, involve risk and danger? Back home we take safety for granted; we're not used to fear. We were off.

Cutajah's expression of pained disbelief as he swayed above us perched among the ropes in his immaculate uniform made me laugh. I forgot my fears and revelled in the sight of the calm, deep blue waters and the tiny, low, white-domed houses

Our car crossing over to Djeiba on the ferry with Cutajah optimistically holding it. The ferry was a little fishing boat!

dotting the distant island. We landed and I hurried off the boat to the safety of land, disturbing two large camels peaceably chewing the cud on the jetty.

Djerba had one of the oldest Jewish communities, living there, they claimed, since Babylonian times. There was just light enough for us to visit an ancient synagogue. An old watchman with a long beard and white turban greeted us, unlocked the building and ushered us in, together with a crowd of his womenfolk and children. They all chatted volubly but in a language we could not understand so we waved our arms, nodded and smiled. There was no electric light; we had to peer around and completely forgot to take off our shoes and cover our heads, but no one seemed to mind. We gazed at the famous Tora, dating from the time of the destruction of the Temple in Jerusalem. How impressive! It had been in use all that time! Forgetting that it was the Sabbath, Alan tried to tip the old man but he shook his head and pointed to one of the urchins, who accepted the money. I distributed toffees among the children but there were not enough to go round. I showed them my empty hands, the children laughed and the whole company escorted us to the car. It was too dark to sightsee any more.

All fears forgotten next morning we drove slowly across the island. The vast, clean beaches sparkled in the sunshine, a cool breeze rustled the palm fronds and there was deep shade in the olive groves. We watched with delight a whole string of Jewish ladies, their backs straight, trotting side-saddle on donkeys. Their thin, brown faces were uncovered. Long veils hung from under broad-brimmed straw hats peaked like those of witches. How wise of the Jews to settle in such a beautiful spot, I thought. They would not make fortunes here but they were able to live decently.

We crossed back to the mainland by the Roman-built causeway. The sea was so still that it reflected the fishing boats with their long harpoons.

I felt in holiday-mood as we reached Ben Gardane, where the celebrations were in progress. In the market-place, festooned with bright-coloured carpets and banners, officials sat on a dais backed by an enormous curtain. We joined them and, looking down at the packed crowd of Tunisian men below, I realized that the curtain must conceal their women.

The last of the cavalry galloped past and the speeches started. The crowd was festive and restless, the loud-speakers kept going on and off, so only occasional words burst on to the square but they were applauded enthusiastically. Young men in white gowns and red caps were making stealthy gestures which brought forth from behind the curtain that strange sound women make by blowing through their fingers as they flap them rapidly against their lips – 'ululating'. Since the speeches were incomprehensible, whom were they greeting? I looked round. Behind the speaker sat a heavy man, middle-aged in a blue uniform with epaulettes, horn-rimmed glasses, his red tarbush set at a jaunty angle – Prince Chedley, the Bey's eldest son. So, the Bey's family had begun to appear in public.

'It's the Nationalists,' Alan whispered, 'greeting Chedley Bey and the Tunisian Prime Minister, Ben Ammar, next to him.' Monsieur Seydoux rose to speak, or rather to read as the French usually read their speeches. In spite of his imposing gold-braided diplomatic uniform, and the blue burnous slung nonchalantly over his shoulders, he looked thin and vulnerable. The crowd started milling around, the ululation grew louder, fiercer. There were bangs behind us. The curtain swayed. I looked nervously round. It bulged ominously behind Seydoux but as French officers moved quickly closer to him, he waved them away. The crowd seemed to have grown enormous. We had heard that Mendé-France's government had fallen. Perhaps, I thought, the Nationalists had given up hope. They had relied on him to keep faith and now they might think their only recourse was to violence. One bomb here would get us all. I was at the edge of the dais and the young men were pushing up against it. The women now drowned Seydoux's words completely. There was no way to escape; the women behind, the crowds in front.

'It's all right,' Alan whispered. 'They won't start anything, not with Chedley Bey present. It's just those ladies behind the curtain who are out of control! Women are fiercer than men!' Before I could protest, Seydoux finished his speech, stepped quickly down and was whisked away with the Prince and the Prime Minister.

We also hurried into our cars and drove away to Sidi Touil in convoy. We followed a track between two sand banks keeping well distanced from the car in front to avoid the whirling dust it raised. At one sharp turn a car skidded, ran up a bank and overturned. The convoy stopped, someone shouted, 'Doctor!' and two doctors hurried up as a man and woman were dragged out and laid down on the track. The

Fête du Chameau, at Sidi Touil.

doctors bent anxiously over the woman. She sat up and directed a flow of the most obscene abuse at her husband.

'Can't be that badly hurt,' one doctor remarked and everyone laughed. The car was righted, the couple climbed back in and we drove on.

At Sidi Touil the camels were assembled on a mountain side and black Bedouin tents had been set up for the *diffa* or lunch. Our hosts were once more the de Giullebons. Madame de Giullebon led us ladies to a small tent, and announced with a straight face '*For Madame la Consul-Général Britannique!*' She was teasing me but I did not care. It had been a long morning and there was not a palm tree or tuft of grass in sight. I hurried in, grateful for the privacy and the hole in the ground. The other ladies queued up.

Protocol was ticklish. Seydoux, Prince Chedley and the Prime Minister, were of equal rank and to place any one above the others would put paid to the General's career. We watched to see how he would cope. The three arrived in an open car sitting at the back side by side. They were led, walking abreast into the first tent and were seated on identical cushions at a round table with Calista, Madame de Guillebon and myself between them. We women were delighted to be the guests of honour and Seydoux was grinning, enjoying the General's predicament.

Over the cous-cous and the brics Calista and I wanted to

learn something of the life of the Touazines. Prince Chedley concentrated on his food and ignored our questions. Watching him sucking up huge mouthfuls, I thought, he's gross. Ben Ammar, a big, impressive man, sighed deeply and began, 'They're nomads, but some have settled down as shepherds or farmers . . .' His voice trailed off; he was evidently very tired. He had been touring the country, trying to persuade the nationalists to co-operate with the French over the new agreements and at the same time trying to extract as much as possible from the French. Seydoux came to his rescue and kept up an amusing flow of conversation.

'On my first trip to America after the war I had to fill in a form and the first question was 'Have you been to prison and if not, why not?'' I explained that the Americans thought if you had not been in prison you must be a collaborator and we joined in his laughter, even Prince Chedley, though I noticed that the two Arabs never even looked at each other.

Outside, a whole roasted sheep was laid out on a trestle table together with other meats and suddenly formality was discarded, everyone was joking, laughing and rushing around snapping photos, and pushing and shoving to get at the table to tear off the juiciest bits. A three-man band, two drummers and a flutist in long white robes over baggy turkish trousers, circled around playing a haunting tune, whose notes hovered on the hot air and occasionally doing little dance steps like Scottish pipers. Seydoux turned to Ben Ammar

'I see Arab influence has extended to Scotland!'

Waiters then offered us Palmolive soap and poured water over our hands.

The camel races began. Police lined the visitors up on either side of the race track. The huge, magnificent camels raced towards us across the flat sands, their tribal riders looked sensational, dark against the white of their flowing robes over black turkish trousers, heads swathed in white cloth with only fierce eyes showing. As one, we rushed forward with our cameras. The camels, terrified, reared up, foaming at the mouth, but their riders with harsh cries forced them on through the crowds. We scattered. They were supposed to do the track twice but as they approached our cameras a second time the camels swerved and refused to advance and the race was declared over. Two men rode up to the prize-giver who asked Seydoux to whom he should give the prize. Seydoux replied, 'Whichever you prefer!' and he shook the disappointed

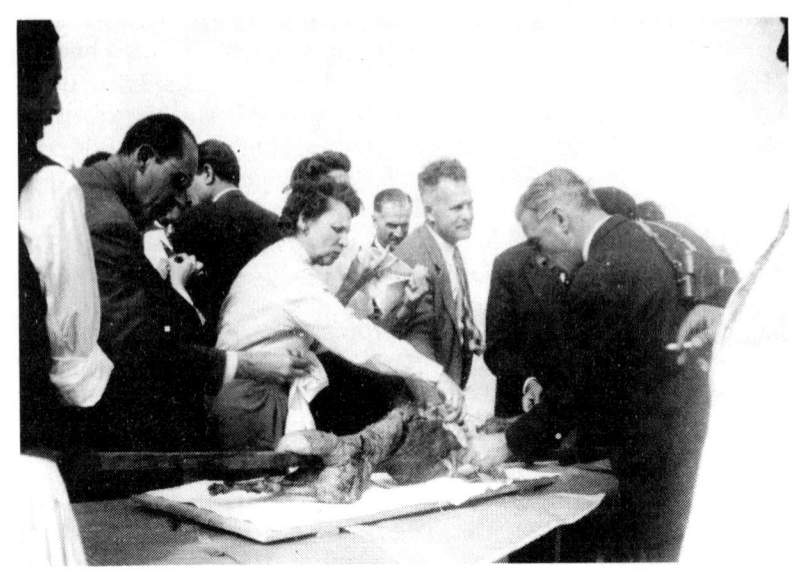

Sidi Touil Camel festival. Guests eating mutton. Alan in centre.

Alan, Mme Seydoux, M. Seydoux, Col. de Guillebon eating roast mutton.

Local Three-man band.

man's hand.

The camels were led off to the side while the fantasia took place – horsemen galloped past firing their rifles. This terrified the camels who stampeded right into the crowd. Their yellow teeth and great hoofs were everywhere as their riders struggled to control them. The horsemen then decided to give another showing of their prowess. This time they charged straight into the camels, whose riders, to save themselves, dashed straight at us. There was pandemonium. We fled amid shouting, laughter, screams, while police and officers tried to catch the brutes. When order was restored, and fortunately no one was hurt, we were all dishevelled and my normally elegant companions glared at me. I had advised them to be prepared for cold weather and had been about to add that they must also be prepared for heat and therefore to dress in layers but, as usual, I was not given the chance to finish my remarks and so they were all dressed in heavy wools and the sun was beating down on us. In the desert, it seems, it is either boiling or freezing.

Exhausted but pleased with the day's events, we drove to Gabes for the night.

Next morning Alan suggested, 'It's only an hour, I'm told, to Matmata, a village of cave-dwellers. Let's go there on our way. The General suggests we call at the Bureau for Native

Affairs.' A good idea, I agreed. It was pleasant country with little patches of barley in the valleys and olive trees wherever water would rest but then the going got rougher, the land more desolate. Now we were in mountainous country, savage and rugged, circling round precipitous rocks and crevasses. We saw dark holes scooped out of the rock where troglodites lived but we dared not stop to investigate. The road was just wide enough to take the car but what happens if we meet another? I wondered. I could feel my heart pounding. I was on the outer edge, inches from oblivion. Up and up. On a corner, miles below, the whole countryside suddenly lay spread out directly below me.

'Look at that view!' Alan cried and Cutajah, as he swerved round, looked down. The car hovered on the very edge. 'Oh! No!' Sick, head spinning, I gazed down into space; but Cutajah pulled the wheel round sharply and we turned the corner. I did not dare ask Alan not to talk. He might laugh – he had no nerves – and again distract that fool Cutajah. I sat very still. Matmata, we were told later is a mountain range, not a village. A horseman trotted towards us. He raised a hand in greeting and pulled in at the side of the road under the rock-face. Cutajah was forced to crawl along the very edge of the road. I did not dare breath or even glance down the precipice at my side. I sat wretchedly silent.

'Look!' This time Alan pointed upwards. 'The Bureau for Native Affairs.' Perched on the mountain's summit, stood a white fort with the Tricolor waving in the wind. Below stood a Tunisian special constable in a white gown falling in graceful folds and a blue burnous. He climbed into the car to show us the way in. At the entrance stood two more constables with drawn swords and between them a young French officer. The garrison had turned out to meet us! It took us three minutes to inspect the fort, then over coffee, the officer told us he lived here alone and ran the district with his three constables.

'It's a grand life, in superb country and with a great people,' he told us. I sympathized. It was exhilarating so high up above the world, the air crisp and clear. There was no room here for meanness or pettiness; everything was on a grandiose scale.

He set us on the way back, assuring me that we were to follow another route not as hair-raising as the one we had come by. 'You pass two villages so it can't be that bad,' he added. It was! We crawled down glued to the cliff-face and I sat speechless, hot and cold in turn. When at last the road widened, I gasped, 'He lied! It's just as bad!'

Alan was amused. 'He had to or he would not have got you down again!' I thought – never again! but now we were out of danger and I could enjoy the rugged scenery and the mountains rising to bald red domes. The villages were a mass of holes in eroded ravines but we saw few people. Those we passed waved and smiled with dignity, in the manner of countryfolk. A fine people, yet they lived in holes!

'This soft stone is probably easier to dig into than to build with,' Alan remarked, 'and they must keep nice and cool in summer.' The troglodytes grew dates, olives and a little barley but we saw no water. Richer villages built of the same stone as the mountains, blended into them and we only spotted them by their gaping doorways. They were safe, well camouflaged.

We drove straight back to Gabes. The trip had taken three hours. After a late lunch we took off back home but our adventures were not yet over. All at once the clouds above us turned black, lightning streaked across the fields, thunder roared and rain pelted down on to the road. Cattle and goats bunched together while shepherds squatted bundled up in their burnouses. When the storm passed, Bedouin women ran out to fill their water-bottles from the puddles. Their children will be drinking this filthy, oily water, I thought! How primitive! and I remembered French protests, 'How can they govern themselves? We have trouble enough doing it ourselves. With the women still veiled, railway workers' wives can't be photographed for free passes, and their schools, hospitals, wells, roads, we built them all.'

Suddenly we skidded across the shiny, wet surface of the road. I clutched the car seat. We landed up beside a bank.

'It's too slippery,' Cutajah cried out.

'Well, try driving on, but slowly,' Alan suggested. Cutajah started up and the car skidded across the road to the opposite bank.

I was thrown up against Alan. 'What's the matter?' I was frightened. I seemed to be frightened the whole time!

'The threads on the wheels are worn down,' Alan explained.

'Alan! and you knew that up in the mountain!'

'I didn't know it was going to be a mountain.'

'I'm getting out. I'm walking.' I was indignant. Alan got out too.

'Crawl along,' he told Cutajah. 'It's quite dry ahead.'

Further on Alan drove. It was getting late and Cutajah was

incapable of hurrying. I held on to my seat and dared not speak as Alan hurtled along. No use arguing. I gave up.

When we finally drove in through our own gates, he grinned.

'Well, that was fun, wasn't it? We covered over a thousand miles.'

'Fun, but nerve-wracking,' I protested.

26

'You must call on the Prime Minister's wife, Mme Ben Ammar,' Alan told me. Call on a Tunisian! Enter an Arab home! I was both excited and taken-aback. The French had seen to it that we only associated with their protegés, like the Tahar Maouis. 'Things are moving. The negotiations are still on in Paris in spite of the change of government. Roger Seydoux says it's now just a matter of '*Trouver la formule!*', find the right formula. We want to give them a prod. You can mix with Tunisians but make sure the French know where and when. We mustn't offend them.'

No, indeed for, as I had boasted to Alan, we had at last stormed the bastion of French inhospitality. We had made French friends, through the children mainly. Our children had been afraid of the French 'gangs' as they called them until Pierre Héritier, the Air Force General's twelve-year old son, whom I invited one afternoon, knocked Lawrence down and snatched his bicycle. The next morning Pierre, a slim, fair child stood before me. He drew himself up to attention and announced,

'Madame, I have come to apologize for my bad behaviour yesterday. I am very sorry.' Lawrence laughed, seized his hand and they rushed off together. From that moment our children were no longer afraid of French children. The two Seydoux boys, Eric and Pierre, and other French youngsters careered around the garden with the dogs, and played with our new donkey, Ouggie (Miss Bourke had exchanged our troublesome Shaggy for her baby donkey), with the new baby rabbits, with Cutajah's baby goats and with my pride – the minutest tortoise, an inch long. The egg I had protected had hatched.

Our children were invited back to French childrens' parties and, judging by their squeals of laughter, they felt part of the 'gang.'

Mothers came to fetch their children. Madame Héritier, her elegant figure perched on a stool, started a painting of our palace and Jacqueline Seydoux dropped in for a gossip over coffee. At our dinner parties I began to enjoy the quick and apt French repartees and I no longer felt excluded.

Now I had to storm another bastion – the Tunisians! I knew little about Arab women or the kind of behaviour they would expect from me. My only contacts with them were at a charity tea when I sat at a table with Tunisian ladies, huge and fat, dressed in layers of bright coloured brocade and swamped in gold, with pleasant faces peering out of it all and eyes, enormous in their circle of kohl. The French, congregated at a central table, had failed to notice my arrival so I sat down in the first empty seat. When Mme La Tour realized I was with Tunisians, she beckoned for me to join her, but I felt it would be rude to leave my companions and to her annoyance I stayed where I was. We could not converse but we nodded, smiled and together enjoyed the delicious, cream cakes.

I had also attended a charity film with Tunisian women present. They came this time in tight-fitting black dresses – 'the little black dress' was the rage of Paris – but few of them had the slim figure of the French. In European clothes they lost their natural dignity and looked dreadful. One enormous women tried to fit into the seat in front of me, but was too fat. An attendant placed two chairs in the gangway and there she sat, bursting out of her 'little black dress.' All this was not encouraging.

'Mme Ben Ammar is receiving tomorrow. You'd better go then.' Alan told me. I rang Mme Héritier and in passing dutifully mentioned that I was calling on Mme Ben Ammar next day.

I dressed up for the occasion, though not in a little black dress – I did not have the figure for it either – and told Cutajah to drive to Mme Ben Ammar's. He stared at me instead of opening the car door.

'Mme Ben Ammar's?'

'Yes. The Prime Minister's wife.'

'But she's an Arab! The British Consul-General's wife cannot call on an Arab!' Poor Cutajah! For him the heathen Arabs were hardly human.

'I have to Cutajah. Let's go!' We drove off, Cutajah's solid neck a protesting red. I felt exhilarated. This was a challenge for me personally. No trailing behind Alan for a change. I was on my own, free to use my own wits. As we approached Tunis Cutajah slowed down.

'Madame, she lives in the centre of the Arab quarter.'

'I know. Drive in as far as you can.'

The narrow twisting lanes between high white walls were difficult to negotiate. Finally Cutajah stopped. 'It's too narrow. I dare not go further.' Police appeared and beckoned me to leave the car and follow them. It was muddy and dirty under foot. Cutajah's lip curled in disdain. Strange that wealthy Arabs should live in the midst of such filth, but perhaps it was better that rich and poor should exist side by side.

A heavy door in the wall swung open and I stepped into luxury, thick carpets, beautiful tapestries, sparkling brass ornaments. Next moment I was enveloped in my hostess's warm, soft arms as she kissed me over and over again as though I was a long-lost friend. With my Russian background I took this in my stride. Still holding my arm, she led me into a large drawing-room and announced, 'My nieces!' Some twenty women, all in tight black dresses, sat on hard-backed chairs in a semi-cirle along the wall. I glanced quickly at the smiling faces, the dark, hennaed hair, and deep eye-shadow. Some were mere girls, others elderly. I walked down the line greeting each one. The older ones kissed me, the younger ones shook hands. I settled on a chair at the end of the line and we sat in silence, complete silence. No one even whispered. It reminded me of how Lawrence took me to Joseph the gardener's house to congratulate him on his wedding. There the Maltese guests sat similarly on chairs along the wall, all silent. After bowing to them, Lawrence and I sat down too. No one spoke as we sipped orangeade.

But I was not used to being socially silent and I began to fidget, wondering whether anything was expected of me. As I glanced at my neighbour, an elderly woman, she smiled and said in good French, 'You are surprised. Yes, we are all nieces, some of Mme Ben Ammar, some of her husband and we range from seventeen to sixty!' Of course, I thought, from different mothers. Other women smiled too but evidently they only spoke Arabic.

More Europeans began to arrive and they made straight for me. Tea and lemonade were served with rich, greasy cakes. I wanted to get to know my hostess so I left the Europeans huddled together and sat down beside Mme Ben Ammar. She was telling those around her in perfect French about a difficult confinement, presumably hers, but she was giving such gruesome details that I was embarrassed and shocked and had to push away the chocolate cream cake I was eating. I was not accustomed to speaking of such private matters, especially in public. She did not notice and again kissed and hugged me when I decided it was time to leave. I had, I decided, little in common with these ladies, yet in their presence, I felt content, at peace. They're warm and emotional, I thought, like Russians, and families are closely knit. I liked that.

The police led me back to Cutajah and the car.

Later Alan informed me, 'The French say your Tunisian tea was part of a campaign to prove that Tunisians are as capable of entertaining as Europeans, and are capable of being independent and of coping with 'internal autonomy'.' I was amused. Could a tea party prove anything? But then I thought, trivial events often do lead to momentous happenings. Tolstoy believed that Napoleon's cold lost him his campaign in Russia. And remembering the Holocaust in Europe, I decided the Tunisians could hardly do worse! I was dithering as usual between two sets of feelings, pro-French and pro-Tunisian and I burst out

'Then who is in the right?'

'No one,' Alan replied. 'There's no right or wrong about it. It's a question of finding what is best for the majority and the least harmful for the rest.'

27

'You're cheating!' I shouted. 'I got there first.'

'Mine's underneath!' Alan flung my card off the table.

'Don't do that! I won't play if you cheat!'

Beside me Libet sniffed.

'It's all right, darling.' I hugged her. 'We're tired and scrappy!' The Ambassador (HE, His excellency, as we referred to him), our boss, Sir Gladwyn Jebb, was about to descend on us. Alan's future, his whole career could be at stake, let alone Anglo-French-Tunisian relations.

All day we had worked to put the finishing touches to the house and a game of racing demon, I had thought, would help us relax but it was no use. We gave up.

The past few days workmen had crawled everywhere and had mended the roof. Torrential rains had followed the drought and water had again poured through our ceilings and even on to Alan's desk, soaking his guest lists for HE's parties. I hung them on a radiator to dry. The telephone rang continually and Alan kept driving to Tunis as the French, vague as usual, kept changing plans. Also the Franco-Tunisian negotiations were now ending and Government officials were flying back and forth to Paris so we did not know who or how many would be coming to our parties. We planned for three hundred and fifty for cocktails and thirty for dinner to follow on the same day so the preparations for the first would also carry us through the second.

The servants always left things to the last moment, not allowing time for unexpected crises, so as soon as the house was dry I bullied them into cleaning well in advance. Hassin hosed down the tiled walls, Mahomet polished the furniture and Fatma cleaned the silver. Soon the tiles were shining, the furniture gleamed, the silver shone. Mavis did the flower-arranging and our palace looked its best.

Alan and Lawrence had their hair cut in the office. 'Why, are we going to be seen?' Lawrence asked. He disliked grown-

Our Ambassador, Sir Gladwyn Jebb, and Alan.

up parties but was afraid of missing the motor-cyclists roaring in or the police drinking surreptitiously in the corridors. I rushed to buy myself the smart A-look costume in light grey flannel I had seen, while Mavis took the children to visit poor, little Pong. He had been run over and his legs were paralysed but there was hope for his recovery. During the ambassadorial visit he was to remain at the vet's. Poor Ping had also been run over and did not recover.

On the morning of the great day we were tense but ready. A tremendous blast shook the house. I remembered – Alan had unthinkingly given two RAF jet pilots permission to photograph the house from the air. We hurried up to the roof. The jets roared round the house, shaking the very atmosphere. Libet and I clung to each other, Hassin pulled Lawrence down and leant protectively over him while Ali and Mahomet clung to the parapet and laughed hysterically. Finally the jets screamed past on either side of our flagpole, or so it seemed to me, though Alan maintained that I exaggerated. They boomed off towards the sea, scattering the bathers who, we were later told, thought civil war had broken out. We kept quiet about the pilots being RAF. My legs were trembling as we climbed down off the roof. What a start to the day!

HE and Lady Jebb flew in that evening, with their daughter

Sir Gladwyn and Lady Jebb and Alan with French and Tunisian officials.

Vanessa and Jebb's secretary. Jebb was met with full military honours and then Alan brought them all to us for an informal dinner.

As he stepped into the Grand Salon, Sir Gladwyn, tall, broad-shouldered with a high, intellectual forehead and a surprisingly unlined face, looked the true Ambassador. Lady Jebb, with her small features and neat figure was doll-like beside him, but she stepped out with dignity. Wrapped in a soft, white coat, a black and white hat perched sideways over meticulously permed hair, a large corsage adding a finishing touch for elegance, I thought, she can hold her own with any of the French. As British representatives I felt proud of them both.

'It's a museum! I can't believe you live here!' Lady Jebb exclaimed as they gazed at our colourful tiles and brightly painted ceilings.

Ali excelled over the dinner. I had taken the navy's hint that where C-in-Cs were concerned, 'informal' meant laying out the red carpet.

Lady Jebb began coughing and sneezing. 'My cold is much worse,' she complained, though she continued to smile ravishingly and Hassin, serving her, bowed lower and lower. That cold was a disaster at the very start of the visit . . . They were

217

officially guests of the French and were not even staying in our house.

Hassin suddenly exclaimed, 'A tisane, Madame! that will do you good!' and he hurried away, returning with a hot infusion of herbs. 'I've added plenty of lemon,' he told Lady Jebb. She drank it gratefully while HE chatted good-humouredly and they left early for the French Residency in Tunis. So far all had gone well. Our home had been admired and our dinner appreciated.

The Jebbs had a dreadful night. The La Tours were in their La Marsa Residency so the Tunis house was unoccupied and unheated. The night was bitterly cold. When Jacqueline Seydoux plugged in an electric fire, it fused the lights. The Jebbs went to bed by candlelight. The Secretary described how he met the Ambassador raiding bedrooms, his large figure staggering through the dark under loads of blankets. When Lady Jebb, cold and coughing, finally fell asleep in the early morning she was woken at regular intervals by military buglers blasting away in honour of HE.

While Alan took HE to lay a wreath on the Unknown Soldier's grave and to call on the Bey and other dignitaries, I visited Lady Jebb. She was huddled under the bedclothes.

'It's icy cold! I'm freezing and my temperature's up.' She sounded hysterical. This was embarrassing. In the Resident-General's house I could not interfere but nor could we risk Lady Jebb falling seriously ill. I hurried to Jacqueline, demanded to see her immediately and told her what was happening.

'It's none of my business, but please do something and quickly!' Jacqueline fidgeted with an ashtray, apparently as embarrassed as I was.

Then she said, 'I'll call the Secretary to the Cabinet. Tell him what you have told me.' When the young man came I repeated what I had told Jacqueline, and added, 'None of us want Lady Jebb to go away feeling ill-used, so it's best to be frank, isn't it? You don't mind?'

He nodded and promised to put things right. A strange way, I thought, to go about such a simple matter, but Jacqueline explained. 'Madame La Tour has had a relapse after the birth of her baby (she had had a son, at last, after eight girls) and is in bed at La Marsa. She did not delegate authority to look after the Jebbs to anyone else.' How formal, I thought, how unfriendly.

I borrowed a woolly bed-jacket from Mrs Pell, picked up some light reading and returned to Lady Jebb. The heating was on, she had a hot-water bottle, and was propped up on several pillows. She looked comfortable and very decorative, though rather flushed. She thanked me and fortunately did not blame us for their discomfort.

At the Resident-General's dinner that night in HE's honour Tunisian Ministers were prominent in their red sheshias. Princess Zakia, the Bey's daughter, seen in public for the first time, was chief lady. Things were truly moving fast. I was on our host's left. I was delighted but tried to appear modest, to make it plain that I realized I was merely replacing Lady Jebb, for the Ministers' wives were senior to me. On my left was Admiral Laurin from Bizerta. He started teasing me, 'So you're promoting your husband's career, I see!' We continued joking though occasionally I turned to the Resident-General. I sat inclined towards him in silence. That satisfied him. Women should be present but not obtrusive.

Next day was our party. That morning the Consulate produced eight helpers. Each did his job well but they ignored each other. I was the link between them. Ali had to produce food both for the cocktail party and the dinner. I issued instructions, left Mavis to cope with any crisis and attended a luncheon at the Seydoux. Roger was away but Jacqueline kept the conversation flowing. However, my thoughts were back home.

Afterwards I hurried to Lady Jebb with flowers, chocolates and more light reading. She felt better, was sitting up, and looked much more like her usual self. When I left, I forgot my bag in her room. I opened the door again without knocking. Lady Jebb was smoothing out with her fingers the smile-lines on her face! She must be feeling better, I thought.

By six we were ready to receive. HE stood at the entrance with us and shook every hand. Alan introduced the guests and when he could not remember the name he murmured 'His Excellency . . .' The Tunisians, Ministers, past and present, imposing in white robes and sheshias, settled down in arm-chairs at small tables laden with food and fruit juices which, knowing they liked to be seated comfortably, we had placed around the room. The Europeans liked to bunch together in the centre.

A crisis in the negotiations caused French officials to dart back and forth to the airport while Jacqueline was almost

Alan.

continually on the phone. Ali kept sending messages, 'What time dinner?' but since no one knew when the Resident-General would arrive, I kept changing from '7.30' to '8' to '8.30'. The Tunisians were eating and drinking their fill, the French were competing as to who could shout loudest and HE had a chance to talk to Tunisian Ministers, French officials and local businessmen, so I decided all was going well. Vanessa Jebb proved a great asset and was the centre of an admiring circle. With her slight figure, round face, dark mop of hair, and a beaming, friendly smile she looked most attractive. There was such a crowd that one lady remarked, 'You'll have to build on to the house for your next party!'

A slight tug on my sleeve. Lawrence was whispering 'Mummy! Come! Ali is throwing saucepans in the kitchen.'

He took my hand and we threaded our way through the crowds, smiling and nodding. In the corridor I could hear shouting, bursts of laughter and the clanging of metal.

Ali, red-faced, beads of sweat on his forehead, leant on the kitchen table and was hurling the pans and saucepans on it at a whole crowd of police and chauffeurs standing around, drinking and laughing at him.

'Out!' I shouted. 'Everyone out!' They poured into the corridor. 'No! . . . Outside! Ali can't cook with you all under his feet.' They dispersed quickly. I hurried back to my guests. Would we get any dinner? I wondered. I was stupid, mad, to expect Ali to prepare for a huge cocktail party and a dinner at the same time. I had only thought of myself – so much easier – the rooms, flowers, our clothes all served for both occasions but for him . . .

The French were still rushing in and out and there was still no Resident-General. At last motor-cyclists, more police, numerous cars, all swept up to the steps and the Resident-General arrived. I could hardly greet him for the crowd of hangers-on that invariably surrounded him.

'Madame, my apologies! I have to leave immediately for Paris. The plane is waiting.'

'Then a quick drink!' I insisted. Hassin stood by with a glass of wine and then the General took off again and Seydoux replaced him.

I told Hassin that Ali could now serve dinner. Most of the cocktail guests had left. Hassin returned shrugging and looking helpless. I followed him to the kitchen. Ali was mopping his brow and doing nothing about serving up the food.

'Come, Ali! I will help you. Hassin get the serving dishes.' I started dishing out the food while Ali watched. Then suddenly he snatched the serving spoon from me. I was evidently hopeless! As he dished out I stood beside him, and said, 'That's good. Thank you!'

Hassin carried the dishes in and I followed. No one had noticed my absence and I led HE and Seydoux into the dining-room for the buffet supper.

'You have an expert cook!' Roger exclaimed and HE added, 'I could do with him in Paris.' Good for Ali, I thought. I sat in a daze but everyone was chatting away and because of Lady Jebb's illness HE left with Roger soon after coffee was served.

When the last guests had gone, I collapsed on to the couch.

28

'The press are very rude about our party,' Alan announced next morning as he handed me *La Depêche Tunisienne* and I read' . . . because of the intimate nature of the occasion – 250 guests were invited – the press was excluded.'

I laughed. 'I think that's rather funny!'

But Alan frowned. 'They asked for permission to attend and I refused. Presumably the office used the term 'intimate' as an excuse.'

Alan was suspicious of the press and always tried to exclude it whereas, having worked for Reuters during the war, I enjoyed meeting reporters and hearing their views even if I did have to keep silent myself.

The Ambassador now left on the usual three-day tour of southern Tunisia, escorted by Alan and several watchful French officials. I was left to minister to Lady Jebb, though not very successfully for another migraine caught up with me. She lay in the French Residency and I in the British. Diplomatic wives, I thought bitterly, are not supposed to have normal bodies that break down occasionally and, like everything else, need mending. But I had provided Lady Jebb with eau de cologne, and more flowers and books. She thanked me prettily, smiled in a friendly way but the aura of an Ambassador's wife remained between us. Fortunately, the local doctor fascinated her as he held forth on Middle Eastern civilization.

I was up again by the time the Ambassador's party returned. Sir Gladwyn was relaxed and smiling – a good omen. Alan remarked that in Gabes in his bath he counted sixteen flea bites but he added, 'I couldn't find the offender. I hope the ambassador didn't take him off me!'

The French had decided to allow Lady Jebb into a Tunisian household and a suitable family had been asked to hold a reception. Vanessa took Lady Jebb's place and arrived with Madame La Tour. The Tunisian ladies were delighted to have the chance to display to us, their European guests, their gorgeous native dresses, more exquisite, more striking than ours – brocaded two-piece gowns, scintillating with silver and gold embroidery, a flimsy bit of lace over brown bellies and a full, long skirt fitting low over the hips and intriguingly slit at the side over lace trousers.

My French neighbour whispered, 'Much as they dislike it, they have to wear our hateful European clothing in public; theirs is too seductive, especially with those revealing décolletages! They can only show it off in private!'

A gramophone spilled out urgent, sensual music. The ladies started swaying. Then as it gathered momentum, their bodies began vibrating. Their bellies fairly pranced around, yet each dancer formed one perfect, graceful whole. They're natural dancers, I thought.

My neighbour went on whispering, 'This is a censored type of dance' and she gave a meaningful nod. 'They spend their days practising to please their husbands, and these are educated women!' I imagined myself gyrating before my husband. Would he bother to lower his *Times* or would he just enquire, 'What's the matter with you?' Yet, I thought ruefully, these wives must be more exciting, more fun.

We sat transfixed, music filling our heads and the dancers whirling before us till they stopped and, laughing, dropped bright-coloured silk scarves into our laps.

'Come, dance with us!' Enticed by the hot rhythm, several French women got up, their scarves were tied round their hips and to the resounding beat, they started wiggling their stomachs. But the effort made their arms and the rest of their body stiff as pokers. I longed to join in the fun but, I thought, it would not do for Britain to look ridiculous and I remained seated. Vanessa pranced around but less stiffly than the French. She looked very glamorous dressed in Tunisian clothes, very charming, with her father's regular features and a generous, smiling mouth, a tribute to Britain. As the Tunisians tried to show the French how to loosen up, they looked funnier and funnier till I burst out laughing but everyone was too excited to notice me.

Driving home Cutajah remarked, grinning, 'That was a wonderful show!'

'How do you know?'

'We could see through chinks in the curtains.' Well, servants did not count in Arab eyes, it would not matter.

Alan was waiting for me back home. I tied the red scarf round my hips, spread my arms out gracefully and with chin held high, I floated into the drawing-room and started wiggling my stomach. Alan glanced round his *Times* and exclaimed, 'What on earth are you up to?'

The Ambassadorial visit was over. 'It's been interesting,' he told us. 'They let me talk to the Néo-Destour and Seydoux was most helpful, thanks to you, Alan!' Promotion? Alan escorted Sir Gladwyn to the airport, where he was seen off with full military honours. Rain poured down and did not help the influenza he had apparently already caught and with which he went down in Algiers, his next port of call. He must have been feeling ill on the plane for his highly complimentary note of thanks to Alan written during the flight referred to the good time he had had in 'Algiers'.

'Thank goodness he didn't fall ill earlier,' Alan exclaimed. 'Here, as far as I can tell, all seems to have gone well. Actually I enjoyed it all. HE has a caustic wit and an objective attitude to things.' He heaved a great sigh of exhaustion. 'Tonight I'm going to bed early whatever happens.' So am I, I thought, contentedly. Alan's career was safe although we still had Lady Jebb on our hands. We both visited her regularly and she continued to smile and thank us.

Two days later Lady Jebb insisted that she was sufficiently recovered to follow. We got up at five to drive her and Vanessa to the airport. It was a cold, damp morning so the French allowed us to drive right to the plane to protect Lady Jebb from the wind. I was only half awake, or that was my excuse, for, having led Lady Jebb to her seat, without thinking, I leant towards her and kissed her soft, scented cheek. Quickly I drew back. What was I doing.? She wasn't Russian! I was far junior to her and perhaps she had only leant towards me in order to shake hands. Embarrassed, I hurried off the plane to Alan who stood waiting for it to take off and was in no state to worry about anything more.

On our return home, we found Pong lying on a rug under the front porch. He was very thin but he licked my hand as I bent down to stroke him. Ali was standing over him. 'His back legs are still paralysed,' he told us, 'but when he saw me he wagged the tip of his tail. He can do that,' and Ali beamed, his normally gloomy face happier than I had ever seen it before. 'He greeted me! He was pleased to see me. He's a better friend that most men.' So Ali was fond of animals. So few Arabs were.

Hassin, Herta and Pong.

If Pong could wag the tip of his tail, his legs might recover too. We looked hopefully down at him. He stared up at us and the tip of his tail was wagging again.

Mahomet with Pong.

29

The negotiations were completed! We could hardly believe it. The Tunisians had not trusted the new Faure government but what had seemed impossible had now been achieved! What a relief! No more *Fellaghas*, no more murders. We were safe.

'The negotiators are pleased with themselves,' Alan told me and he was beaming too. 'The Tunisian Prime Minister returned from Paris yesterday praising everyone and he gave a solemn promise that Frenchmen and their property would be protected.' Excellent news! Alan went on, 'But troops are everywhere as there'll be howls of rage from the local French. But things should go quietly now, provided that the Faure government does not fall before August when the agreement should be ratified.'

At Miss Bourke's picnic luncheon in her shady garden suddenly a local French guest started shouting, 'We've been sold out! We don't recognize these negotiations and we won't accept them. You'll see, we'll stop them being ratified!'

I could not eat. Such deeply held feelings, such bitterness. As we drove home Alan remarked, 'It's worrying this attitude of the *colons*. Evidently we're not out of the wood yet, not till the conventions are ratified. I won't be able to take leave if there's trouble.' We were due for home leave that summer. 'But you can always go ahead with the children.' No, I thought, if there's trouble we stay together.

We gave a luncheon for the Bishop of Gibraltar who was visiting Tunis. Roger and Jacqueline Seydoux arrived late, bringing with them the tension that was always so close.

In the dining-room the French ladies sat down firmly whereas I had to ask the Bishop to say Grace. They quickly realized and got up but Miss Bourke remained seated. As we teased her the tension eased. She insisted that in Irish families visitors had to make a really good *fauxpas* before being accepted into the family. So she now hoped to be accepted.

Roger was his usual loud-voiced, cheerful self, flinging jokes

Left to right. Bishop Morris, Mrs Dunbar, Archdeacon and Alan.

around. 'My compatriots have pelted us with rotten vegetables; they can't attack the Residency, so next they'll be shooting us!' But he kept throwing up his long, wiry arms to stroke his hair, and with thin fingers he fiddled with the cutlery. A French official beside me whispered, 'Seydoux is off his head with work and worry.' Then he laughed. 'Actually he loves both and even hates taking time off for meals.' He told me that Roger only allowed himself a couple of hours' sleep. 'He takes sleeping pills at night, and pep pills during the day and to keep up with him, we have to take all these pills too!'

Roger suddenly turned to his Minister of the Interior, 'My friend, what exactly are you up to? I telephone my wife. There is silence. I ask the exchange why I can't get through to her. And what answer do you think I get? 'The censor is out to lunch. I'm waiting for him to return.' You are censoring my calls?' the Minister stared down at his plate. There were titters from some junior officials. Roger laughed and everyone started talking to cover the Minister's confusion.

Local French officials were in disarray. Would they retain their jobs or what was to happen to them? The Headmaster of the *Lycée de Carthage*, a new school, light, airy and cheerful, where we hoped to send the children in the autumn, had no idea whether his school would still exist. 'It may become a

228

Tunisian school,' he told us, 'whatever that means!' And as everyone was flying to and from Paris one never knew who would or would not appear at one's table.

'What's the latest?' Alan asked Roger.

'The Néo-Destour have declared themselves satisfied. But the *colons* are still trying to stop the agreement going through Parliament. They accuse France of betraying her sons abroad. They're trying to stir up trouble between the Néo-Destour and the extremist Salah Ben Youssef faction. Then they can say that the Néo-Destour cannot speak for Tunisia.' He laughed. 'We've bartered differences with the Tunisians for difficulties with the French! They're holding a monster protest meeting now in the Sports Palace.'

We had to go on to an art exhibition which the Resident-General was to open. We waited but he did not turn up. 'The monster meeting!' Alan whispered. 'Perhaps Roger will come instead.' But he did not come either. At last when our feet were about to give up a young, rather scared and entirely inaudible secretary came, opened the exhibition and scuttled back to his office.

Later we heard that at the meeting the *Collectivité Française*, as the *colons* now called themselves, had condemned the conventions, had booed General la Tour and called him a disgrace to his uniform. They only dispersed on the decision to hold another meeting on the anniversary of the Liberation of Tunis. A rumour spread through Tunis that Bourguiba would be allowed to return – we knew that Roger had felt his return would calm things down, but now that was postponed in order not to provoke the French community.

That evening at the Italian Consul-General's party only the Residency wives arrived and they looked glum and kept whispering in corners and falling silent when we foreigners approached. We continued dancing but half-heartedly. All the time we wondered what dreadful thing had happened. Rumours spread of shootings, assassinations . . . Alan would not dance with me; he clung to his glass of whisky. He was worn down by late office work so we went home early.

Next morning over breakfast we read in the papers that French youths had attacked and beaten up the eighty-two-year-old President of the Committee for Franco-Tunisian Co-operation. Fortunately he was expected to recover. They also shot at the secretary but he escaped. Our normal cheerful sun-lit breakfasts, were now spoilt by depressing news in the papers.

Every evening Alan came home very late. More Frenchmen had been attacked by young Europeans and the Resident-General decided to expel from Tunisia the President of the *Présence Française*, a retired general. At the meeting he had used grossly insulting language about La Tour – in itself an incitement to violence – and he was in touch with Moslem extremists. The French community reacted by announcing that they were behind the general, 'Expel us all!' they cried. Youths painted 'Resign' on walls all along the road from General La Tour's Residency to Tunis.

'The Resident-General is faced with the problem that broke Voizard', Alan remarked, 'how to cope with extremist compatriots without rousing Parisian reaction.' It was frightening.

Then we heard that Paris had allowed the French community to hold their meeting to commemorate the Liberation of Tunis in spite of the ban on open air demonstrations. 'Presumably to avoid a head-on collision,' Alan remarked. 'It looks like weakness but then a first class set-to with fire hoses and all that might stop the ratification. Quite apart from the fact that the police and firemen would be local French too!'

They marched several thousand strong in silence down the main street of Tunis and laid a wreath on the Unknown Soldier's grave. Some started shouting insults and tried to climb into the Residency grounds but the police and army were ready and the crowd were forced to disperse. When we drove down later to a British Legion celebration, we could only advance slowly in the main square through the massed ranks of troops. Roger told us that he had been worried as the demonstrators were armed and the local police were not entirely trustworthy.

Next morning was the Liberation of Tunis and V-E day parade. As we drove out in our Sunday clothes, Libet with her hair loose in flowing waves to below her waist, the children were excited by soldiers with rifles on guard outside our wall. The Resident-General would pass that way. By 7.45 am Alan was seated on the dais and we on chairs to the side. The children joined their friends on the pavement while Lawrence took up a strategic position under the elbows of two military policemen.

It was a picturesque parade. The sun shone, a slight breeze played among the palms and to the rhythm of numerous bands, the troops swung past, rifles over their shoulders; dark-blue beretted *Chasseurs Alpins*, turbanned Zouaves in turkish

Left to right. M. Seydoux, Gen. La Tour, Gen. Tahar Maoui, The Bey of Tunis, Turkish C.G., Italian C.G., Spanish C.G. and Alan.

trousers, dark-faced Senegalese in red tarboushes. Black turbanned Goumiers in brown striped gowns padded past on bare feet, Spahis, white-cloaked trotted on white steeds, and white turbaned *Tiraillers Tunisiens* beat enormous white drums. Tanks and gun-carriages lumbered past in between the famous regiments.

After watching for a while I suddenly noticed that the troops lining the street were not facing the parade. They were facing us and they carried machine-guns! They seemed as numerous as the troops parading. I looked back. Behind us stood the massed ranks of sullen-faced ex-servicemen, the extreme element of the French community! We had been deliberately placed to forestall trouble. Even these fanatics would not attack through a crowd of women and children, especially diplomatic

Liberation of Tunis parade, above Sengalese troops, below Goums.

Tiraillers Tunisiens, Liberation of Tunis parade.

families, at least I hoped not. I no longer watched the parade. I kept glancing at the grim faces behind and the determined faces in front and I remembered what all these young men were trained to do – to kill! I called the children to me and waited for the end.

At last the parade was over. Alan came off the dais towards us. Suddenly there was a loud explosion. Everyone started, then froze, the troops, police, dignitaries and the crowd, all stood motionless till a voice shouted, 'It's a tank back-firing' and I heard Roger's loud, nervous laughter from the dais. We hurried away.

30

Bourguiba was coming home, back to Tunis – the man the French had banished and imprisoned for so long that they repeated, 'He's forgotten. He can come back, and in any case he approves of the conventions.' But now he electrified the whole country. His name was flung passionately around.

Our French *colon* friends cried, 'Murderer! Allow the murderer back!' and a French Parliamentary mission visiting Tunis were so moved by their eloquence that they determined to fight the conventions, the government's policy of 'scuttle'. Alarmed, the French postponed Bourguiba's return.

It was difficult to follow events. The Old Destour party, rivals for power, also denounced the conventions – Defence and Foreign Policy were to remain in French hands – and appealed to Tunisians to oppose them. So did Salah Ben Youssef, Néo-Destour's Secretary-General from his exile in Cairo. He was stirring up support among members of the Arab League and he had become Bourguiba's personal rival.

'Better Bourguiba than these extremists,' Roger Seydoux decided and Bourguiba's return was at last fixed for June 1st. By then the conventions would have been initialed.

The Néo-Destour were jubilant. They announced in the press their plans for a triumphant entry for their leader into Tunis with a twenty-one gun salute. They proclaimed a general strike, so that workers would be free to cheer Bourguiba on his way. Bourguiba would land at La Goulette, call on the Bey (Prince Chedli had already tactfully laid a foundation stone for his villa in Tunis) and in the evening would address the people in the Medina. There would be public entertainment and feasting.

'Who would have expected all this?' Roger demanded, 'but we can hardly forbid them to celebrate.' Tunisians poured into the city. 'How are we going to control them? They're all hot-blooded, *colons*, Tunisians, the lot. Goodness knows what may happen.'

'Murder!' the newspaper headlines suddenly cried and we read 'The Old Destour leader, Professor Abdullah Gamra, has been murdered in Sousse, and Tunisians have been beaten up and robbed on the Algerian frontier and in the Kef.' Roger remarked 'The Néo-Destour has evidently ordered that the Old Destour should be silenced.' Next day a bomb exploded and destroyed the Néo-Destour office.

At the parties we attended guests looked tense and their laughter sounded false. 'All this excitement can so easily turn to trouble,' a French official said. 'Tunisians are already waiting in Marseilles to sail back with Bourguiba. How are we going to protect everyone? The non-Moslem population is scared.' So was I but I did not admit it.

At the Seydoux' I consoled Jacqueline by telling her that, 'Men love challenges and Roger is having the time of his life!' She merely sighed. Her boys were ill with both mumps and whooping-cough. Monsieur Le Mire, down from Bizerta, was sure 'Some madman will shoot Bourguiba and if he doesn't get shot, once in front of a Tunisian crowd, he'll forget his Parisian moderation and he'll become the usual rabble-rouser.' Tunis bristled with police and soldiers.

Meanwhile the *Comédie Franaise* staged Racine's *Esther* in the Dougga Roman theatre. Culture drew the French, however tense the political situation. Three thousand spectators, sitting on the stone seats, filled the amphitheatre, their bright summer clothes forming a colourful spectacle. Spahis, in red and blue uniforms and white cloaks, poised on the sky line, looked deceptively romantic till one saw the tommy-guns in their hands. Through the pillars on the stage we gazed across the green valley and over to the misty hills. Such a peaceful, beautiful setting, but all entrances were barred by police and troops. The actors played it as a melodrama rather than a tragedy and, as the crowd was out to enjoy themselves, they roared with laughter whenever an actor made a mistake.

Dark clouds suddenly massed above us. As the heroine cried out in anguish:
'*From this sacred throne encompassed in thunder*
I thought you were about to crush me . . .'
and ended with '*. . . flashes of lightning from your eyes,*' thunder drowned her words and lightning rent the sky. The audience burst into yells of applause.

Across the other side of the theatre, ladies began to squirm, lift up their feet and giggle, while others hissed. First one line of spectators, then another and so on round the theatre, nearer and nearer. Suddenly a lizard slithered across my bare legs! I sprang up, then quickly sat down again as the lizard slid away to cause havoc further on.

On May 27th the Resident-General and the Prime Minister left for Paris to initial the conventions. The signing would take place a few days later by President Faure and Prime Minister Tahar Ben Ammar.

On May 28th a student was shot and killed. Seydoux wanted to postpone Bourguiba's return once more and we were told that the Prime Minister and the Bey both felt that the celebrations should be damped down. But the Néo-Destour went on with the preparations and now they even demanded that the security forces should not be in evidence.

'But the Young Destour will never be able to keep order,' our French friends exclaimed. 'They don't have the experience, and in any case Bourguiba will not be allowed into the French part of Tunis. Our troops will see to that.'

On the thirty-first it poured with rain – unusual for the time of year. 'Too bad it was today and not tomorrow,' Alan remarked. 'That would quieten things down!' I did my shopping. Europeans had been advised to remain in their houses on June 1st, 'the day of mourning' as the French called it, and after that, who knew what would happen? We kept our fingers crossed for our French friends. 'It's a bitter blow to French pride,' Alan remarked.

June 1st. Loud rumbling woke us. The sky was streaked with the first bands of light. Alan and I rushed up to the roof. Tanks were lumbering past. We watched them turn the corner and disappear behind a hillock, where their noise ceased. The French were taking precautions and I imagined troops marching to other secret strategic posts.

As we were finishing breakfast we heard shouting. We all hurried to the roof again. Lorries roared past, crammed with young men carrying palm fronds and shouting '*Yah Ya Bourguiba! Yah Ya Bourguiba!*' (Long Live Bourguiba!) Cars and lorries streamed past, their klaxons ringing out 'Hoot, Hoot, Hoot-Hoot-Hoot!' The little train running through our estate shrilled 'Peep, Peep, Peep-Peep-Peep. All around us the world was shouting out this rhythmic greeting to Bourguiba as the populace hurried to the port of La Goulette, and our children danced on the roof shouting '*Yah Ya Bourguiba!*' Alan and I smiled with relief: so far it was a joyful, peaceful reception.

Bourguiba was returning on the Ville d'Algiers. Sailing vessels were congregated in the port ready to greet him. Prince Chedli, his sister, the Princess Aicha and Tahar Ben Ammar were to board his ship. Four hundred thousand people, we later read, lined the docks and the road to Tunis. Hassin gave us a graphic account. The Néo-Destour youth and the Moslem Boy Scouts lined the route and kept order. An excited procession of cars, horsemen, buses, lorries and camel riders with Bourguiba in their midst in an open car waving madly headed for the Bey's Palace in Carthage. Everyone hooted jubilantly '*Yah Ya Bourguiba.*'

Then on to Tunis, national flags – a Red crescent and Star on a White Orb against a Red Background – waved in the breeze. 'The first time for seventy-four years,' Hassin said, shaking his head. The whole Arab city was garlanded with flowers, decorated with colourful carpets and triumphal arches, and in an uproar of '*Yah Ya Bourguiba.*'

An incident had occurred that morning at the Porte de France, the dividing gateway between European and Arab Tunis. Someone during the night had pulled down the French flag and put up a Tunisian one. In the morning the gateway was surrounded by troops who lowered the Tunisian flag, and with great tact, amidst the applause of onlookers, hoisted up the French and Tunisian flags together with military honours.

That night Bourguiba addressed his people. Alan brought the text from the office. With great emotion he had called for national unity and he spoke of the conventions as a stage on the road to Independence. He wanted collaboration with the French and respect for the rights of others. He spoke of interdependence and of Tunisia's debt to France. He would not enter the government, but wished to remain leader of the Néo-Destour. We were thoughtful; this was no rabble-rousing speech.

Dancing and singing went on all night. Bonfires dotted the countryside as sheep were roasted and people feasted. If only we could have taken part! But we had to keep out of the way.

'What a day!' Alan remarked. 'And how wrong we all were! There was no trouble. Tunisians showed that they could keep law and order and the Néo-Destour proved to be a disciplined party. With all those tremendous crowds only one person was killed and a few injured in road accidents.'

It was a wonderful day, I thought, a joyful day! and how I longed for a glimpse of Bourguiba!

☆   ☆   ☆

The Princesses were organizing a charity 'Tea' to which I took my school-girl niece Maya, a solid girl with a round, beaming face who was staying with us, and Joan Cavell, Alan's secretary, all long and thin. We were the only non-Tunisians present and I wondered at the French not attending. We were seated at little tables in a lush garden in front of a stage. The place was full. Monumental ladies displayed fabulous jewels on their ripe figures that bulged out of the low bodices of their tight French dresses. My two girls in neat, cotton frocks, stared goggle-eyed.

We were offered ice-cream and sweet cakes while an all-male orchestra played the usual wailing Arab music, strange and nostalgic to our western ears. The women were unveiled but the musicians, like the waiters, being of a lower order, presumably did not count. Periodically another orchestra outside burst into the Beylical hymn and in came a Princess to join her sisters in front.

A singer mounted the stage. As she sang the women nodded approval, cheered and clapped and some, in their excitement, rose to their feet. This must be political, I thought. I must not be seen to approve of what might be criticism of the French. The girls were smiling and laughing so as I composed my face, I hissed at them 'Look neutral!' which made Maya giggle all the more.

Next an Egyptian dancer began gyrating, wriggling and squirming. Every part of her body rotated under her skin-tight scarlet dress – an erotic dance and quite unsuitable, I thought, for young Maya. She, however, watched intently the dancer's every movement, while Joan stared wide-eyed. I was embarrassed but I had to admit it was brilliant dancing, in fact thrilling! The Tunisian women went on eating, hardly glancing at the dancer, presumably used to such sights.

Mme Ben Ammar was offering us more sweet cakes when there was a roll of drums. She looked up, gasped, 'Bourguiba!' and rushed forward. He stood there, neat and elegant in a dark suit and bright red sheshia, face bronzed, deep blue eyes gazing round, as handsome as a film star. We gaped as a gasp went up, like an electric shock. Bourguiba smiled, showing brilliantly white teeth. The older women dived for their veils and cloaks and covered their faces but the Princesses ran to meet him, the 'Supreme Warrior' as they called him. He embraced them and then advanced between the tables, thrust from one pair of arms to the next, the women hugging and kissing him, laughing and crying at the same time, while he waved his arms and grinned like a favourite brother come home. He is attacking the purdah system, I thought, and some of these women are hastening onto his band-wagon.

I kept to the side well out of his way but I suddenly saw that Jacqueline Seydoux had arrived and was out in front. Bourguiba was advancing towards her. What would she do? He had just come out of a French gaol. Would he ignore her? Surely he would not try to kiss her! I was too far to join her. She stood alone, tall and slim, a French woman. Bourguiba stood before her. She extended a long arm. All eyes were on him. He smiled, bent down and kissed her hand. What a gallant gesture, I thought. What a generous nature! He spoke a few words, then moved on.

'We had better go,' I whispered to the girls. 'I don't think I should be here.' We crept away.

31

The girls and I could not stop talking about our sensational
'Tea' and above all, Bourguiba. Maya was bubbling over with
excitement and Joan's long, serious face lit up as she burst out,
'He's an historical character and we're probably the first
Europeans here to see him!' Lawrence named the new kitten
Miss Bourke had given him, Bourguiba, and he told us
proudly, 'He's an Arab leader!' We were the envy of our
consular colleagues who wanted to know every detail; they
were annoyed that their wives had not bothered to go to the
'Tea'. The Turkish Consul-General said his wife would certainly have kissed Bourguiba.

The Uzels were leaving and we were sorry to see them go. At
official dinners I was always seated, according to protocol,
beside him and as we had exhausted religion, politics, literature, nature and human relationships as subjects of conversation, at a French Residency dinner, I suggested we should
decide what animals our consular colleagues resembled. M
Uzel hesitated, then laughed and we looked round the table.

'Morrie Hughes – a fox, don't you think, with that little
moustache, thinning, reddish hair, and small, inquisitive eyes?'
M Uzel looked embarrassed. Better not describe colleagues, I
decided. We would just point out the resemblance. 'The sleek
Krugger, a leopard? Tiny M Guillaune, a mouse?' M Uzel
nodded, grinning. 'M Martig a retriever?' Then I stared at M
Uzel's long, heavy face; a basset hound? and then I realized he
was staring at mine. We burst out laughing and dropped the
game. I would miss him.

With the conventions signed, and peace throughout the
country, I was able, in between parties, to get on with
preparations for our leave. We were to fly home on July 11th
and spend our holiday in Wales where we had inherited a
house. Apart from the packing, there were arrangements to be
made for our household. Alan calculated it was twenty-two
persons, excluding Ahmed's family, who lived somewhere else,

seven dogs, one donkey, one horse, four cows, four goats, four cats, three tortoises and sundry rabbits and chicken. As for the house, AP Vella had agreed to move in. I also had to make plans for our arrival in Wales.

Meanwhile another niece arrived from New York, Katiousha, a round-faced girl with big grey eyes and hair hanging loosely to her shoulders. It was a relief, after so much political tension, to have the house resounding with carefree, young voices, Katiousha arguing loudly with Tunisian youths over politics, Maya romping around with the children – 'The two fatties' Lawrence called Maya and Libet – Mavis on the phone organizing tennis parties, beach parties and dances, and hordes of young persons pouring in. They rushed off in cars to visit Roman ruins, went sailing with the Mrosovsky young, or dived into the souk. Their parties went on till morning and ended up on the beach. I did not interfere.

Alan now had time again to escape into the garden, where he was building a pergola and training honey-suckle along it. Soon Katiousha had to leave and we were sorry to see her go. She was a sweet-natured young thing. Maya decided to return to the UK with us.

Alan and I went to the motor races. Round me everyone yawned from boredom as cars roared past round and round the same course. But I had never seen motor-racing. It was nerve-racking when the cars overtook each other, and then there was the excitement of General de La Tour's arrival in his gold-braided kepi. Bugles sounded and arms were presented, a colourful scene. Then more excitement as the General hurried forward and the Bey arrived.

As the whole stadium rose to their feet, Colonel Meric beside me, whispered 'He's old and decrepit and for the past years has refused to take part in anything, but he is pleased with the turn of events and is beginning to appear in public.' A frail, benevolent, elderly gentleman, with steel glasses, dressed in a European suit with the usual red sheshia on his neat grey head, he was supported on all sides as he climbed out of the car. He carried a golden-headed walking stick and wore a thick gold bracelet and a large ring. As he took his seat, he gave little signs of recognition to the populace who clapped half-heartedly, but then the crowd was mostly French. Once he was seated, all I could see – we were in the same row – was a mass of sheshias with long, black tassels belonging to the Ministers and officials surrounding him, and Tahar Maoui's big bulk protectively in front. They kept making loud, excited comments and were evidently enjoying themselves.

When the cars had done their seventy-six turns, the winners were escorted up to the Bey, who presented the prizes. We stood up as numerous hands were stretched out to help him off his seat and to support him. Then he left, followed by the Resident-General and the VIPs including, flag flying, ourselves.

This restful period was suddenly shattered when a bomb went off one night in the USA Information Service office in Tunis, causing considerable damage though no one was hurt. Then an unexploded bomb was found in the garden of the USA Vice-Consul who was away with his family. The servants did not live on the premises so no one was hurt here either. The French as usual accused the communists but it was noticeable that the French local newspaper, *Tunisie France*, accused the USA Information Service of being an anti-French organization and suggested that the Americans deserved the bombs. They also accused us of helping the Tunisians to Independence.

'It's curious,' Alan remarked, 'that the bombs were put where everyone knew no one would be hurt.' And Roger Seydoux' explanation was, 'I think the bombs were placed by Tunisians in the pay of the French community.'

As a result, guards were posted at all offices and houses of USA officials and a posse of soldiers with rifles turned up at our house in a lorry and jeep stating that they would now be guarding us during the night hours. Alan thought it unnecessary but he could hardly protest since the French were responsible for our safety.

Mavis and the children had to hold the dogs off the soldiers and to coax them into accepting them as together they would be prowling around our premises all night long. They brought Herta and Pong up to the young men to be stroked, while the soldiers kept thinking up excuses to keep Mavis up later and later. One night Alan and I were woken by a young tenor singing, '*J'aime my petite . . . J'aime my petite*' (I love my little one) outside our window. It overlooked a field where cattle grazed and I had once woken to a loud snort and said, 'What darling?' only to face Alan's indignation as it was a bull snorting! Maya wanted to sing back, '*J'aime mon petit*,' but she never found an appropriate moment. In the mornings the children rushed out to greet the guard and to wave them off.

There was no more trouble and we prepared to leave. The sirocco was blowing, it was hot and muggy, and we could not bathe. We longed to get away and to get back home. Maya objected to our constant counting, 'Only seven more days! Only six more days!' and Mavis looked sad. She had done her two-year stint with us and would not be returning. Parting is a sad business, I thought.

We were ready and packed for next day's early morning start when Alan spotted a wasps' nest under the eaves of the house.

'I'll just get that down,' he said. 'They might sting the children.'

'Must you?' I protested, but he was already calling, 'Hassin! A ladder!' We stood watching, Mavis, the children, Hassin and I, as he climbed up. The next moment wasps poured out and whirled round his head and body.

'Darling, what on earth are you doing?' I gasped. Shaking himself, he started slithering down. He lost his footing, and though Hassin tried to catch him, he fell with a thud. Wasps swarmed round him. We all seized bath towels and beat them off, the children prancing around with excitement.

'Ouch!' Alan cried as he tried to get up; he had twisted his ankle. Supported by Hassin and me, he staggered up the steps and inside and collapsed into an armchair. He tore off his shirt. We backed away as wasps cascaded out, but they were dead wasps. Then we counted the stings, the children shouting, 'Here's one!' and 'Here's another, look!' Fourteen in all! I could not remember what to put on stings, something for wasps stings and something else for bee stings but what? None of us knew. I put a cold compress on Alan's swollen ankle and bandaged it up. He began shivering and his head was hot. I gave him two aspirins and wrapped a blanket round him. He looked like a woebegone Indian. I fussed around him with tea and soup and Hassin tip-toed out of sympathy but we forgot the obvious – to get the doctor!

That night I thought what a typical way to start a holiday! and would he be well enough by morning?

I woke up to find him sitting up in bed, grinning. We were off at last.

Alan.

32

September. The holidays were over and we had to get back to Tunis for the start of the school term, something the children had forgotten and I did not want to face yet. They had been accepted by the *Lycée de Carthage* and I was afraid of that French school.

We had had a grand time. The house we inherited near Llandudno Junction, our first home, was spacious enough for my mother, my parents-in-law, my sister Vava's family and all of us. It was such a pleasure having the family all together and everyone got on well. The extensive grounds allowed the older generation to rest near the house while the youngsters rushed around elsewhere. After a short drive we could brave the sea, scramble up mountains and picnic beside lakes. I was free to do what I liked, when I liked and how I liked, and Mavis, with two interesting suitors in tow, was able to stay with us for the first month.

I told the children that this was our own home, where they were free to do what they liked. That first night we were woken by hammering. The point of a nail appeared in the wall above our heads. Lawrence was drilling a hole through to us. I ran to him, 'What do you think you're doing?' I demanded.

'You said this was our own home and we could do what we liked,' he complained, but with a cheeky grin on his pixie face.

We had been told that we would be posted to Tunis for another two years at least so it was worth taking out our carpets – the long marble corridors in the residence were icy cold in winter – our favourite books and our pictures, all of which would follow us by sea.

I had to find someone to replace Mavis. An advertisement in *The Lady* brought numerous applications. I replied asking for details, confident of finding a suitable young woman. Then suddenly the BBC started broadcasting daily reports of bombs exploding in Tunis, stories of soldiers patrolling the streets, of attacks on cars, of Jews leaving the country and young

Frenchmen being expelled. One by one the girls withdrew their applications. The latent anxiety about the French school was now replaced by the fear that no one would agree to accompany us.

'The conventions have been ratified and it's only disgruntled French extremists causing trouble,' Alan remarked, but though I assured the girls that we British were not threatened there were no more applicants. I applied everywhere I could think of. At the same time I had to pack and try to remember what had to be settled in Wales before our departure, and foreseen for Tunis for the next two years. The result was a heavy migraine. Then just before we were due to leave a girl called Pauline applied and I took her on without an interview. She was pale, and quiet with thick glasses and evidently fearless.

I wondered whether the children would accept her; Mavis was such a favourite. They kept referring to her and I kept looking round for her but on the plane Lawrence showed Pauline the treasures in his suit case and when we changed planes Libet hung on to her arm.

Back at the residence both children rushed for Pong. They cried 'Mummy! Daddy! Look!' and together, with Pong in fine shape leaping round us, we admired the cats who purred lustily as they rubbed their soft, fat bodies against the children's legs.

'Look! There are four more tortoises,' Libet was beaming, 'and look tortoise eggs!' I was already blasé about those.

'And chickens! Five chickens!' Lawrence was amazed and so was I. Ali had given them a hen before we left but I had expected it to be eaten by now.

But the greatest surprise was Ouggie. We had left him a bad-tempered animal who kicked and bit. Now Ali led him up, a thin little donkey, who nuzzled the children in the friendliest way and trotted quietly beside them.

'You can ride him,' Ali said proudly. 'I spent a lot of time calming him down. I took him to the market with me every day.' The children ran off into the garden, their arms round Ouggie.

The house was in order and the garden showed signs of last minute industry. We started unpacking and settling in once more. The children had to show Pauline what to do and lead her by the hand as she could not find her way around the house. After a few days I asked her how she felt and she exclaimed, 'It is all wonderful and so fascinating!'

Libet and Ouggie.

Politically all was quiet. The split in the Néo-Destour between Bourguiba and Salah Ben Youssef had come to a head and Salah Ben Youssef was threatened with expulsion from the Party. A Party Congress was to be held in November. Meanwhile Salah Ben Youssef condemned the conventions in the Zitouna Mosque, while Bourguiba urged 'unity' and created a 'Benevolent Society' for former *Fellaghas* which gained him the support of most leaders.

It was good to be back but I could not control those fears that kept creeping up on me. How would the children manage in this French school? French children were rougher and though ours had had French lessons before our holiday, their French was minimal, and the teachers, I had heard, often struck the children.

'Don't fuss so,' Alan kept saying. 'You'll make the children nervous. They have to start school sometime.' I wondered whether other mothers worried too.

The great day was upon us. School started at eight in the morning. The children were up at first light but after breakfast Lawrence clung to me and whispered, 'I don't really want to go!' Quickly I brought out their new satchels and when Ali produced large ham and salad sandwiches for the break, Lawrence ran to the car with Libet. Cutajah drove us to

The Author and Lawrence, with his new school satchel.

Carthage.

At the school there was chaos. Tunisian children poured in as well as French and obviously there were not enough classes for them all. We were directed from one official to another, the children clinging to my hands and I holding them tight. We trailed up and down staircases; I dragged the children in and out of classrooms. We got completely lost, and standing in a long corridor, suddenly we all three started giggling. Finally a teacher directed us to class 10B, with the seven-year olds. It was a relief to learn that the children would be together because half the school studied in the morning and the rest in the afternoon. I watched my two little ones sitting down side by side at a desk and then I had to leave.

I could not settle to anything that morning. At last it was eleven o'clock and time to set out to fetch them. Pauline and I took our little train and had to change once. At Carthage station a swarm of squally children met us pushing each other as they rushed on into the station.

'I don't think we should let the children travel alone like this,' I remarked just as Libet and Lawrence appeared holding hands and skipping along.

'Did you have a good time?' I asked.

'Yes,' they exclaimed together.

'Who else was in your form?'

Libet pointed to the blackest little Negro. 'That one is ours. And the Tahar Maoui twins.'

I seized their hands and they chatted excitedly all the way home.

'All right?' Alan asked over lunch. I nodded.

The children were in the afternoon classes from one to five. They were given a great deal of homework, both reading and writing. Libet could soon read in French but Lawrence guessed wildly. If anything began with an 'a', he read 'Air France'; if it began with 'au', he guessed '*Haut les mains!*' (Hands up!) I spent at least an hour every day helping them and Pauline also tried to learn with them. Usually they came back smiling from school, but one day, when they had to learn twenty lines of poetry, Lawrence could not quite remember the whole poem.

He sighed, 'School is quite nice but I don't feel quite up to it today!' He looked pale and his normal sparkle had gone. He was on the verge of tears.

'He'll be put in the corner if he doesn't know it!' Libet whispered in my ear.

Libet and Lawrence with Pong.

'Will you be all right tomorrow?' I asked.

'Yes,' and he sighed again. I let him stay at home. I did not care what Alan thought, but he did not protest.

'We must start going out again,' was all he said.

33

Alan was on the phone. 'Masha! we're in a fix. What's FAO?'

'FAO? I've no idea. Why? Anyway where are you?'

'I'm on board the *Forth* and it's all too embarrassing.'

Rear Admiral Holland-Martin, flying his flag in *HMS Forth* had arrived in Bizerta. His imposing title was Flag Officer Flotillas Mediterranean. He was accompanied by HM Ships *Battleaxe*, *Contest* and *Comet*.

Alan rushed on, 'I've had a call from the Prime Minister's office. It was a bad line but I understood his secretary to say that in view of Britain's FAO attitude the PM is boycotting this naval visit and he's cancelled his dinner for the Admiral. The Tunisians are apparently very angry; they're broadcasting virulent statements against us.'

'FAO? What can we have done? And how extraordinary that the Foreign Office hasn't informed you.'

'The Admiral doesn't know, nor anyone else here. We can't ask the French. That would be admitting that we haven't been warned. It's obviously something important to the Tunisians. We'd better prepare for trouble. Get Hassin to put up the shutters round the house and let the dogs loose in the garden.' I was recovering from a migraine and had stayed at home. I sighed. Inside me was this longing for Britain to be always in the right!

We had planned a grand reception for the Admiral, and it was a great opportunity at the same time to receive and entertain the new Tunisian Ministers and now this FAO, whatever it was, was spoiling everything! I warned Hassin, and with Mahomet, they began putting up the shutters. Herta and Pong were already outside. Herta had a nasty habit of rushing at strangers, crouching beside them and if they moved spring-ing for their throats. The locals waited at the gates for one of the servants to rescue them. Pong barked so furiously he also frightened intruders away.

Hassin came running up. 'Madame! There's someone in the

official dining-room! I can hear someone moving around.' I hurried with him across the Grand Salon, we crept up to the dining-room door, and listened. Yes, I could hear something too. Every now and again. Tiny, stealthy movements.

'Get a stick,' I whispered. Hassin tip-toed away and returned with one of Alan's golf clubs. We stared fearfully at each other.

'Come! Open the door and stand back!' Hassin grasped the golf club and flung the door open. The room was empty! Across it a window was open, and the draught was rustling papers on the table. Hassin shook his head as we both laughed with relief.

Alan had not returned. I waited, feeling let-down and frightened. Then I sat down to dinner on my own. Still no Alan. Hassin cleaned up and went home; Mahomet and Ali retired. Alone I hovered, hands clenched, by the front door. An accident? The *Fellaghas*? What should I do? How long should I wait? The same fears, the same thoughts raced through my mind.

It was midnight before the door opened and Alan hurried in.

'Oh Alan!' I clung to him, close to tears. 'Where have you been? Oh, darling, you're safe!'

'I stayed to dinner on board,' and, as I still held him, 'You mustn't keep worrying.' Yes, my cursed vivid imagination! But I still clung to him. 'All right, I should have phoned. I'm sorry. Everything all right here?'

'Yes, and your end?'

'Yes, it all went very well. The French didn't change plans, so we made our Bizerta formal calls. Then I got cold feet. Perhaps I should have sent the ships out to sea again? But the Admiral was all for carrying on. So we lunched with Admiral Laurin. At the ship's cocktail party the first to arrive was the Bey's representative, then the local Caïd and the Tunisian Mayor of Bizerta. No one mentioned any trouble. Perhaps the news hadn't reached them.' We went to bed puzzled and anxious. What could FAO mean? 'It's all too ridiculous!' Alan murmured before he fell asleep.

Next day was our luncheon for the Admiral and the four Commanders. Tunisians had not been invited so there was no embarrassment over their refusing our invitation. All thirty-four guests arrived safely. Although the Admiral was reserved and talked little, the navy made it a friendly and cheerful occasion. Only one French lady mentioned FAO; she whispered, 'Shame about this FAO business.' I replied, 'Yes, too bad,' and willed her to say more, just to give some hint but she only smiled.

The children had gone with the Seydoux boys onto the *Forth*. They came back just as we returned from taking the Admiral on a quick round of our nearest sites, Carthage and the famous blue and white Moorish-style village of Sidi Bou Said. They bounced in, Lawrence exclaiming,

'We went all over the ship and talked on the phone from all different parts and we saw torpedoes and guns!'

'We saw a guinea pig on the *Battleaxe*,' Libet added 'and we lunched in the Admiral's cabin.'

Then Lawrence said proudly, 'We went to sea in the Admiral's launch, and I drove it!'

The Admiral interrupted. 'My launch? You steered it?' Lawrence glanced quickly at the thick gold stripes on his sleeve, realized who he was, hesitated, then nodded. 'Did you steer it alongside the *Forth*?'

'Oh no!' Lawrence exclaimed. 'I wasn't allowed to do that.' The Admiral leant back, relieved, as we all were. Later the Admiral reassured us that there was no visible damage to the launch.

The Admiral was staying the night. Before dinner I saw that he was seated in an armchair and was showing Lawrence pictures in *The Illustrated London News* of the ships he had commanded. Lawrence was leaning up against him. 'And here are the *Agincourt* and the *Eagle* . . .' he was saying and Lawrence asked, 'Did you fight real battles . . .' he hesitated 'and you know . . .?'

The Admiral was silent a moment, then he said 'Yes, Lawrence, I did, but only gentle ones.' Lawrence smiled and pressed his cheek against the Admiral's shoulder . . .

By evening we were all controlling yawns over family bridge till the clock struck ten when Alan decided we could decently go to bed.

After breakfast next morning Lawrence disappeared with the Admiral. 'I helped him with his uniform,' he told me. 'He has a terrific sword! Mummy I keep getting so muddled up with Admirals and Ambassadors and things!'

The Admiral was to lay a wreath on the Unknown Soldier's grave in the centre of the town.

'I'm going to drive there first,' Alan told me, 'in uniform and flag flying to see whether there's any hostile reaction from the locals. I don't want the Admiral to be insulted or attacked. I'll drive slowly through town.' He came back grinning. 'The Tunisians smiled and waved. I didn't meet with any resentment. Perhaps they don't know what FAO is either!' It's all so stupid, so unnecessary, I thought. Alan had wired London for an explanation but there was no reply so far.

They set off, the Admiral laid his wreath, the local crowd stood respectfully round and he then started on his Tunis formal calls. The French C-in-c cancelled his, with many apologies; his office was in the midst of the native city. 'But the Bey was most affable,' Alan reported. 'The Prime Minister stood, according to protocol, beside him, looking very sheepish.' Tahar Maoui returned the Bey's call. Then lunch with the French at which no Tunisians appeared; a visit to the souk was cancelled as the police refused to accept responsibility and then they returned for our cocktail party.

'Alan, any news?' He shook his head. 'I feel such a fool. Suppose someone asks me about FAO?'

'And how do you think I feel?' he retorted and we laughed. 'But it doesn't seem to bother the Admiral.'

We wondered, as we waited for our guests, would this mysterious FAO affect our party? Would Tunisians turn up? Alan and I exchanged glances as a Tunisian was the first to arrive, an ex-Minister too. He was the local historian, Abdul Wahab. He and his wife disappeared among the white uniforms, beaming at the attention immediately surrounding them. We stopped worrying. Not all Tunisians were ostracizing us. Later other appears, Tahar Maoui and his assistant General Bahri, followed by five other ex-Ministers, but none from the present government. All wore European clothing, perhaps to be less conspicuous. We were touched that they had come but, 'It's a shame this FAO business has landed on Holland-Martin' Alan whispered. 'It's one of his first visits as Rear-Admiral. He has only just been promoted.' Then to crown the proceedings Prince Chedli arrived, the first time he had visited us. The Admiral and the officers crowded round him.

The strain of FAO must have affected our guests too for they were hungrier and thirstier than usual. When our larder and drinks cupboard were empty we asked the navy to leave in order to encourage the others. Some of the elderly ladies had to be helped into their cars.

Next morning Alan was shouting and waving a bit of paper as he jumped out of the car. 'Come here, Masha! Look!' I ran down the steps. 'FAO is the UN Food and Agricultural Organization!' We laughed with relief. 'France proposed membership for Tunisia and we voted against. Stupid thing to do! Tunisia got in anyway by thirty-three votes against four with twenty-six abstentions. We might at least have abstained!' The riddle was solved and the explanation was there too in the paper. Britain wanted Tunisia at first to become an associate member since the required thirty days's notice had not been given. 'Nit-picking,' Alan exclaimed. 'We're France's ally and it was France who proposed membership! Why vote against her and why insult the Tunisians? Unless there's some deep intrigue we know nothing about.'

We drove to Bizerta to Admiral Laurin's cocktail party with light hearts. At last we knew what to say. Laurin placed a room at our disposal so we could brush up. What luxury! For once, after that journey up, we could appear calm, relaxed and, we hoped, elegant.

After Laurin's party we drove to the *Forth* for Admiral Holland-Martin's dinner and Alan was able to explain about FAO. We sat down at a big round table. As acting hostess, I sat opposite the Admiral. The Tunisian Prime Minister did not turn up. The low ceiling and confined space produced a feeling of intimacy while at the same time the uniforms and the smart white-coated waiters introduced a pleasing formality. It was an excellent dinner, and with no more worry over FAO, and in such jovial company, I enjoyed myself thoroughly. We in Bizerta had met so often that we felt at home with each other. I protected my wine from M Le Mire who had drunk all mine by mistake at our first meeting and poor pretty, fastidious Madame Le Mire was teased about the narrow skirts she now wore. As she had stepped abroad on her first naval visit, all eyes on the charming picture she made, her wide, pleated skirt had billowed up around her head and while the navy tactfully turned away as she fought to hold it down, her husband looked on fascinated. 'He did nothing to help! Absolutely nothing!' she kept remembering.

As hostess, according to naval tradition, I had to uncork the port, pour it into a silver cup, drink from it and hand it round. And a naval privilege – we drank the toast to the Queen sitting down.

After dinner I led the ladies to the Admiral's cabin. They giggled delightedly at this 'British custom.' '*Ah, c'est delicieux!*' French ladies are never supposed to want to go to the bathroom. There was an embarrassing moment when the guests were leaving. A drunken Irish officer approached the new French C-in-C, General Baillif, who was saying good-bye to me, and came out with a very indecent joke. We both looked away and after a moment's pause the General said, 'The weather seems to be clearing up, don't you think?'

After the guests left the Admiral presented us with a picture of the *Forth* and two cap ribbons for the children. He also gave us the *Forth* ship's badge, a golden bridge over a blue striped sea and white sky, an addition to the *Surprise* and *Trenchant* badges. Our collection was growing. He said he had thoroughly enjoyed the visit and thought it very successful and well-planned. We left clutching the mementoes of a happy naval visit.

Next day, when the *Forth* left, we received official thank-you letters in which the Admiral said it had been a very instructive visit, since he had learnt the meaning of FAO. We were relieved that he had taken it in good part.

Now what to do about the Tunisians? I was invited to a tea by the new Air Force General's wife, Mme Debernardy.

'Madame Ben Ammar is sure to be there,' Alan told me. 'You go, and ignore any insults. Tunisians are proud, so to heal the breech it's easier for us to take the first step. You might have a chance there but don't do anything too blatant!'

At the tea I sat among a group of French ladies. As usual the Tunisians were at the opposite end of the room. Several Ministers' wives were present. There was an air of expectancy and though we sipped our tea no one touched the sweet cakes. Mme Debernardy kept glancing at the door. At last Mme Ben Ammar's ample figure swept in, and she joined the Tunisian group. She had not looked my way but after she had kissed her friends, her neighbour whispered in her ear and she turned quickly round. I looked away. We both started talking in loud nervous voices in our respective groups, ignoring but acutely conscious of each other.

When we had finished the sweet cakes I got up and started examining a series of engravings round the wall. A moment or two later, Mme Ben Ammar got up too and studied the engravings at her end of the room. I moved her way, she moved mine. The room was hushed; everyone watched us. We drew closer and closer to each other. Then Mme Ben Ammar faced me. As I looked into her magnificent, dark eyes, I could not help smiling.

'How are your children?' she asked. '*Les petits*, are they well?'

Eagerly I replied, 'Yes, very well, and how are yours?'

'Well. All well, thank you,' and she added, 'I have a photo of us eating cakes together at our charity tea.' She smiled, nodded and we returned to our tables. Easy!

34

'Vava is at the end of her tether,' my mother wrote. Michael, her son, had been desperately ill, Vernon, her brother-in-law, was dying of cancer and just as Michael was recovering, Geoffrey, her doctor husband had a knee operation.

'It's too much all in one family,' I exclaimed. 'Perhaps one of Mother's bad Stars was passing over the Whittalls.' My mother-in-law practised astrology. Alan smiled that superior masculine smile.

But now Michael, was back at school, Vernon had died and Geoffrey was out of hospital. We wrote and invited poor Vavotchka and Geoffrey to recover with us. I hardly dared hope that they would accept but they did. My sister was coming again!

I planned their stay. 'We'll let them sleep, and sleep and sleep. They must get a complete rest, both of them, at least at first. Then, once rested, Geoffrey can try short walks in the countryside he loves so much and Vavotchka can get her bit of flightiness!'

Then Katia, my eldest sister, who lived in New York, wrote saying that she and her husband, Kapa Nebolsine, would like to stay with us and she gave their flight number from Rome. We did not believe it. Kapa, a consultant engineer flew around overseeing his works in the most inaccessible parts of the world. Usually a telegram announced their arrival, another cancelled it. It was impossible to pin Kapa down.

'By now they're probably on their way to Australia or Iceland,' Alan remarked. But if they came, I would have two sisters with me, an incredible luxury! I could not rid myself of this longing for the family. And, I thought, I could give Katia a good rest too. Kapa must be exhausting, always on the go.

At the airport a tired Vava was only just able to smile. I noticed dark patches under her eyes. She was thinner but her face still had its soft roundness. Geoffrey, I realized with amusement, fitted into the Tunisian scene with his black hair,

259

heavy black brows and slightly hooked nose. His family had lived for generations in Turkey.

Back home the servants beamed as they shook hands with Maya's parents. Geoffrey insisted on first admiring our tiled walls, brilliantly-coloured wooden ceilings and delicate, white stucco work, reminders of his childhood in Istanbul. Then they collapsed into bed.

We continued our usual round of functions while our guests slept, ate large meals and lounged in the sunshine. We avoided all talk of sickness or of problems, ours or theirs.

Before driving to the airport to meet the Nebolsine plane, Alan took me aside, 'Kapa might be put off coming as a Néo-Destour cell in Tunis was gunned down from a passing car and two people hurt. These are troubles between Bourguiba and Salah Ben Youssef. The two sides are murdering each other.' He was whispering. The Whittalls must not be worried in any way. 'And that's not all. The Prime Minister's car was mobbed and, in the south a train was machine-gunned. Salah Ben Youssef has some fifteen hundred armed supporters. Seydoux is anxious. He is High Commissioner now, and Tunis is tense once more.' Oh, no more violence! I prayed, and with the children going back and forth to school by train.

The plane from Rome flew over Tunis and went straight to Algiers. But later Alan received a message that it would return to Tunis next day. So no Nebolsines so far.

That evening we took Vava to Marchiori's, the Italian Consul-General's. She could never resist a party but Geoffrey stayed at home. The noisy crowd was in fancy-dress. Some French women had come as sirens, and were able to display long, wavy tresses. They were accompanied by triton-husbands. Others wore magnificent ball gowns of past centuries, their décolletages as revealing as the period demanded. Each lady was enchanting. Then the Americans arrived, the women disguised as kettles, and dustbins – amusing but hideous beside their French rivals.

'It's not fair,' young Mrs Hill was angry. 'We thought we had to be funny, but we look ridiculous!' And seeing the disdainful, self-satisfied glances at the lid wobbling on her head, tears sprang to her eyes and she cried, 'I'm going home.' Her husband tried to dissuade her and I chipped in with, 'We weren't even told it was fancy-dress, and anyway what does it matter?' But she rushed out of the house, followed by the other American women. The husbands, embarrassed, stayed behind.

We danced.

'Look at them!' Vava murmured. 'Snuggling up like that to their partners!' The women were disappearing into the men's arms. I knew I was considered 'cold' and I noticed that Vava held her partners firmly at a distance. But she was beaming and laughing and I was pleased. It was late when we left but Vava could sleep on in the morning.

Next day Alan drove once more to the airport. To his astonishment Kapa and Katia were on the plane. To Alan's, 'Sorry you were carried on to Algiers,' Kapa replied, 'Oh that was all right. We were able to explore Algiers and go to the opera.' Of course, Kapa would never miss an opportunity.

'Well!' Kapa exclaimed as he looked up at our home. 'It really is a palace! I want to see everything. Alan lead on!' He rushed from room to room, his loud voice echoing, 'This really is something!' and in the Grand Salon, 'Magnificent!' They were in good form, Katia elegant as ever in a grey matching costume, blouse and jacket. She was the beauty in our family, with classic features and big, grey eyes. Kapa was good-looking too, with expansive gestures. He had a tiny cast in one eye.

It was late. We showed them their room, where the servants were waiting to greet Katiousha's parents. Now we were three sisters together.

'Alan isn't it wonderful?' I exclaimed. He smiled but seemed puzzled. What was so wonderful?

Up early next morning, Kapa was shouting, 'Alan I'm ready. I'm coming with you, and here's Geoffrey. Come on, Geoffrey, we'll explore Tunis.'

Back for lunch, Kapa went off with Lawrence into the garden. I heard Lawrence saying, 'Uncle Kapa, Mummy told me I must learn to take a joke. How do I do that?' Kapa came in saying, 'Your son is adorable!' After lunch he was off again. 'I have to arrange my flight tomorrow to Tripoli.' He would at least have stayed with us two nights.

That evening it was, 'Come on everyone – the local sights.' Alan drove us through Sidi Bou Said perched blue and white against the green hillock, then to Carthage, where we picked up Libet from school; she skipped out shouting, 'I was best in Arabic today and got a picture of a donkey!' Kapa was delighted 'In Arabic! Well, say something in Arabic.'

Libet wound plump arms round Alan's neck and said, 'My *Bou!*'

'My little *bint*,' Alan murmured back. 'She certainly has

Left to right. The author, Katia, Vava, Alan and Geoffrey on our back terrace.

charm,' Kapa decided and Libet giggled.

Kapa charged ahead through the ruins of Carthage gesticulating and explaining, 'Phoenicians . . . Queen Dido from Tyre . . . Romans . . .' He was a walking encyclopaedia.

'Stop a moment! Look!' I said. We gazed across the pinkish, sun-lit stone to the blue waters that merged into the blue-mauve of the twin peaks of the Bou Kornine, and these rose up against a light blue cloudless sky. Even Kapa stood still for a few moments.

Next morning he flew off to Tripoli. It was like entertaining a whirlwind. Once at the ticket office in Rome airport, Kapa had asked, 'What planes have you got going where?'

Without him we calmed down. At a lunch for the Dunbars, Katia, normally so reserved and shy, blossomed and chatted away. My sisters promised to attend that evening's meeting of St George's Society. After coffee I still insisted that the Whittalls retire for their siesta and Mrs Dunbar agreed to 'have a little snooze too', before returning home to bake scones for the meeting. This was a great success. Katia and Vava liked the religious talk Mrs Dunbar gave and the Dunbars beamed. My sisters were so impressed by the work the Dunbars were doing that later they visited their Jewish school. Katia brought bags of sweets for the children, who sang and acted for them.

Vava had regained some of her colour and was now itching

to go out socially so we began taking our guests round with us. At cocktail parties and evening functions Vava talked without stopping to generals, diplomats, French functionaries and old friends like the Hughes family while Katia, to my amazement, remained relaxed too. At Mr Mangano's, the US Consul's, she was standing, laughing arm-in-arm with a young American Vice-Consul. If only Kapa could see her now, I thought; In New York she refused to go to parties. Geoffrey meanwhile was happy talking Greek to the Greek Consul and Turkish to the Turk.

Geoffrey was not a cocktail man but at the weekend Alan took us on trips through the countryside. We three sisters chatted in the back and the two men sat silent in front. We drove to Korbous, famous for its hot-water spring. It was an enchanting sight – little white houses, some domed, nestled around a square, white minaret. The village was perched between the blue seas and high pinkish rocks. We sat on a wall at the water's edge while Geoffrey looked for plants. Then we drove back across the hills, dark against the setting sun. Bands of orange and yellow crept up the greying sky while above ominous deep purple and crimson storm clouds hung over the hill-tops.

Next day Alan drove us to Teburbo Majus, the Roman city whose slender twenty-eight foot columns dominated the countryside. Then we wandered over the Zagouan mountain and tried to find the temple housing the source of the waters that supplied Tunis. We reached a Tunisian village with narrow, cobbled streets and dark mysterious doorways. In a small square I took out my camera. A little boy pointed to it, shook his head then stared at the crowd of men shouting and gesturing. When they saw us they fell silent and stood frowning at us. They did not return our greeting. Quickly I put my camera away. There was a tenseness about them that made Alan exclaim,

'Let's get out of here. Quick. That's some sort of meeting.'

'I'm getting the creeps!' Vava whispered. We hurried down a hillside but Katia fell behind. I happened to turn round. She was just about to sit down on a flat, white tombstone. Men were shouting. Some began running towards her.

'Stop Katia! Don't sit down! Come here quick!' Alan dashed to meet her, took her arm and we rushed down to the car.

'That was a tombstone!' I told her.

Left to right. The authors sisters Katia and Vava with Geoffrey and Alan.

The author and Katia at Teburbo Majus.

'Oh! I thought it was a convenient stone to rest on! But why were they so fierce, so unpleasant?'

'The Tunisians are having their troubles; they don't much like us Europeans, and they now feel freer to express it.' An understatement, I thought, but Alan evidently did not want to cause alarm.

When we reached home Katia said, 'We've decided to leave on Wednesday.' It was a shock. The time had passed so fast; they had only been with us a week. 'Geoffrey needs time to get ready to start work again,' Vava explained.

'We might stay the night in Marseilles,' Katia added 'or we thought we might go to Lyons. Kapa talked of a good restaurant there, and then by train on to Paris.' I knew the truth was that Vava could not resist the lure of Paris now that she felt rested. They want to go, I thought sadly, and I did not dissuade them.

When we had seen them off Alan remarked, 'I'm sorry they've left but there's no keeping them, unfortunately!' Once home he changed, skipped down the veranda steps and went contentedly back to his digging. But I felt let down. Didn't they want us to be together as long as possible? And did our beautiful palace mean so little to them? And I wondered, did Vava and Geoffrey get an inkling of what our diplomatic life meant, day in, day out, to have to be careful of what one says,

265

of what one does? I sat on my bed alone and felt miserable.

I had a head-ache. Next day my throat was sore, my nose was running and I coughed painfully. I've caught the 'flu, I thought. As the day wore on my temperature soared. By evening my whole body ached. When Alan came home he called the doctor. Soon I was burning and I felt that every bone in my body was breaking. I tossed and turned but there was no relief. Alan fed me aspirins with cold fruit drinks and sat beside me, holding my hand. I clung to him. He changed my sheets and wiped my face with a wet flannel. The rack, I thought, was like this, I wanted to cry out.

At last the doctor was beside me. He gave me an injection. 'Opium,' he told Alan. 'That will help and I'll come again in the morning.'

I lay on my back. The pain was still there, but I could no longer feel it. Alan had undressed and sat on his bed beside me in his dressing-gown. I clung to his hand. It felt strong and cool. I did not dare move. Alan put the light out but I still held on to him. Time slipped by. I lay still and dozed. A clock chimed and chimed again.

Suddenly I was aware that the darkness was lifting and streaks of grey filled the room. It was morning and Alan's hand was still round mine. I stirred; my bones no longer ached. I could move. I breathed deeply and turned to Alan. My sisters had gone but he sat there, head lowered, still in his dressing-gown. He was dozing. Alan had sat there all night holding my hand! Waves of happiness surged through me. I squeezed his hand, let go, turned on my side and fell asleep.

Alan's bigger sweater was warm and comforting and the heaped pillows soft. I lay back and tried to keep calm.

'Mummy, those snakes, tell us about them again.' The children, goggle-eyed, sat crossed-legged at the end of my bed.

I took a deep breath. 'It was a nightmare! It was like having coils of snakes in my bed, all aching, each one more painful than the others; I couldn't believe it was just one sore back. It went on and on, all these coils aching at once. I've never felt anything like it! But you were such a help, Libet my love, bringing me water and listening to my bell, and as for Daddy, I clung to him.'

Dr Tabone had been and had spoken severely, 'It's a bad influenza epidemic and relapses can have serious consequences for the heart. Madame, you must take it easy. In bed until I say you can get up and then go gently.'

Alan and I exchanged glances. The word 'heart' was alarming, but 'Go gently!' How could I? The fateful telegram that Foreign Service personnel always subconsciously expect had arrived while my sisters were still with us. Orders to return to London and Alan to become an Inspector and start work at the beginning of February. So much for the two years we were to spend here. But we were not allowed to mention the transfer. What a shock! With my head in a whirl, my stomach heaving and bursting with the news I had to control my tongue and carry on normally. It was already mid-December. So little time! 'I can't even book passages on a boat,' Alan grumbled, 'without letting the cat out of the bag.'

My sisters had chatted and assured me, 'You're so lucky to be here . . .' while I could hardly follow what they said. So many things to do! Where to live in London? Vava might find us temporary accommodation if only I could ask her.

'All those heavy carpets, Alan, and the pictures we brought out!' I had exclaimed. The packing, clearing, farewell parties, planning the journey, how was I going to manage? And leaving Tunis, Hassin, Ali, Mahomet. It was heart-breaking. We had many friends among colleagues and the French but Hassin was special, and in our household we had lived through so many excitements together.We slept badly. My sisters and Geoffrey left before permission to speak came so I could not get their help, or advice, or moral support. And now, disaster, here I was confined to bed with warnings of heart strain.

Lawrence had been coughing for some time but suddenly his temperature soared to 103. The doctor called it 'flu. Pauline slept through his coughing and choking so Alan and I hurried to him several times a night. He kept being sick. The second night I slept beside him and tried to rest during the day but I kept worrying about him, and thinking of everything that had to be done. I felt very weak.

Alan sent a telegram to stir the office up in London for more information. Meanwhile I fretted in bed and he attended the seasonal functions alone. We were both edgy but the children's cheerfulness kept us sane.

When it was sunny Lawrence and I transferred ourselves to the sun-bathing area that Alan had built and lay on the camp beds with the dogs stretched out beside us. We watched the trees swaying above and Lawrence asked, 'Mummy, what were the first men like? Funny, weren't they?' And he added, 'I suppose in a hundred years people will laugh at us.' Then he stared at me with knitted brows and asked, 'Mummy, did ladies descend from lady monkeys?'

Libet was a great help. In between Christmas parties, she and Pauline chose the Christmas tree at Hassin's. She got Mahomet, Fatma and Ali to help decorate it and Alan kept falling over mysterious parcels wrapped in Christmas paper. When Hassin went down with 'flu, she kept running to see how he was. She told me, 'I asked him '*Ça va?*' and he said '*Oui*', so he's better.'

Lawrence was better one day and worse the next. His special American friend, a naughty little boy called Alex, came for the day with his racking cough. In between coughing the boys played, quarrelled, fought, made it up and started all over again. The doctor still maintained that Lawrence's cough was the result of 'flu, but why was Alex coughing? I heard Rida coughing too, though Hassin denied it and kept him away from us.

On Christmas day – our last Christmas here – the children received so many presents that Lawrence yelled, 'I'm shouting with joy!' They received parcels from Mavis with an exciting note saying, 'I'm not yet engaged but I'm considering it.' 'I hope it's John Sandy!' Libet smiled. 'He gives us ice-creams.'

Looking at the train from Father Christmas, Lawrence noticed that the scotch tape was the same as ours.

'You must have given it to me, not Father Christmas,' he exclaimed but then he decided, 'I'll write him a thank-you letter just in case he does exist.'

Christmas dinner was on trays in bed for Lawrence and me, but afterwards, when the staff and their families arrived, I got up; I had to be with them this last time. I settled on the couch, while Libet distributed the presents we had bought in the UK, Marks and Spencer trousers and shirts for the men, blouses for the women, cotton suits for the little ones and blue mackintoshes for Cutajah's boys. Smiling, they fingered their presents and then the usual embarrassing silence was broken by the children shouting and jumping up and down as they let off sparklers and crackers, raced their cars with sirens blaring and pulled quacking ducks. It was fun watching their ecstatic faces; Hedia was now at an Arab school; she had forgotten the little English and French she had learnt and kept hiding behind Zora.

Next day, when the office staff arrived for their party, my bed was so laden with bouquets of flowers, boxes of chocolates and stuffed dates that I felt like a queen and munched contentedly. My sole contribution had been writing out fortunes. I heard murmurs of greeting, chairs scraping, then silence as the Maltese, in their usual way, also sat in silence. I could imagine Alan fidgeting uncomfortably till Hassin entered with food and I heard them settling down to the serious matter of eating.

Suddenly doors were flung open, there was laughter, and young voices burst into carol singing, with Liza Mrosovsky leading. When they finished I heard the relief in Alan's voice as he thanked them and offered refreshment. There was more giggling as everyone drew a fortune and then they all left. A pleasant, endearing crowd.

A few days later Alan announced, 'I've had another telegram. It's still secret but I'm to go abroad almost immediately.' Then he added, 'It's as well we're going. The shops are all shuttered today because of the funeral of a chap killed in a riot, and a rumour spread through Tunis that Salah Ben Youssef had been arrested. It proved wrong but it shows how jumpy

Left to right. M. Choiseull-Praslin, General de la Tour du Monlin, M. Uzel, Alan, M. Guillaume, Mr. Krugger, celebrating the New Year.

people are and how bitter the struggle has become between Bourguiba and Salah Ben Youssef. And did you hear about Cutajah's boys? Village children tried to tear their new mackintoshes off them. It's inevitable that law and order should break down at first, so we are well out of it,' but he sighed. I knew he loved the place as much as I did.

At last a telegram arrived giving permission to announce our departure. I hurried out of bed in spite of the doctor's orders. He was in any case too busy, for he was in the Honours List – an MBE – for some thirty years of caring for the Maltese in Tunisia. Alan announced our news at the High Commissioner's New Year reception. He then hastened to book us on to a boat leaving on January 31st and I sent a hurried note to Vava asking her to get us into a boarding house. Lawrence should be well by that time, and so I put away thoughts of illness; there were only three weeks to go; I would manage.

With sadness I broke the news to our household, stressing the exciting boat trip for the children's sake. Hassin's eyes filled with tears and he clasped both children in his arms. Ali shook

Left to right. M. Seydoux, Snr Marchiori, Morrie Hughes, and Alan.

his head while a sniffing Fatma seized paper and pencil and tried to copy out '*La ligne de l'horizon* . . .' The children were teaching the illiterate Fatma their own lessons. Mahomet growled, 'Take me with you!' When I explained that we could not, angry and pouting he rushed away, found out from Pauline that Mavis lived in Leeds and murmuring, 'Leeds eh?' he disappeared.

'Could he really have flown to the UK?' I asked Alan.

'He doesn't have a visa; he won't be let in.' A few days later he reappeared but with a black eye.

'From his father,' Alan decided. 'If he told him he wanted to go away. Mahomet supports the family.' Poor Mahomet resumed his work, subdued and silent, his long face even longer. In the garden Joseph and Ahmed suddenly showed a desire to work and started on the wall round the Folly that Alan was determined to finish.

What were we to do with the pets? The children insisted, 'Mummy, you must take photos of them. Each one of them so that we never forget them.' We now had a family of thirty-six rabbits. The doorman at the Consulate asked for Herta.

Telegrams poured in from London with instructions. The

Fathma and Libet.

Pells were to move into our palace, so we persuaded them to take over Pong, Blanco, the cats, rabbits, hens, tortoises and pigeons.

Noticing the children's gloomy faces, Hassin hastened to promise, 'I'll look after them.'

'You promise? All of them?' Libet insisted.

'Yes, all of them.' The servants were to stay on at the government's expense until our successors arrived. 'It won't be the same without *les petits*!' they kept exclaiming. I went around with a heavy feeling in my chest. Our life was a perpetual series of good-byes.

It was still an effort to move and I kept sitting down, my head full of all that I had to do. We had to finish our entertainment before we could use the Grand Salon for packing. Alan dragged out a trunk, put two pairs of shoes in it, gazed at it with revulsion and announced, 'No, I'm finishing my Folly first!' and disappeared into the garden.

Lawrence's cough was as bad as ever, but apart from that he was cheerful and energetic and the doctor kept repeating that it was nothing, just the result of 'flu, though he took an X-ray of Lawrence's chest, just in case.

'The navy is on the way!' Alan announced and laughed. Of course, any crisis and the navy arrives! He went on, 'It's just as well. We'll have to give a monster farewell party and since we started with a naval visit, we might as well finish with one!' Yes, and I had to admit, the navy lends glamour to a party.

We sent out hundreds of invitations and were immediately invited to farewell parties in our honour. We were in great demand as people used us as a pretext to return hospitality. But when the Hugheses planned a party for us, it made the other C-Gs think they should too.

It's so kind of them all, I thought, but so exhausting, especially as I now also had a kind of permanent tremor inside at the thought of the unknown future. But we still had to go through so much, too much, I thought. If only I were one of the children, and could sail through it all under someone's wing! But I'll survive and then I can collapse back home. A magnificent branch of mimosa in full bloom from the new Greek consul, Migliaressi, gave me courage. We and the Greeks were still not supposed to associate with each other but Migliaressi had lost a leg in the war, had been treated and supplied with an artificial one in Britain and, as he gallantly put it, 'I shall always remember and remain grateful.'

The farewell parties began: a luncheon at General Baillif's, the new C-in-C, a tea in Baroness d'Erlanger's Moorish palace and then I whirled around like a puppet – luncheon, cocktails, dinner, luncheon, cocktails, dinner, with the French, the British, Maltese, our consular colleagues. But I kept going and always with the thought – I'll never visit these friends again. At one party I exclaimed to Jacqueline Seydoux, 'Everybody is so charming, so decent!' What I meant was, then why in public service have they no conscience? I was thinking of the black-mail, the broken promises, the slaughter of Tunisian villagers. But Jacqueline was official; I could not discuss such a question. Also, I wondered, in foreign affairs did we also act unscrupu-lously? I supposed so. Did Alan? No, I was sure he would rather resign.

Miss Bourke combined us with her Christmas party. Her Arab home was bright with wood fires, and festive with greenery and red crackers. We sat at small tables, the Bizerta notabilities in their smart uniforms crowned with comic paper hats. M Le Mire, a tiny figure, the deposed ruler of Bizerta, and the Tunisian Caïd, a monumental Arab and present ruler, teased each other in the friendliest way. Very civilized and most reassuring. After numerous delicious dishes Admiral Laurin rested his head on a cushion, and to his wife's embar-rassment, closed his eyes. Outside, Libet played with Ouggie, Shaggy and a new-born lamb. She was now coughing too.

The Tahar Maouis gave us a cous-cous luncheon with brics. I displayed my talent by sucking up, Tunisian fashion, the whole poached egg, concealed in its triangle of fried, flaky pastry without spilling a drop.

Our host was worried. Peering through rimless glasses, he began, 'Perhaps you can advise me, Madame. My youngest children are at the *Lycée de Carthage*. They study in French. Is this wise? When I speak French I feel French and my morals are French, but when I speak Arabic, I am an Arab and my morals are Arab. I'm two different people. Is this healthy? or will it make my children unhappy?' I remembered my moth-er's gestures with her grandchildren. When she spoke Russian, her arms went round them; when she spoke English, she just smiled. I also remembered how Lawrence had whispered, 'The teacher is always hitting the Maoui twins. They sit and refuse to speak.' No use telling the General, I decided, as with government passing to the Tunisians French teachers will not dare strike Tunisian children. As we left, I wondered, would the General be safe? A French stooge?

There was no reply yet from Vava.

Libet called in the night. Tears poured down her cheeks; she had been sick and her head was hot. At that moment Lawrence started a fit of coughing and ended with a mighty 'whoop'.

36

We called Dr Tabone. 'Lawrence is whooping' I cried. 'Libet is coughing too and she's been sick. It's whooping cough.'

'No, no, it's not. Lawrence's X-ray shows a clear chest. It is the after-effects of influenza. Believe me, Madame.' He looked at me steadily, the stillness of his short, sturdy figure emphasized his words. 'Please, Madame, it's not whooping cough! Trust me! I will give the children injections and the antibiotics will get them well in time for the journey.'

When he left I turned to Alan, 'I think he's wrong. It sounds like whooping cough but I suppose we'll have to trust him.'

'Have you had whooping cough?'

'No, and you?'

'No.' We stared at each other. Then as Alan exclaimed, 'That would be something!' we burst into a nervous fit of laughter.

Five days to go. I have to survive five days and remain outwardly calm and 'diplomatic'. The navy – a mine-sweeping flotilla – was in Bizerta. 'We'll combine their entertainment with the Bizerta farewell parties,' Alan had decided. We instructed Pauline to, 'Keep the children in the garden, away from everyone,' and we drove off to the Admiral's luncheon. The Captain of the *Woodbridge Haven* and his second in command kept up a cheerful flow of conversation.

Lunch over, the Admiral insisted that I should rest upstairs and, 'We'll look after your officers, Madame.' It was Alan who immediately fell asleep while I could not stop worrying. We had to warn Vava that we needed a flat and not an hotel or boarding house and we must just say that the children are not well.

Then over tea at the *Maison de France* we were to say farewell to the Bizerta French colony. But first the Le Mires insisted that we enjoy a last view of the city from the top of the local hill.

Cutajah drove up and up a steep, winding road. Suddenly

he jerked to a halt. A cart piled high with bricks stood in his way and there was no room to pass. The driver, an ancient Tunisian, was whipping a skinny, weak little horse but the cart was too heavy. We waited.

Finally Monsieur Le Mire jumped out of the car and started pushing the cart. Alan followed him. In their dark suits, now covered in white dust, they strained and shoved with the horse while Cutajah reluctantly placed one, superior hand on the cart. Slowly the wheels turned.

'Anglo-French aid to the Arabs,' Monsieur Le Mire muttered. Squeaking and groaning the cart at last reached the top and disappeared. Monsieur Le Mire and Alan dusted themselves, we admired the magnificent view of the bay and drove to the reception.

Later we boarded the *Woodbridge Haven*. I stood among the smart uniforms, surrounded by laughter and good fellowship, a refreshing sea breeze blowing whisps of hair across my face, and thought, this is probably our last ship's cocktail. I love the sea, I love the navy; if only it was not tied to arms and warfare!

As we drove back home Alan was chuckling to himself.

'What is it?' I asked.

'There's another naval visit looming up for Pell! He's not at all pleased!' But Alan added, 'Actually it won't be too bad as he'll have our lists and he's seen what we do.'

Back home a letter from Vava awaited us. London was in the grip of bitterly cold weather. In the flat she had found the pipes had frozen, there was no water and the deal had fallen through. She could not find anything else.

'We can't ask her to take us in with Michael convalescing.' I cried.

'No,' Alan agreed. 'We'll just have to phone when we pass through Paris and see what she has arranged.'

We prepared for our farewell party. Four hundred guests packed into the Grand Salon. Most Ministers came – Tunisians now – and Prince Chedli represented the Beylical family. The navy were decorative and the girls fluttered round them. Roger Seydoux was dealing with trouble on the Algerian frontier but he managed to look in towards the end. This was our farewell to Tunisia; everyone with whom we had had dealings was present and I wondered about our French friends. Will they be safe here? If they return to France, what will they do? How will they live? I will never know. I sighed.

Jacqueline was watching me and smiled. I told her that I

had not had time to do my official farewell 'calls'.

'Don't worry,' she said. 'I'll make it known that I shall be seeing you off on the boat and people will follow my example. Arrange a cocktail party on board and that will make it all right.' I thanked her – a real friend.

That night Pauline was already with the children when in the night I went to attend to them.

'I'm sorry I've slept through their coughing,' she apologized. 'I'll leave my door open and then I'm sure to hear them.' I went back to bed, relieved. In the morning Alan was beaming, 'What luxury! A whole night's sleep! I feel a new man!' Just as well, I thought, as we rushed through the packing in the Grand Salon. Packers dealt with the furniture and the heavy goods. The servants gaped as a mountain of cases drove off down the alleyway for eventual storage in the UK. We dealt with the clothes and everything still needed here, needed for the journey and at first in the UK. Next the inventory – hundreds of plates, cups, saucers and loads of linen, but Mrs Pell helped me.

The crowning party was that night at the Seydoux'. Instead of their usual casual dinner, a magnificent flower arrangement took up the centre of the table and silver candle-sticks lit up the length of the gleaming white damask cloth. Crested menus were headed 'In Honour of the British Consul-General and Madame Williams.' Dare I take one as a souvenir? I wondered. No, the French would never miss such an instance of 'vulgarity!' The Prime Minister, Tahar Ben Ammar was present with his wife as well as the Tahar Maouis, prominent Britishers, including the Dunbars, the Italians, the Americans and numerous French officials. The atmosphere was friendly and not as it had been previously at the French Residency when, generalizing – a fault I had to admit to – I decided that the French were rude and self-centred.

Roger Seydoux rose to speak. It was a flattering speech. He praised us for our 'contribution to the Tunisian scene', referred to Alan's British sense of humour and stressed the great honour of Alan's new appointment. He spoke of our work together in New York against 'American Imperialism'. Everyone laughed and stared at Morrie Hughes, except, I noticed, the Tunisians. The Prime Minister looked down at his plate and I realized that Roger wished to remind the Tunisians that Britain should not be despised, that she had always been a good friend to the Arabs and he was reproaching them for their insulting behaviour over the FAO vote.

Alan, speaking in French, said how much we had enjoyed our posting in Tunisia and our conviction that her future would be peaceful and prosperous. Roger then leant across to the Prime Minister and said, 'What a shame that FAO marred the British Admiral's visit'. The Prime Minister smiled; Roger was certainly rubbing it in.

The Seydoux' had done us proud. Next day I paid for it with a migraine. I lay on my bed in the dark. I could hear the children coughing and choking.

'When we get home you must have a proper rest,' Alan said as he went off in full uniform, gold braid, feathers and sword to take leave of the Bey. 'I'll call at the office on my way back. There may be news from Vava.' As I nursed my head I decided: I must talk to the FO. The Foreign Service needs temporary accommodation in London. We would pay for it, so they won't lose out and they must consult wives; they must recognize that we're doing a job too. We need to be healthy to do it and not worn out as I was when we arrived here.

Alan had returned. 'Feeling better?' I nodded. 'We British mustn't show feet of clay after those eulogies last night!' I laughed, I was much better. It had been a slight attack. I sniffed. 'Sorry about the scent. It's pretty potent; the Bey held both my hands in his. He was easy this time and seemed a very nice sort of chap if only one could get to know him.' Alan was waving a telegram. 'News not so good. I'll be going abroad in the middle of February,' and Alan made a face. 'Sorry!' I would be left to hunt for accommodation alone; so much for a proper rest.

Our last day and the consulate farewell drinks party. When Alan entered they produced his portrait and hung it ceremonially in the gallery at the end of the long row of bearded and ancient Consuls-General who had served from 1860 onwards. I gazed at it with pride and a heart overflowing with emotion, but among these British I had to conceal my feelings, so I started chatting to the women beside me. I did not realize that Mr Pell was making a speech; he had such a quiet voice. When I did notice and fell silent, someone else talked on, so we never heard Mr Pell. Alan replied and the ladies all gazed lovingly up at him, but I was used to that.

One last duty – a call on the Prime Minister's wife, Mme Ben Ammar. It was always nerve-racking hurrying along the narrow high-walled alleys of the Arab quarter, pursued by beggars and urchins clutching at my clothes and now no

French policeman to chase them away. At last a magnificent doorway. I knocked and a black, curly head appeared and let me in. Two others peered out but were whisked away. Slaves now renamed 'orphans', I thought. Curly-head took me upstairs, slipped out of his sandals and led me into Victorian-style, sumptuous apartments with red damask sofas and gilt mirrors. Mme Ben Ammar greeted me with a kiss and we sat down facing each other on red, plush gilt chairs. She asked after my children, I replied and asked after hers. Then she leaned towards me, pressed her plump hands together, her whole figure tense and in a low voice exclaimed,

'Madame, it is all so difficult. My husband is exhausted, he's ill. Everything is going wrong and all this violence . . . We're dreading the elections. I'm at my wits' end how to keep him fit! He never has a moment of peace and quiet or a single day off . . .' I made sympathetic noises; I understood only too well and I felt for her and reached for her hand, just as curly-head led in two French ladies. Mme Ben Ammar immediately changed back into her cheerful public self.

All three ladies began flattering me in true French-Arab style – my French was excellent, we entertained so graciously, my children were so well-mannered. I found it difficult to shed my reserve and reply similarly. 'You have all been so hospitable,' I stammered and got up. Mme Ben Ammar put her arms round me and kissed me over and over again. With promises that we would keep in touch, I left.

On our last morning I photographed the whole office staff on our terrace as well as Doctor Tabone who whispered, 'Madame, wrap the children up warmly. On the boat take them straight to their room and don't let anyone in. *Bon voyage!*' It was very cold and suddenly it began to snow. Mahomet ran down the stairway and we had to laugh as we watched his sturdy figure prancing around trying to catch the flakes. It broke the tension.

'We have never seen snow,' Hassin explained. I wrapped my long fur coat round me. Alan was wearing his heavy overcoat and the children were well wrapped up in woollen coats and trousers.

Shivering I remarked, 'It doesn't feel like Tunisia anymore!' and with a last look at our beautiful palace, we drove off, followed by a van with our luggage and cars with the servants and some of the staff. On the quay, I clutched a large bouquet covered with flakes of snow, and after the last farewells we

Goodbyes on the quayside with Pauline, Cutajah and Gladys.

hurried on board the El Mansour which was to take us to Marseille.

We left the children and Pauline in their cabin, with instructions to keep the door shut. A large gathering of guests had already collected in the reception hall. Monsieur Choiseul represented the French authorities, General Tahar Maoui the Tunisians. Jacqueline Seydoux had come as promised and I was able to apologize to the officials' wives for not 'calling'. As we drank the champagne, I noticed that Jacqueline had disappeared. I rushed to the children's room. They were both coughing and Jacqueline was there.

'I could not let them go without saying good-bye!' she explained. 'But they've got whooping cough!' I told her what the doctor had been saying.

'Infectious diseases,' she explained, 'have to be reported to the authorities. That is the law and the patients go to the isolation hospital. They rarely come out alive. That's why your doctor refused to admit that they had whooping cough. Keep

281

Lawrence and the author joining the El Mansour.

On board the El Mansour. Left to right, Alan, Mrs Jacqueline Seydoux and the author.

the door locked till you are out of the bay and at sea.'

I told Alan and whispered, 'I hope no one finds out.'

'*Insha Allah!*' he whispered back. Finally guests started leaving. For weeks past Alan had smiled, grinned and nodded over farewells so that when Tahar Maoui now stood grinning before him, he produced an incredibly artificial crooked smile that, caught by the press photographer, went down in the family annals as the 'Maoui grin'.

We stood on deck close together, buffeted by the bitterly cold wind. The ship moved off.

'What a sensational transfer!' I cried. 'Christmas celebrations, my 'flu, a naval visit, packing, farewell parties, and on top of it all – whooping cough!' I slipped an arm through Alan's. 'Still alive?'

'Just! I feel held together with bits of string!'

Through the sleet whipping our faces, we made out a long line of dark figures, figures dear to us, waving – the servants were still standing there. AP Vella's generous silhouette stood out and Fatma swathed in white. We waved back.

Then all we could make out was the green coastline dotted with little white domes and slender minarets, and soon only the swelling, white-capped waves against purple hills. The deck

Leaving on board the El Mansour. From left to right, Alan shaking hands with Tahar Maoui. In the background is A. P. Vella.

Farewells on board the El Mansour. The author shakes hands with Mme Benattar with Mme Ros in the background.

heaved under us.

'A lovely little country!' I exclaimed. 'We'll never again have such a beautiful home!' Roger Seydoux with his formula ... Bourguiba, a generous spirit ... sovereignty, peace for Tunisia. Snow whipped our faces but I felt a great calm and deep satisfaction. I shouted above the whining of the storm, 'It was great, wasn't it?'